Teaching in Challenging Circumstances

Cambridge Handbooks for Language Teachers

This series, now with over 50 titles, offers practical ideas, techniques and activities for the teaching of English and other languages, providing inspiration for both teachers and trainers.

Recent titles in this series:

Teach Business English
SYLVIE DONNA

Teaching English Spelling
A practical guide
RUTH SHEMESH and SHEILA WALLER

Using Folktales
ERIC K. TAYLOR

Learner English (Second edition)
A teacher's guide to interference and other problems
EDITED BY MICHAEL SWAN and BERNARD SMITH

Planning Lessons and Courses
Designing sequences of work for the language classroom
TESSA WOODWARD

Teaching Large Multilevel Classes
NATALIE HESS

Using the Board in the Language Classroom
JEANNINE DOBBS

Writing Simple Poems
Pattern poetry for language acquisition
VICKI L. HOLMES and MARGARET R. MOULTON

Laughing Matters
Humour in the language classroom
PÉTER MEDGYES

Stories
Narrative activities in the language classroom
RUTH WAJNRYB

Using Authentic Video in the Language Classroom
JANE SHERMAN

Extensive Reading Activities for Teaching Language
EDITED BY JULIAN BAMFORD and RICHARD R. DAY

Language Activities for Teenagers
EDITED BY SETH LINDSTROMBERG

Pronunciation Practice Activities
A resource book for teaching English pronunciation
MARTIN HEWINGS

Drama Techniques (Third edition)
A resource book of communication activities for language teachers
ALAN MALEY and ALAN DUFF

Five-Minute Activities for Business English
PAUL EMMERSON and NICK HAMILTON

Games for Language Learning
(Third edition)
ANDREW WRIGHT, DAVID BETTERIDGE
and MICHAEL BUCKBY

Dictionary Activities
CINDY LEANEY

Dialogue Activities
Exploring spoken interaction in the language class
NICK BILBROUGH

Five-Minute Activities for Young Learners
PENNY MCKAY and JENNI GUSE

The Internet and the Language Classroom (Second edition)
A practical guide for teachers
GAVIN DUDENEY

Working with Images
A resource book for the language classroom
BEN GOLDSTEIN

Grammar Practice Activities (Second edition)
A practical guide for teachers
PENNY UR

Intercultural Language Activities
JOHN CORBETT

Learning One-to-One
INGRID WISNIEWSKA

Communicative Activities for EAP
JENNI GUSE

Memory Activities for Language Learning
NICK BILBROUGH

Vocabulary Activities
PENNY UR

Classroom Management Techniques
JIM SCRIVENER

CLIL Activities
A resource for subject and language teachers
LIZ DALE and ROSIE TANNER

Language Learning with Technology
Ideas for integrating technology in the classroom
GRAHAM STANLEY

Translation and Own-language Activities
PHILIP KERR

Language Learning with Digital Video
BEN GOLDSTEIN and PAUL DRIVER

Discussions and More
Oral fluency practice in the classroom
PENNY UR

Interaction Online
Creative activities for blended learning
LINDSAY CLANDFIELD and JILL HADFIELD

Activities for Very Young Learners
HERBERT PUCHTA and KAREN ELLIOTT

Teaching and Developing Reading Skills
PETER WATKINS

Lexical Grammar
Activities for teaching chunks and exploring patterns
LEO SELIVAN

Off the Page
Activities to bring lessons alive and enhance learning
CRAIG THAINE

Teaching in Challenging Circumstances

Chris Sowton

Consultant and editor: Scott Thornbury

CAMBRIDGE
UNIVERSITY PRESS

CAMBRIDGE
UNIVERSITY PRESS

University Printing House, Cambridge CB2 8BS, United Kingdom

One Liberty Plaza, 20th Floor, New York, NY 10006, USA

477 Williamstown Road, Port Melbourne, VIC 3207, Australia

314–321, 3rd Floor, Plot 3, Splendor Forum, Jasola District Centre,
New Delhi – 110025, India

79 Anson Road, #06–04/06, Singapore 079906

Cambridge University Press is part of the University of Cambridge.

It furthers the University's mission by disseminating knowledge in the pursuit of
education, learning and research at the highest international levels of excellence.

www.cambridge.org
Information on this title: www.cambridge.org/9781108816120

© Cambridge University Press 2021

First published 2021

20 19 18 17 16 15 14 13 12 11 10 9 8 7 6 5 4 3 2 1

Printed in Great Britain by CPI Group (UK) Ltd, Croydon CR0 4YY

A catalogue record for this publication is available from the British Library

ISBN 978-1-108-81612-0 Paperback
ISBN 978-1-108-81616-8 ebook

Contents

Thanks   iii

Acknowledgements   iv

Introduction   1

I   Creating a good environment for language learning   9
   1   Teaching in your situation   9
   2   Creating a safe classroom   13
   3   Creating an inclusive classroom   21
   4   Making your teaching student-focused   27

II   Being effective in the classroom   33
   5   Planning lessons   33
   6   Managing lessons   40
   7   Teaching inexperienced students   46
   8   Using different languages   51

III   Teaching large classes   57
   9   Managing the seating arrangements   57
   10   Managing mixed-ability classes   63
   11   Managing mixed-age classes   69
   12   Learning outside the classroom   72

IV   Teaching language skills and systems   77
   13   Teaching receptive skills   77
   14   Teaching productive skills   85
   15   Teaching grammar   93
   16   Teaching vocabulary   99

V   Teaching language without textbooks   107
   17   Creating your own resources   107
   18   Using the local environment   114
   19   Using technology effectively   120

VI	**Teaching language with textbooks**	**127**
	20 Understanding textbooks	127
	21 Managing textbook bias	132
	22 Supplementing textbooks	138

VII	**Helping students achieve their potential**	**143**
	23 Motivating and empowering students	143
	24 Checking what students have learned	148
	25 Creating assessments	154
	26 Helping students perform well in exams	158

VIII	**Linking the school to the outside world**	**163**
	27 Involving parents and guardians	163
	28 Involving the local community	167
	29 Bringing the outside world into the classroom	172

IX	**Supporting yourself and others**	**175**
	30 Caring for your students and for yourself	175
	31 Reflecting on your own teaching	182
	32 Accessing development opportunities	186

Glossary	**190**

Index	**200**

Thanks

I would like to express my sincere thanks to Scott Thornbury for his editorial support and guidance in creating *Teaching in Challenging Circumstances*. This is a much better book, and I feel I am a much better writer, as a result of his patient, focused feedback. Scott understood the vision of *Teaching in Challenging Circumstances* from the very beginning of the project, and supported it throughout. Salut!

Karen Momber championed the book at an early stage, and was instrumental in bringing it to fruition. Jo Timerick has been a constant source of support, information and direction throughout the process, and Zoltán Rézmûves brought a kindly but forensic eye to the text as editor. To all three, many thanks. I would also like to thank CUP more widely for being willing to publish such a book as *Teaching in Challenging Circumstances*, the commercial benefits of which may not be as immediately obvious as other titles.

This book has been an emerging project in my mind over the past 20 or so years. I am deeply indebted to the many teachers I have had the pleasure to work with in the Global South, from whom I have learned so much. I hope this book has been able to articulate the challenges which you face, and the incredible ways in which you try to overcome them for the benefits of your students. This book is therefore dedicated to Ahmed and Chen, to Hala and Mim Kaji, to Agnes and Binta, and to all those teachers around the world who are doing phenomenal work in sometimes unbelievably challenging circumstances, whose value is regularly not recognized or rewarded as it should be.

Lastly, I would like to thank my wife Angie for doing the lion's share of teaching in potentially the most challenging circumstances of all – home-schooling during COVID-19 lockdown. I would also like to thank my daughters Livvy and Amy for (mostly) leaving me in peace in my shed during the writing process, and to all three (plus Wilma) for helping me see beyond the text when it wasn't all going smoothly.

Acknowledgements

The authors and publishers acknowledge the following sources of copyright material and are grateful for the permissions granted. While every effort has been made, it has not always been possible to identify the sources of all the material used, or to trace all copyright holders. If any omissions are brought to our notice, we will be happy to include the appropriate acknowledgements on reprinting and in the next update to the digital edition, as applicable.
Key: INT = Introduction; U = Unit.

Text

INT: Greenwood Publishing Group for the adapted text from *The Politics of Education: Culture, Power, and Liberation* by Paulo Freire, p122. Copyright © 1985 Greenwood Publishing Group. Reproduced with permission of Greenwood Publishing Group via the Copyright Clearance Centre; **U2:** Macmillan Education Limited for the adapted text from 'General: controlling lesson time' by Jim Scrivener. Copyright © Macmillan Education Limited. Reproduced with kind permission of the Macmillan Education Limited through PLSclear; **U4:** British Council for the text from 'Planning a grammar lesson' by Tanya Cotter. Copyright © British Council. Reproduced with kind permission; Adapted text from 'Minimal resources: Photocopy-free grammar practice' by Scott Thornbury based on an original idea by Mario Rinvolucri. Copyright © Scott Thornbury. Reproduced with kind permission; **U8:** Yakubu Anas for the text from comment on Facebook page 'Schools do not properly engage parents in schools' decisions and they hardly share critical information about what concerns the children's education except where there arises a problem beyond the school's control' by Yakubu Anas. Copyright © Yakubu Anas, Kano, Nigeria. Reproduced with kind permission; **U9:** British Council for the text from Slides 'Challenging Thinking on Challenging Behaviour Bad Kreuznach' by Sally Farley. Copyright © 2018 British Council. Reproduced with kind permission; British Council for the text from 'Language for Resilience: Cross-disciplinary perspectives' by Beverley Costa. Copyright © 2018 British Council. Reproduced with kind permission.

Photography

The following images have been sourced from Getty Images.
U1: Dimitri Otis/Stone; **U4:** Kateen2528/iStock/Getty Images Plus; **U5:** Kristian Buus/Corbis Historical; BFG Images/Brand X Pictures; **U8:** AVvector/Digital Vision Vectors; **U9:** MicrovOne/iStock/Getty Images Plus.
The following image is sourced from other source.
U1: Copyright © 2003 Pip Wilson and Ian Long www.blobtree.com.

Commissioned Photography

Chris Sowton

Cover Page Photography

Thomas Kokta/Photolibrary/Getty Images Plus

Illustration

Illustrations by QBS Learning

Introduction

Washing one's hands of the conflict between the powerful and the powerless means to side with the powerful, not to be neutral.

Paulo Freire

Background to *Teaching in Challenging Circumstances*

The inspiration for *Teaching in Challenging Circumstances* is Michael West's *Teaching English in Difficult Circumstances*, a work which evolved out of his experiences as an educator in British India during the first half of the 20th century. Despite the six decades which have passed since its publication in 1960, many of his conclusions about English language learning in Bengal feel very familiar today, and there is much which we can learn from his experiences. He noted, for example, that despite students spending around ten hours a week on English study, very few students 'had real reading ability in English, nor were they able to speak more than disjointed sentences, and they could write only very slowly and laboriously', with the effect that their 'results were extremely poor'. This state of affairs is instantly recognizable throughout the modern world, from Afghanistan to Zimbabwe, where millions of students are daily receiving a language education where both the outcome and experience is unsatisfactory.

West's response to the situation he found in Kolkata and beyond was to support teachers in developing a pragmatic, practice-oriented pedagogy. This approach prioritized practices such as the comprehensibility of input, the recycling of new language, and linking language learning with the wider curriculum. His emphasis on a more liberal, democratic form of education was radical in its time, and indeed he purposefully 'stood away from and was opposed to the dominant beliefs and practices of his day' (Smith, 2016). One such contentious area concerned the negative impact which an assessment-focused culture had on classroom practice. This pressure resulted in a situation where teachers 'can't do what they want to do because it doesn't help students pass examinations'. Again, West's critique is as fresh and relevant today as it ever was.

For West, the role of the teacher is nuanced. One particular area which he was critical of was classroom performativity, that is, where the teacher 'is thinking too much of what he does so as to impress the Supervisor rather than of what the pupils are doing'. He challenged the notion of teacher-centredness, and undertook pioneering action research where he measured TTT (teacher talking time) and PTT (pupil talking time) in his classroom, the aim of which was to identify how the PTT could be maximized. He was also critical of teachers whose methodology consisted solely of lengthy explanations followed by written exercises, noting wryly that 'a marked enthusiasm for grammar is one of the commonest symptoms of a bad teacher'. For West, it is the learner who is central. He argued that 'language is a thing which is learnt by practice – it is learnt by the pupils' and that when TTT dominates, students 'will not acquire practice in the use of the language.' In short, West saw the role of the teacher as being to 'help the pupils do the work' because language 'is learnt rather than taught, and too much teaching can be an obstacle to learning.'

The World after West

While we may still recognize many features of the educational landscape that West described, much has changed for the better. This is most evident in terms of access to education. In 1960, global literacy was only around 60%. The comparable rate today is closer to 90%. When West was writing, the Gross Enrolment Rate in secondary schools averaged 29%, a figure which now stands at almost 80%. Educational massification has thus been one of the dominant themes of the post-1960 educational landscape.

Clearly, the expansion of education to the widest possible audience is to be warmly welcomed. However, the speed of the transition – over just a generation – has had significant impact on the quality of education which can be provided. One of the chief successes of the Millennium Development Goals was to massively increase the number of students in school. One of their great failures was the relative lack of support for teachers, institutions and systems to cope with the huge additional demands. The classrooms of the 2020s are crammed full of students who probably wouldn't have been there in 1960. Yet while the numbers have changed in much of the global South, the facilities, resources and pedagogy have not – at least not in a genuinely meaningful way. West's description of lessons being comprised of 'lecture … grammar … textbook-study … written translation' remains very familiar.

Another aspect of education which has not changed significantly during this time is the so-called 'hidden curriculum.' In many classrooms, the main focus of learning has been reduced to the maintenance of control, the consumption of information, and the passing of exams. As a result, in many contexts, education has not been a mechanism for achieving social, cultural, economic or political change. Instead, it has enabled pre-existing hierarchies to reassert their primacy. More than half a century ago, in *Teaching as a Subversive Activity*, Neil Postman and Charles Weingartner (1969) listed several factors that made up the hidden curriculum, many of which remain highly relevant in challenging contexts:

> *Passive acceptance is a more desirable response to ideas than active criticism; Discovering knowledge is beyond the power of students and is, in any case, none of their business; Recall is the highest form of intellectual achievement, and the collection of unrelated 'facts' is the goal of education; The voice of authority is to be trusted and valued more than independent judgement; One's own ideas and those of one's classmates are inconsequential; Feelings are irrelevant in education; There is always a single, unambiguous Right Answer to a question.*

Clearly, in many parts of the global South, educational access and quality has improved. In other parts, however, the needle has barely moved. In Niger, only 1 in 3 women aged 15–24 are literate. South Sudan spends less than 1% of its GDP on education. If you speak a minority language anywhere in the world, the chances that you will be taught in that language are minimal. Such problems of inequity are not confined to the global South. As UNICEF make it clear in *An Unfair Start* (2018), it also affects the world's richest countries:

> *Some children do worse at school than others because of circumstances beyond their control, such as where they were born, the language they speak or their parents' occupations. These*

children enter the education system at a disadvantage and can drop further behind if educational policies and practices reinforce, rather than reduce, the gap between them and their peers.

As we enter the third decade of the 21st century, a global levelling-up of education is needed, both between nation states and within nation states. To quote West, 'We are compelled to face realities'.

What are 'challenging circumstances'?

The shift from West's use of the term 'difficult' circumstances to 'challenging' circumstances is a conscious and deliberate one. As Harry Kuchah Kuchah (2018) argues, the 'use of the word "difficult" may itself be patronizing and limits ELT professionals to pathologizing these contexts'. Kuchah (2016) further notes that in such situations context is crucial, asking the foundational question: 'Who decides what is "difficult"?'. Educational contexts are often conceptualized in positivist, binary, outcome-oriented terms, where specific inputs inexorably result in specific outputs. The reality tends to be very different.

The issue of 'large classes' is one such area where this dichotomy is apparent. West himself talked about the difficulties of class sizes of '30, 40, 50'. Some 15 years later, Paul Nation (1975) suggested an increase to this figure stating that a large class was one which – specifically – contained '50 or more learners'. Having such a seemingly arbitrary cut-off point, however, does not make sense. Can we conclude that a class of 49 is not a large class? What even is a large class? Is the term 'large class' itself a social construct? By implication, the connotation of the term 'large class' is one which contains more students than can be taught effectively. But if a teacher uses a transmissive, teacher-fronted pedagogy and the students are demotivated, hungry, tired and barely understand the language of instruction, it may be difficult to teach a class of five students. On the other hand, if they develop a 'pedagogy of partnership' which entails 'involving students in the sourcing and selection of teaching materials from the local environment as well as involving them as partners in the teaching process', in Harry Kuchah Kuchah's description (2016) of his experience in Cameroon, then it is possible to teach 'a class of 235 students in a classroom meant for 6 students with fewer than 20 textbooks and temperatures of up to 46 degree Celsius.'

This example is indicative of the prevailing 'deficit model' often found in challenging circumstances. This term refers to the widespread practice of focusing on *obstacles* and that which *cannot* be done rather than on *opportunities* and that which *can* be done. This does not mean being naive or utopian: it simply means providing people with the best education possible within the context. Seeing education in relative rather than absolute terms will help enable this process. The spectre of this deficit model, which is haunting the global South, has to change. The repeated use of negative language about weak, fragile, helpless educational institutions will not lead to the step changes which are necessary. Whilst the class struggles faced by teachers around the world must be recognized, it's also crucial to recognize their inherent strengths and resilience, and that what teachers are able to achieve in many challenging circumstances is remarkable. Otherwise, teachers in challenging circumstances may feel downtrodden, marginalized and fatalistic. Returning to our example of large classes, we should therefore not be asking questions such as how we 'deal with', 'cope with' or 'handle' large classes, but rather how we can empower and give responsibility to students, how we can draw on the wide range of experiences and knowledge in this group, and how students can use outdoor space in order to optimize their learning opportunities.

This said, there are clearly certain factors which directly affect the ability of the institution or the teacher to be effective. Several such factors, each of which can have a significant impact at the institution and classroom level, are listed below. This is by no means a comprehensive list, and as noted above, context is crucial. However, as a general rule, we can say that when several of these factors co-appear, the more challenging the circumstances are likely to be. Typical contexts include those where:

1   There is conflict between the official language of instruction and the teachers' / students' ability in that language, and where as a result minority languages may be sidelined or even discriminated against.

2   There is a clear mismatch between the educational philosophy of different stakeholders. For example, whilst the head teacher / inspectorate prefers a 'chalk and talk' approach, the classroom teacher may wish to be more student-focused.

3   Institutions and teachers are not involved in the process of shaping policy which directly affects them. This denial of agency can mean that they have to implement policy which has been made without proper understanding or appreciation of the context in which they are working. Educational non-specialists and bodies are allowed to unduly and negatively influence how education takes place (e.g. private capital, political parties, powerful individuals).

4   Textbooks and other learning resources are insufficient – whether in terms of content, condition, level or number.

5   Teachers are not sufficiently trained and supported to be the most effective teacher they can be within their context.

6   Institutions and teachers are not permitted to take initiatives which they believe would optimize their students' learning experiences and outcomes.

7   Funders don't appreciate the situation in which learning is taking place, and set unrealistic, short-term time frames for interventions to succeed.

8   Teachers and institutions are on the front line of challenging political social change (e.g. mass migration), but are not supported in managing these situations.

9   The presence of different educational models (formal / informal / non-formal institutions, low-cost private schools, religious schools, etc.) creates a confusing and volatile educational landscape for stakeholders.

10 Teachers are expected to be a 'catch all' for wider problems in society (e.g. psychologists, social workers, medical doctors and so on), but they do not receive the necessary support in this, and few / zero service providers are locally available.

11 Teachers and other staff are paid poorly, late, or not at all, and their position at work is precarious – e.g. they don't have secure, strong contracts which are fully recognized in law, or aren't allowed to join a trade union.

12 Absenteeism is high, of teachers but also of students and other members of staff, potentially as a direct result of lacking job security.

In education systems, one size rarely fits all. The importance of context means that the contents of this book should not be treated as a set of specific answers, but rather as a series of suggestions – suggestions based on good practice from around the world. The constant across all these suggestions is that *Teaching in Challenging Circumstances* seeks to increase the agency of teachers and students, addressing the following central concern expressed by Ian Kidd et al. (2017):

> *Who has voice and who doesn't? Are voices interacting with equal agency and power? In whose terms are they communicating? Who is being understood and who isn't (and at what cost)? Who is being believed? And who is even being acknowledged and engaged with?*

The importance of language teaching

Although many of the suggestions made in *Teaching in Challenging Circumstances* could be applied in classrooms of different subjects, its primary focus is the language classroom. Language is vital in terms of human development. As Suzanne Romaine (2013) notes, it is 'at the very heart of significant fault lines in the development process'. The ability to use languages provides opportunities for people to 'contribute to their full potential and be active participants in breaking out of the poverty cycle' (Wisbey, 2016). The absence of this ability is a significant barrier to sustainable and equitable individual and societal development.

In *Pedagogy of the Oppressed*, Paulo Freire (1970) is explicit about the centrality of language in challenging the 'culture of silence', through which learners acquire a negative, passive and suppressed self-image from their oppressors. The continued inability of students in challenging circumstances to develop language skills (in particular of dominant national and international languages) ensures that economic, political, social and cultural marginalization continues. That said, and despite the best intentions of educators and other stakeholders, systemic inequalities are not automatically erased by language learning. As Marr and English (2019) point out, 'the gates to symbolic and cultural capital do not swing open to anyone who just happens to learn a second language'. This echoes Bruthiaux (2012), who argues that for the 'severely poor … the global spread of English is a sideshow compared with the issue of basic economic development and poverty reduction.' Nevertheless, for many learners in such circumstances, functional literacy in a language like English is difficult to separate from the acquisition of other 'life skills', such as digital literacy and higher education. As such, it is surprising that this is barely mentioned in either the Millennium or the Sustainable Development Goals. It is even more incredible when one considers the high percentage of classroom time which is spent learning languages, most particularly English.

Who is this book for?

This book is primarily for teachers who are working in some of the challenging circumstances identified above, recognizing them as key workers in the battle against political, social and economic inequality. Even in 'favourable' circumstances, where there are sufficient resources and support systems in place, teaching is a demanding and complex job. In challenging circumstances, these demands and complexities are even harder to manage.

However, as noted above, *Teaching in Challenging Circumstances* acknowledges and celebrates what teachers can do. It views them as the fundamental building blocks of the whole educational process. It argues that even when there may be policy or institutional level barriers, they still often have the power to make significant changes in their classroom practice, to support their students in the best possible way. This is not to say that such changes will be easy, and often changes which you try to implement will not work as expected. As West (1968) notes, 'you should keep on experimenting'. Learning, and developing as a teacher, is an ongoing process. The key thing is not to be discouraged, but to learn as much as possible from the challenge. To echo the Irish writer Samuel Beckett: 'Ever tried. Ever failed. No matter. Try again. Fail again. Fail better.'

What's in this book?

Part I begins by examining the importance and (economic, social and cultural) value of language learning in challenging circumstances (Chapter 1), and the general ways in which teachers can create a good environment for language learning so that it is safe for the students (Chapter 2), and education is inclusive (Chapter 3) and interactive (Chapter 4). It argues that whatever else is being expressed through policy or institutional norms, there is usually a way in which the teacher can make their own classroom a model for positive social change.

Part II looks at the day-to-day reality of teaching in the classroom in challenging circumstances, and how you can be effective in terms of planning (Chapter 5) and managing lessons (Chapter 6). It then looks specifically at two particularly pertinent issues, namely teaching inexperienced students (Chapter 7) and using different languages (Chapter 8).

Part III concentrates on the issues of teaching large classes, exploring how teachers can manage the seating (Chapter 9), manage students of different abilities (Chapter 10) and of different ages (Chapter 11). In addition to discussing how different seating layouts and systems can facilitate this, the chapter looks at how outside space can be used effectively and responsibly to maximize learning (Chapter 12).

Part IV turns to the specifics of teaching language skills and systems, and identifies some of the main challenges of teaching receptive (reading and listening) skills (Chapter 13), productive skills (speaking and writing) (Chapter 14), grammar (Chapter 15) and vocabulary (Chapter 16) in challenging circumstances. It includes a wide range of different interactive, effective and zero-resource activities which can be used.

Learning materials and resources are often in short supply in challenging circumstances, meaning that teachers have to teach language without textbooks. **Part V** explores solutions to this difficulty, including creating your own resources (Chapter 17), using the local environment (Chapter 18) and using technology (Chapter 19).

Part VI analyses the flip side of this, identifying how language can be taught most effectively when textbooks are available (Chapter 20), whilst also noting some of the inherent problems this poses, such as bias (Chapter 21). Furthermore, it looks at when and how textbook materials can be supplemented (Chapter 22).

In challenging circumstances, institutions are often not optimized to help students achieve their potential. This can lead to a negative mindset and culture of learned helplessness. **Part VII** addresses these issues, specifically: how you can motivate, empower and give agency to your students (Chapter 23), how you can check their learning effectively and humanistically (Chapter 24), how you can create assessments (Chapter 25), and how you can help students perform at their optimal level in exams (Chapter 26).

A good educational institution is embedded within its community. **Part VIII** looks at how you can make these specific links with key stakeholders such as parents and guardians (Chapter 27), and the wider local community (Chapter 28). Then, we look at the flip side of this process, and how the outside world can be brought directly in to the classroom (Chapter 29).

Finally, **Part IX** looks at how you can support and care for yourself and others within your place of work (Chapter 30). It also makes suggestions about how you can reflect on your own teaching, so that you can become the best teacher that you can be (Chapter 31), and how you can access wider development or training opportunities (Chapter 32).

How is each unit structured?

Each of the 32 chapters is structured in a similar way. Each is introduced with a relevant quotation which sets the scene. This is followed by **The short version**, in which five key points summarize the key information presented in the chapter. Several questions are then posed in the **Introduction**, to enable you to reflect on your current practice. A short lead-in then sets the scene more generally, prior to the main content of the unit, which looks at typical *challenges* which you might face, and particular *techniques* which can be used in the classroom to address them. Activities and examples are scattered throughout. At the end of each unit, a short **Reflection** section looks at what next steps you can take to apply this knowledge to your classroom setting.

As far as possible, *Teaching in Challenging Circumstances* is written in straightforward English. At times, however, the use of the specific term is both needed and helpful. In such cases, the term is marked with ▶ as well as highlighted in bold, and a simple definition is provided in the ▶ **Glossary** on pages 190–199.

References

Beckett, S. (1989) *Worstward Ho*. in: *Nohow On*. New York: Grove Atlantic.

Bruthiaux, P. (2012) 'Hold your courses: Language education, language choice, and economic development' *TESOL Quarterly 36(3)*. p. 291.

Freire, P. (1970) *Pedagogy of the Oppressed*. New York: Continuum.

Freire, P. (1985) *The Politics of Education: Culture, Power, and Liberation*. Westport: Greenwood Publishing Group. p. 122.

Kidd, I.J., Medina, J. and Pohlhaus, G. (2017) Introduction to: *The Routledge Handbook of Epistemic Injustice*. Abingdon: Taylor & Francis. pp. 1–9.

Kuchah, K. (2016) 'ELT in difficult circumstances: challenges, possibilities and future directions', in: Pattison, T. (ed.) *IATEFL 2015 Manchester Conference Selections*. Canterbury: IATEFL. pp. 149–60.

Kuchah, K. (2018) 'Teaching English to young learners in difficult circumstances' in: *Routledge Handbook of Teaching English to Young Learners*. Abingdon: Taylor & Francis.

Marr, T. and English, F. (2019) *Rethinking TESOL in Diverse Global Settings: The Language and the Teacher in a Time of Change*. London: Bloomsbury.

Nation, P. (1975) 'Teaching vocabulary in difficult circumstances'. *ELT 30*. pp. 21–4.

Postman, N. and Weingartner, C. (1969) *Teaching as a Subversive Activity*. Harmondsworth: Penguin.

Romaine, S. (2013) 'Keeping the promise of the Millennium Development Goals: Why language matters' *Applied Linguistics Review 4(1)*. pp. 1–21.

Smith, R. (2016) 'Michael West – extracts' Available online at: https://warwick.ac.uk/fac/soc/al/research/collections/elt_archive/halloffame/west/extracts [Last accessed 3 November 2020]

Tickoo, M. (1988) 'Michael West in India: a centenary salute.' *ELT Journal, 42(4)*. pp. 294–300.

UNICEF (2018) 'An Unfair Start: Inequality in Children's Education in Rich Countries'. *Innocenti Report Card 15*. Innocenti, Florence: UNICEF Office of Research.

West, M. (1960) *Teaching English in Difficult Circumstances*. London: Longmans Green.

West, M. (1968) [untitled message on the sixtieth anniversary of Teachers' Training College, Dacca, dated 18 December 1968] in: *Dacca Teachers' Training College Annual, Sixtieth Anniversary Issues, 1968–9*. Dacca: Teachers' Training College. p. 9.

Wisbey, M. (2016) *Mother Tongue-Based Multilingual Education – the key to unlocking SDG4 – quality education for all*. Multilingual education working group Asia-Pacific. p. 3.

Follow Chris Sowton's Twitter feed (@TeachingInCC) on https://twitter.com/TeachingInCC

I | Creating a good environment for language learning

1 Teaching in your situation

The limits of my language mean the limits of my world.

Ludwig Wittgenstein

The short version
1 Your main focus as a teacher is to maximize your students' learning experiences and learning outcomes. You need to identify the most effective way to do this in your institution and context.
2 Understanding what your students want from education should influence your classroom practice.
3 Understanding what other educational stakeholders want from education is also necessary – but this may be different from what your students want.
4 There is often a wide gap between why people learn languages and what or how they learn about languages in the classroom. This gap needs to be bridged.
5 When teaching languages, consider both *what* you teach and *how* you teach.

Introduction
1 Think about your teaching situation. What do students, teachers and parents think is the purpose of education?

2 What do these groups think is the purpose of language learning?

3 How closely does your ▶ curriculum (including materials, methodology, assessment) reflect this purpose?

What is the purpose of education?

Whilst there is no clear, simple answer to this question, it is important nonetheless to think about it. It's too easy to focus on the 'micro' (what happens in the classroom on a day-to-day basis) without thinking about the 'macro' (the big picture). However, the macro *should* influence the micro. Therefore, it can be useful to understand the views of all your institution's ▶ educational stakeholders. Common responses by some of these different groups in challenging circumstances are given below.

Students	Teachers	Parents
It's where I feel most safe.	*It's a job.*	*They can pass exams and get a job.*
I like playing with my friends.	*It's the right thing to do.*	*They can get a certificate.*
It's better than being at home.	*I can help the community I'm*	*School makes them feel better about their life.*
I want to get a good job.	*living in.*	*I have time to myself when my children are*
I like learning new things.	*There's nothing else to do.*	*at school.*
	I love teaching.	*I feel proud when they go to school.*

The views and attitudes of different stakeholders towards education will depend on the type of institution you teach in. Stakeholders are likely to have different expectations about the purpose of education depending on whether they work in a formal, an informal or a non-formal institution. As a teacher, you need to be aware of all these different views – as well as your own personal opinions. In your classroom, you will often need to balance these different views.

Note: the role of the state

In ▶ **formal education** systems, the nation state is also a key stakeholder. Depending on its priorities, it may see education as:

- a way to build national unity, or to advance a particular ethnic or social group;
- a mechanism to promote a wide curriculum, entrepreneurism and life skills, or to give people just enough knowledge to participate in the economy at a low level;
- an instrument for genuine change, or to reinforce existing social divisions.

What is the purpose of learning languages?

Developing language skills, as well the process of learning a language, are both extremely valuable. There are many direct and indirect benefits arising from this, especially in challenging circumstances. Some of the main economic, social, cultural and psychological benefits of learning and acquiring languages include:

- helping people assimilate in different communities, and brings people together;
- improving people's general opportunities to get work, as well as the quality of the work they can do;
- helping people manage their trauma, for example by providing the mental and physical space needed to process it;
- enabling people to pass exams and obtain qualifications and certification;
- empowering people to access learning and training opportunities which might otherwise not be available to them.

If displaced people cannot use the language of school, work and/or society then, as with many less privileged groups in society, their chances of socioeconomic mobility and social integration are greatly reduced. This means that the disaster of having to flee their home country is often followed by a lack of access to basic rights for displaced adults and their children, compounding trauma and disadvantaging their life chances.

Tony Capstick

When talking about 'learning languages', this is often interpreted as 'learning English'. Although English is, by far, the most common language learned by students around the world, it's also important not to ignore other languages. In some challenging circumstances, it might be more useful to learn a dominant regional or national language as opposed to English – e.g. when students need to acquire the school's ▶ **language of instruction** in order to participate fully, or where the language of business and commerce is neither English nor the student's ▶ **L1** (first language).

What kind of language?

It is important to make a distinction between 'language knowledge' and 'language ability'. In challenging circumstances, it is often the former which is prioritized. In reality, however, it is language ability which would really benefit students in some of the ways listed above. As a result, there is often a significant gap between *the reasons why people learn languages* and *what / how they learn about languages* in the classroom in terms of:

- *what* students learn: curriculums and ▶ syllabuses often focus on knowing about grammar (e.g. how to form the present perfect continuous or when to use a definite or indefinite article), remembering long lists of vocabulary, and imitating text structures and text types (e.g. writing compound vs complex sentences, or letters of complaint). One of the main reasons for this is that such language is easy to test (e.g. using ▶ cloze or ▶ matching tasks). Whilst some of this language is useful, in general it is not an accurate reflection of the kind of language which they would need in their everyday lives.
- *how* students learn: the process is often based on memorization, ▶ rote learning and repetition. Students are passive recipients of knowledge, rather than active agents. They learn language individually rather than collectively. Accuracy is valued above fluency.

Note
The 'natural way' to learn language is similar to the way in which you learned your L1. The emphasis is on communication, and the kind of language which you need in your daily life. There is less focus on areas such as formal grammar and writing. Developing ▶ L2 follows a similar path to developing L1, that is, listening – speaking – reading – writing. This approach decreases the stress and anxiety which many students feel when learning languages. Furthermore, what is learned is generally of more relevance and use.

What kind of English?

If you teach in formal education systems, you may not have any choice in terms of what English you teach. It will be determined by the curriculum, the textbooks and the assessment which you have to follow. Teachers often worry about whether they should be teaching British English or American English, or some other specific form of the language. However, if the goal of learning language is the ability to communicate meaningfully with others (as it should be), differences in certain words, or accent, or minor grammatical issues, are unimportant. English should therefore be seen from a multilingual perspective. It should be considered as an additional language resource which complements the student's existing language resources (see ▶ Chapter 8).

Ideally, the kind of English you would be teaching your students is English as a Lingua Franca (ELF). This form of English prioritizes the use of English as a tool of international communication, rather than the accurate imitation of British or American English, or indeed any other variety. It is more democratic, and focuses on what speakers of English do in real life (rather than prescribing what they 'should' do). Whilst there is no universal agreement about what ELF is, some of its key features include:

- an accent which can be generally understood (but is not 'native-like');
- reduced vocabulary (including greater reliance on general verbs such as *do*, *have* and *make*);

- simplified verb usage (e.g. not using third person -*s*);
- non-standard use of articles, prepositions and pluralization.

You may have greater flexibility to teach this form of English in informal or non-formal situations. However, even if this form of English is not considered acceptable in formal institutions, as a teacher you can make choices in your own classroom (e.g. about what you correct and how you correct).

Reflection

- How similar are the views of the educational stakeholders in your institution about the purpose of education? Are your views similar or different? How can you manage these different views?
- What kind of English do you teach in your institution? What influence can you have over this?

2 Creating a safe classroom

[The focus] is very much on creating a safe space for learners, but we had to introduce the idea that we could allow risks to be taken within that safe space.

Fiona Robertson

The short version

1 'Safety' can be understood in many different ways – for example physical, mental and emotional safety.
2 There is a very close relationship between how safe your students feel and their learning outcomes.
3 Closely involve your students in discussions about safety – they are part of the solution, not part of the problem. So too are parents, other teachers and school management.
4 Recognize and understand all the factors (e.g. social, ethnic, cultural) which influence why students may not feel safe.
5 You don't necessarily need to make big changes to make your students feel safer. Sometimes seemingly minor changes can have a significant impact – e.g. what language is spoken, where learners sit, or how playtime is organized.

Introduction

Imagine that you are a student in one of your classes. Answer the following questions.

1 What makes you feel safe in your classroom?
2 What makes you feel unsafe in your classroom?

Now, as yourself, reflect on the answer to 2 and think about the following:

3 Is there anything which *you* could do to make your students feel safer?

Why is it important for students to feel safe?

For some students, school can be the most amazing experience of their lives. It can be the place where they feel safest in the whole world. However, for others, the experience of school can be very negative. Students can feel lonely, sad, confused and scared. This can significantly affect their ability to learn. There may be several reasons for this – e.g. they might have very little experience of going to school, might not know the way they are supposed to behave, or might speak a different language from the one used in the classroom. In challenging circumstances it may not always be possible to create a classroom or school which is 100% safe, especially if the school is in a conflict or post-conflict area. However, there are many things which you can do to make your class a 'safe space', and to show students that they belong.

Note
A 'safe space' is somewhere that students feel they can speak and act freely, without being judged unfairly by you or their fellow students.

Making your classroom a safer space

2.1 *Physical dangers in the classroom*

Challenge: You and your students have the right to learn in a classroom which is safe. In challenging circumstances, classrooms are often in a poor state of repair due to a lack of resources. This can present a physical threat to both you and your students.

Solution: Although you might not have the money or resources to make your classroom *completely* safe, you may be able to make it safer. Ask yourself: *What can I do to manage or minimize the physical risk in the classroom?* For example, there might be places where students shouldn't sit, or you could set up a system for how students leave the class at the end of a lesson. It may be useful for you to create a checklist of potentially risky areas in your classroom, such as broken chairs or uneven parts of the floor. You should do regular checks to ensure that no new problems have emerged.

2.2 *Students' names*

Challenge: Although it might seem unimportant, for a student it makes a huge difference if the teacher knows their name. For a student, it's very motivating if a teacher knows who they are, so they may feel proud or valued. In contrast, if a teacher doesn't know a student's name, that student might feel unwelcome, and think that school is not a place 'for people like them'.

Solution: If you have a large class and it's difficult to remember everyone's names, ask the students to wear name badges at the beginning of the academic year. Students can also write their names on pieces of paper, and put them on their desk in front of them. You should also ask students what name they would like to be called (which might not necessarily be the name in the register) and use it in class. They might prefer a short form of their name, or a nickname, or another name completely! If the teacher respects this, it shows they are listening to the student, and valuing what they say and think.

2.3 *The language of instruction*

Challenge: Some students may speak one language at home but use a different one at school. The language used at school could be a national or international language. Indeed, students might not use their L1 at any point during the school day. For some students, especially younger students, this may feel strange, and even frightening. In some schools, students may even be punished for using their L1, or other students might bully them for speaking it.

Solution: Encourage your classroom to be a multilingual space, where different languages (or language varieties) are accepted and respected. Be more tolerant of students using their L1 in class (e.g. to explain things to each other). From time to time, you could also speak in these languages to those students, if you can. Even just a few words can make the classroom feel a much safer place for them. If there are several different languages in use in your classroom, you can also encourage students to teach each other words from their own languages. This could even be turned into a learning opportunity, e.g. they can make posters and put them up in a ▶ class gallery. Based on these, you could lead a class discussion about the similarities and differences between these languages and the ▶ target language. Talking openly about these languages makes them more normal and acceptable, which is especially important for speakers of minority languages. See ▶ Chapter 8 for more details.

2.4 The teacher's voice or physical presence

Challenge: If you sound bored, annoyed or angry, your students are likely to feel nervous or scared. Both what you say, and the way that you say it, has a big influence on how your students feel. Your physical presence also has a significant impact on whether students feel safe in your class, specifically in terms of:

- **movement:** e.g. marching up and down the class in an intimidating way, or towering over students and being in their 'personal space';
- **gestures:** e.g. pointing, clicking fingers at students;
- **touching:** e.g. even if the intention is positive (e.g. to hug a child who is upset), the student may misinterpret the action, or it might be a ▶ **trigger** for a traumatic experience in the past.

Solution: Don't just think about *what* you say in class, but *how* you say it. You shouldn't shout (unless in an emergency), keeping the volume as natural as possible (but ensuring that all students can hear you). Maintaining eye contact with students, especially when they are talking to you, can also make them feel valued. If students are being noisy, you could use a small bell to get their attention, or else clap three times (to which the whole class should also respond with three claps).

You should also take the time to be friendly, and be interested in your students' lives. For example, when they come into your class, ask them questions like: *What did you eat for breakfast? How are you feeling today? What class did you just have?* If you show genuine interest in your students, they may trust you more, and see you as a person as well as their teacher. Taking this further, you could also share more about your own life with them, by asking them questions like: *What do you think I like doing in my free time? What do you think is my favourite food / drink / book,* etc.? *How many brothers and sisters do you think I have?* You can then say if their guesses are right or wrong. This is also a good opportunity for practising language (e.g. question forms or specific verb forms).

2.5 Bullying

Challenge: Sadly, bullying is a problem in many schools. In challenging circumstances, bullying may be more common or more serious. People may be bullied or discriminated against for many different reasons, e.g. gender, sexual orientation, social class, ethnicity, race, nationality, religion, HIV status, disability or home language.

Solution: As a teacher, you must make your classroom an open, welcoming space. If students see you doing this, they are more likely to copy this behaviour outside the classroom. You can do this in small, subtle ways (e.g. making sure you divide classroom jobs, such as helping the teacher or collecting homework, equally between all students) or more explicitly (e.g. directly addressing textbook ▶ **bias** in the class – see ▶ **Chapter 21**). It is also important to be aware that discrimination is sometimes accidental and unconscious, and may reflect your own bias or background. See ▶ **Chapter 3** for more on creating inclusive classrooms.

2.6 Stereotyping of particular ethnic or social groups

Challenge: Some students may not feel safe if their classmates are of a different ethnicity, nationality or from a more privileged or less privileged social group. Depending on the context, students may have a ▶ **stereotypical** opinion towards people from particular groups. If this is the message which they are getting from home, it may be very difficult to change their view.

Solution: Ensure that you make your classroom as fair and equal as possible, and treat everybody in exactly the same way. Don't be afraid to explore differences in class, but ensure this is done in a respectful way. One way to achieve this is to get students to sit or work together with people who are different from them. This might be difficult when students don't know each other well, e.g. at the beginning of the academic year. It is best to mix students in larger groups (five students or more) rather than small ones. If students have the opportunity to work with a wide range of classmates, they will find that they are more similar than they think. See ▶ **Chapter 4** and ▶ **Chapter 9** for more on how to do this successfully.

2.7   Natural disasters

Challenge: If your institution suffers (or might suffer) from natural disasters, your students need to know what to do in these situations.

Solution: Where possible, consult expert opinions about what to do in case an earthquake, flood, landslide, windstorm or tsunami occurs. Useful information which you can adapt to your local situation can also be found online (e.g. from the Ready campaign of the US Department of Homeland Security: www.ready.gov or from the American Red Cross: www.redcross.org/get-help/how-to-prepare-for-emergencies). You should regularly rehearse what to do in an emergency situation. As students do this more often and gain a deeper understanding of what they have to do, they can take over leading the sessions. This is a good way of developing their ▶ **soft skills** (e.g. leadership, organization, giving instructions).

2.8   Physical violence

Challenge: In challenging circumstances, low-level violence may be a regular occurrence. As well as being physically dangerous to students, this creates a negative atmosphere for learning. Students may be scared or nervous about the potential for violence, raising their ▶ **affective filter** (see below). Such poor behaviour can be caused by many different factors, such as trauma or teasing, or potentially even something minor (e.g. a student sitting in the wrong place, or taking something without permission).

Note
The **affective filter** is a concept outlined by Stephen Krashen. He argues that if a student has a high affective filter, their ability to learn language will be lower (and vice-versa). A high affective filter is caused by stress, anxiety and low levels of motivation.

Solution: If fighting starts, try to stop it immediately and make sure other students are not in danger. You should also try not to put yourself in physical danger. Try not to get angry, but rather to understand why the fight began. If you can work with students to understand this, and identify ways in which they could have addressed the problem differently, it may be less likely to happen in the future. One way to help students with this is to model the conversation which they could have had, and to give them the language which they would need (e.g. *Can I sit here?* / *No, you can't, someone else is*). Whilst you may need to repeat this many times, at least it gives them an opportunity to find another way of managing the issue. See ▶ **Chapter 30** for more on this.

Poor behaviour, and subsequent violence, is often the result of students feeling bored or unengaged in class. Make sure you don't spend too much time on the same thing in your lesson – it's important to keep it moving. Try to anticipate when students are starting to feel bored, and either do something different, or directly involve them (by giving them a task to do, or getting them to come and 'help' you).

2.9 Error correction regarded as a threat

Challenge: Although it's important to correct mistakes, you should not correct too often. If you do, your students might be afraid to say anything at all, or they might feel embarrassed or stupid. This may lead to them 'shutting down' and remaining silent.

Solution: In large classes there isn't time to correct every mistake, and it isn't the best use of classroom time. 'Collect' rather than 'correct' mistakes that you hear in class. At the end of the lesson, discuss some of the most common errors which your students made. This is a quick and efficient way of managing mistakes. It also anonymizes the mistakes, so students don't feel embarrassed.

2.10 Bare and unwelcoming classrooms

Challenge: Classrooms which don't have anything on the walls are not welcoming spaces. Often, there is no culture of doing this in classrooms. Teachers also often say that as soon as they put anything up, it gets ripped down by students.

Solution: Putting some of the students' own work and pictures on the wall makes the classroom feel less intimidating, and hence safer. They feel they belong to the classroom, that they 'own' it. It is motivating for students to see their own work, and the work of their friends.

Some solutions to the issue of students' work being taken down are shared below in a teacher's online teaching group.

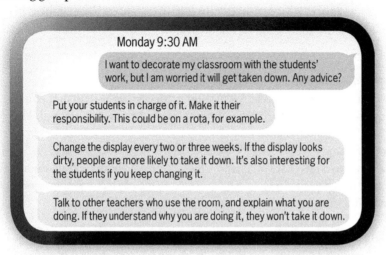

Monday 9:30 AM

I want to decorate my classroom with the students' work, but I am worried it will get taken down. Any advice?

Put your students in charge of it. Make it their responsibility. This could be on a rota, for example.

Change the display every two or three weeks. If the display looks dirty, people are more likely to take it down. It's also interesting for the students if you keep changing it.

Talk to other teachers who use the room, and explain what you are doing. If they understand why you are doing it, they won't take it down.

Creating a safer school

As a teacher, you are generally able to control what happens in your own classroom. However, it is important that students feel safe everywhere in the school. Below are five suggestions for how you, other teachers, the head teacher and other stakeholders can make the whole school a 'safe space'.

1 **Work closely with students' families.**
Parents and guardians, in particular, can help their children feel that school is a safe place. One way to do this is to invite them to sit with their children in the classroom for the first (or last) ten minutes of the day. You can also encourage them to talk to their children at home about what they did and what they learned at school.

2 **Discuss problems with other teachers.**
If you notice that one student doesn't feel safe in school and is having a difficult time, ask your colleagues to see if they behave in the same way in their classes. If that's the case, discuss how you can help this learner together; if not, talk individually to the student to understand what the problem is.

3 **Ask students if they feel safe.**
Don't be afraid to talk directly to your students about whether they feel safe. You can do this as a whole-class discussion, or through class representatives (who have to talk to other students and then share their views with you). If students are nervous about or unwilling to discuss the issue openly, you could put a 'comment box' in your room. They can write how they feel on pieces of paper (in whatever language they like), either with their name or anonymously.

Variations
If students find it difficult to talk about these issues, try using images to see whether students feel safe.

Your students may be familiar with **emojis**. Pointing at which ones they feel like can open up a conversation. This can be especially helpful if students feel so unsafe that they find it difficult to say what they want to say.

The Blob Tree was designed to help children to express difficult emotions. Students can point to the blob(s) to say how they feel. If they point to blob 12, for example, they are struggling to hold on. If they point to number 3, they feel like they are falling. This may open up a conversation.

4 **Have a clear complaints procedure.**
If learners feel unsafe, or in danger, do they know what to do? Who do they talk to? It's important that students have this information. It can be shared with them at the beginning of the year (and then regularly throughout), as well as publicized around the school, for example through posters on noticeboards.

5 **Manage playtime more effectively.**
Playtime is a very important aspect of school life, especially for younger students. The playground can provide amazing opportunities for physical, social and emotional development. It can also be a place where learners feel unsafe if it is not managed well. Make playtime safer by:
- **having breaks at different times for different ages:** This can be particularly useful when there is a significant age difference between learners (e.g. five-year-olds can feel threatened by the presence of twelve-year-olds).

- **thinking about the space itself:** Some children may prefer more enclosed spaces with a clear perimeter (e.g. a wall or fence) as this makes them feel safer. Others may prefer the freedom to run around. Find out about your students' preferences. If possible, offer both types of spaces so that the students can choose themselves.
- **doing regular physical checks:** Are there any unsafe places where children play? Check for broken glass, dirty water, litter, broken fences, etc. What can be done about it?
- **monitoring playtime:** The presence of a teacher during playtime can have a positive impact on behaviour, and makes potentially nervous students feel safer.
- **using locally-available resources:** Children don't need expensive equipment and resources. They are very creative and can be very imaginative with items such as tyres, tree trunks, large stones, etc.
- **managing the 'desirable' resources:** Don't let particular groups dominate any desirable items, such as balls, nets, popular toys, etc. Think about creating a rota so that all students have the opportunity.
- **creating a 'playground friends' programme:** Older, responsible students in the class could be asked to play with and look after younger students. This is good for both.

Reflection

- How do you make your students feel safe in your classroom? What could you do differently to make them feel safer? Are there any particular students that you think don't feel safe?
- Does discrimination exist in your school, whether direct or indirect? If yes, what can you do to change this?
- What could be done in the whole school to make the learners feel safer?

3 Creating an inclusive classroom

Inclusion and equity in and through education is the cornerstone of a transformative education agenda.

World Education Forum

The short version

1   Economic and social pressure means that in challenging circumstances, classrooms are often not inclusive, and in certain situations may actually be anti-inclusive.
2   Creating an inclusive classroom can be challenging, especially if students, teachers, school management, parents and even you have strongly-held views.
3   Inclusivity must be considered from multiple perspectives – e.g. students' physical disability, gender, sexual orientation and age, as well as their ethnic, racial and religious identity.
4   Inclusivity is a critical issue in terms of both student retention and student assessment.
5   Inclusive policies are most effective when supported by all the institution's educational stakeholders.

Introduction

1   Think about your institution. What specific challenges do your students face if they
   - have poor eyesight / are blind?
   - are deaf or hard of hearing?
   - are physically disabled?
   - are HIV positive?
   - are a member of a minority ethnicity / race?
   - are female?
   - are a member of a minority religion?
   - are lesbian / gay / bisexual?

2   Think about your answers above. How inclusive is: (a) your institution, (b) your own classroom? What views do the stakeholders have on these issues?

What is an inclusive classroom?

An inclusive classroom is one in which all students have a chance to participate equally and to the best of their abilities. Students recognize and accept each other as equal partners in learning. An inclusive institution is one which has fair, open and full access, and where all students are supported equally in their learning. Inclusivity means that no student is discriminated against, whatever their age, level of (dis)ability, gender, sexual orientation, ethnicity, HIV status, race or religion.

Note
Managing multilingual and mixed-age classrooms are discussed in detail in ▶ **Chapter 8** and ▶ **Chapter 11**, respectively.

Creating inclusive institutions and classrooms can be difficult. Individuals and communities can have strong views about particular groups or identities. This can affect whether they are allowed (or if they feel comfortable) to learn. These views may be held by the students, teachers, school management, parents – or even yourself. These views may be strengthened, reinforced or even shaped by the textbook, which may contain biases and represent the views of dominant groups (see ▶ **Chapter 21**). Inclusivity, therefore, must be viewed as a process. At first, it may only be tolerated, but in time, it might actually be celebrated.

> *Strive for equity, diversity and inclusion, not as a one-off exercise but continuously, from one class to the next, one cohort to the next, and from one generation to the next … We need to be constantly vigilant to counter the prospect of backsliding, the emergence of new prejudices or the persistence of those that endure.*
>
> Jo Beall

An inclusive classroom provides social and emotional benefits for all students. This can have a positive impact on their learning and psychological development. Inclusivity can be a very powerful weapon. Your classroom can be a vision for what you want your community and society to look like. In so doing, you can change long-held attitudes – for example, the belief that poverty is caused by people's *lack of capacity*, rather than their *lack of opportunity*.

Finally, since inclusivity is a very sensitive area, take care about the language that you use. In English and other languages, many negative and derogatory words are used to talk about people with a different sexual orientation, or who are from a minority ethnic or racial group. This language might be intentionally or unintentionally offensive. You should also be careful when describing groups of people in collective terms (e.g. 'the disabled', 'women'). Although there are things these individuals have in common, there will also be differences. Avoid using the word 'normal' when referring to dominant groups of people, as this suggests that there is a particular 'correct' standard which all students should try and meet.

3.1 *Students with physical disabilities*

Challenge: Classrooms and institutions are often not optimized for supporting students with physical disabilities, therefore they do not have equal opportunities to learn. Furthermore, staff may not have received training, or there may be no overall policies, about how to support students who require particular assistance.

It's also important to think about whether your institution fairly and equally promotes access for all potential students in your local area. Often, students with physical disabilities are denied the opportunity to even apply.

Solutions: Suggestions are given in the following table according to specific physical challenges which students may have.

Helping students who		
are deaf or hard-of-hearing	**are blind or have poor eyesight**	**are physically disabled**
• Encourage them to sit where the acoustics are best (e.g. away from the door). • Speak loudly and clearly, and direct your voice towards them as often as you can. • Try to decrease the ambient noise in the classroom. • If playing audio on a machine, provide them with headphones. If this isn't possible, ensure they are sitting close to the machine.	• Ensure the classroom has clear pathways (e.g. bags are stored under desks). • Ensure they sit near the front so they can see the board as clearly as possible, or so that you can provide any necessary support more easily. • Write in large letters on the board, and ensure your boardwork is clear – and also say aloud everything that you write on the board. • Encourage them to sit next to students with good eyesight, who can help as necessary – but don't put too much pressure on the students to provide help. • Ensure the classroom is as light and bright as possible. • If possible, photocopy materials so they are larger and easier to read.	• Discuss with them the best place to sit (e.g. quite close to the entrance, not at the end of a row). • Have a system for how they come into the room – i.e. before or after the other students, so they are not pushed over. • Identify whether any specific seating provision is needed. • If an activity involves physical movement, plan ways in which they can play an active role that doesn't necessarily involve much movement.

The development of a ▶ **class contract** (see ▶ 30.4) can create an environment in which the strategies above are more likely to succeed. The process of creating this kind of agreement can be a valuable learning experience in itself. Such a contract might include:
- a 'responsible seating' rule based on some of the points above, so students with particular requirements can sit where they need;
- a 'responsible toilet' rule, which allows students to go if they need to without having to ask permission (not all physical disabilities are visible);
- a 'responsible running' rule, which forbids or restricts running in and near the classroom.

3.2   *Fairness and equality for girls and women*
Bias against girls / women is common in education systems across the world. In challenging circumstances, this bias may be strong, for a wide range of social, political, economic, cultural or religious reasons. In the classroom, this bias is often unconscious, and the teacher may not even be aware it is happening. To minimize these problems, teachers need to use a ▶ **gender-responsive pedagogy**.

Challenges and **Solutions**: Common examples of **gender-related challenges** are presented below, alongside **gender-fair strategies** which can be used to combat them.

In mixed-sex classes, the teacher focuses attention on the boys / men, and involves them much more than the girls / women.
- If the seating is divided into male and female sides, ensure you direct your voice and attention equally to both sides.

- Ask questions in equal number, and of equal difficulty, to both sexes.
- Give equal praise to both sexes.
- Actively encourage girls to ask you questions, or say if they don't understand something, especially if the culture is one where this is not the norm.
- Create extra or co-curricular sessions which are only for girls, where they can discuss particular questions in a safe, welcoming environment.

There are assumptions about what subjects or areas of learning that girls / women are good or not good at.
- Break the cycle of repeatedly telling girls what they can and can't do – or what they are good and not good at. Too often, they are conditioned to believing these incorrect opinions or attitudes as facts.
- Provide educational and career advice in a non-biased and non-judgemental way.

Girls / women may not feel safe in the classroom, feeling threatened by male students and/or teachers.
- Where possible, encourage interaction and cooperation between male and female students. This can be done in a sensitive but effective way (see ▶ Chapter 4). This will hopefully be a positive experience for both sexes, and may empower young people to challenge the gender hierarchy in wider society.
- If it is necessary (or desirable) that classrooms are segregated, ensure that the quality of education received by both sexes is the same.
- Develop school-wide policies about ▶ gender violence, and about providing training and support for all educational stakeholders.

Classrooms and textbooks commonly use gender-biased language.
- Use gender-neutral language – e.g. *police officer* (not *policeman*), *firefighter* (not *fireman*), *humankind* or *humanity* (not *mankind*) and *businessperson* (not *businessman*). Challenge ▶ gendered language in the textbooks, and make a specific learning point of it.
- Don't use male pronouns as a default. Alternate between male and female pronouns (or use *they* as a neutral singular form).

Female sanitary facilities may not be appropriate or sufficient, and teachers may restrict when girls can go to the toilet.
- Be sympathetic to female students' toilet or bathroom requirements. Not allowing them to go when they need to can have a serious negative impact on their health. In turn, this can affect their education experience and attitude towards learning.

Girls / women may not be encouraged to play sport or do physical activities.
- When students play sport or games in the playground, female students should have an equal opportunity to participate. This may require teacher involvement, or else dividing the time when males and females can play.

Girls / women may have less exposure to other languages because of restricted mobility, meaning they have difficulties in understanding the language of instruction.
- Be considerate about how female students use their L1 in language learning, and use more multilingual strategies in your teaching (see ▶ Chapter 8).
- Be clear in giving instructions, and in checking understanding of the target language.

Girls / women are presented in fixed, traditional roles in textbooks.
See ▶ Chapter 21.

3.3 When students feel they don't belong

Challenge: Some students may begin school with a negative ▶ **mindset**, especially if they come from families or communities who have historically not had much experience of education (especially formal education). This can be reinforced by the textbook contents and common classroom practices.
Solution: If possible, identify mentors or role models in your institution who can support these students – e.g. by giving them advice or just providing general support. Ideally, these mentors / role models would be other students (in a ▶ **'buddy** system') who have been socialized into the school culture. If other students cannot fulfil this role, it may be that teachers or members of the wider community could.

3.4 Fair and equal chance for every student in testing

Challenge: The challenges which some students face in the day-to-day learning in the classroom may also be present when being assessed, for example in exams. This can have a negative impact on whether they can perform to the best of their ability.
Solution: Whilst you should create the best possible exam environment for all students (see ▶ **Chapters 24–26**), there may be specific additional things you can do to help students with specific needs. For example, some students may need additional time to do reading exams (for example if they are partially sighted, or have ▶ **dyslexia**), or you may need to check that the audio is of sufficient quality for deaf and hard-of-hearing students, or provide large-print materials for students with poor eyesight.

3.5 When homework excludes students

Challenge: In many societies, females have to do more household tasks than males. Even from a young age, they may have to cook, clean, care for the family animals or look after younger siblings. This can seriously affect the time they have available to do homework. Homework can place additional pressure, and widen the education gap between the sexes.
Solution: Don't place too much emphasis on homework. You can also create different levels of homework – for example, with 'must', 'should' and 'could' tasks. (See ▶ **Chapter 10** for more details and an example.) As long as the 'must' homework is minimal, it will not put too much pressure on the students (but it will also allow students to do more work if they can and if they want to). You should also ensure that classroom lessons don't require students to have completed the homework, otherwise they will be doubly disadvantaged.

3.6 Less inclusive classrooms

Challenge: Whilst you might be working hard to create an inclusive classroom, other teachers – or indeed the institution management – might not. Additionally, you may also be getting some negative feedback from parents, or the wider community, about what you are doing. This can be confusing for students, as they are getting different messages from different people. As a result, they may lose confidence in what you are trying to do.

Solution: The best way to make your classroom inclusive is to make the whole institution inclusive – e.g. through the development of a ▶ **school charter** or agreement which focuses on this issue. Ideally, a member of staff would also be given the responsibility for inclusivity across the whole institution. This would ensure consistency and that good practices are being followed. If getting this support is difficult, you might begin with your own classroom, and try to make it a model of inclusivity. Your students can then also be advocates for what you are trying to do.

If there are barriers to inclusivity which you cannot move, you could consider running before-school or after-school clubs (or on days when there is no school). These clubs should be free, and open to everybody. These could be held within your institution, or another public (or indeed private) space, and could focus on conversation, film, music or whatever else interests the members. The focus would be on developing their language skills (whether English or other languages spoken locally) in a friendly, non-judgemental environment.

Note
These kind of clubs might be especially beneficial where education is organized in a ▶ **double-shift** system, that is, where one group of students attends in the mornings, and another group in the afternoons. These clubs can be an overlap between students in both groups. These clubs can be especially positive when there is the risk of division between the morning and afternoon groups – e.g. in situations where ▶ **refugees** attend one shift, and students from the host country attend the other.

Reflection
- How can you make your classroom more inclusive? What specific strategies could you implement?
- How can you make your institution more inclusive? Who would you need to speak to, and how would you convince them?

4   Making your teaching student-focused

Traditional education ignores or suppresses learner responsibility.

J. Scott Armstrong

The short version

1   In challenging circumstances, the most common teaching approach is 'chalk and talk' or 'sit and listen', where the students are generally passive.

2   There are several social, cultural and political reasons for this; however, it is a wasted opportunity not to actively build on students' energy and curiosity.

3   Students are not blank slates. They have rich knowledge and experiences, which can add considerable value to the classroom.

4   Whilst group work enables students to work together in interesting, effective ways, it has to be done well to be successful.

5   It's important to see your students not just as a 'class', but as a collection of individuals, who have their own personalities, issues and challenges.

Introduction

1   Which of the models below best describes your teaching?
  • teacher speaking at the front of the class
  • students working in groups with the teacher monitoring
  • a combination of these two models

2   Would you describe your teaching as student-focused? What are the advantages and disadvantages of the students being more active in your classroom?

What are the challenges in making your teaching student-focused?

In challenging circumstances, a ▶ 'listen and sit' or ▶ 'chalk and talk' methodology is often used in the classroom. That is, the teacher monopolizes the classroom interactions by lecturing the class and using the board as the main teaching aid. The students sit and listen silently except when being called on to answer questions or to repeat in chorus. Not only were teachers often taught in this way themselves, they may also have been trained like this. As such, it feels natural and appropriate. Furthermore, students are also familiar with this approach, and it is often expected by parents as well as by management, who see it as the 'normal' and 'correct' way of teaching.

   Many teachers, especially those who lack experience or confidence, feel more secure when they can control what is happening, and when they have the 'safety' of the textbook in their hands. They may worry that allowing students to work together, or giving them more responsibility, could result in chaos. These feelings are likely to be even stronger if they have large class sizes, or if they face classroom management issues.

   However, there are many reasons why a ▶ student-focused approach to learning is better and more effective. Generally speaking, a student-centred approach:
  • maximizes the opportunities for language practice;
  • engages the students more deeply and more effectively;

- channels their energy and their natural instincts to be cooperative. It reduces the gap between 'the playground' and 'the classroom', which is particularly important for younger learners;
- mirrors real-world interaction and relationships. The classroom feels like an extension of their everyday lives rather than a completely different and unfamiliar space;
- is a more natural, 'normal' way of acquiring language (because it is similar to how students learned their L1);
- creates more trust, and a better relationship, between teacher and students, as well as between students. This contributes to better learning experiences and outcomes.

4.1 Students' preference for teacher-centred lessons

Challenge: Students can be conditioned into thinking that they prefer being passive in lessons. Or, when asked if they like the teacher-centred model, may feel that they should answer yes. Furthermore, in many cases, many students might not have experienced any other kind of teaching model. If we were to flip the question, and ask students whether they would like to be more active in class or to work more with each other, the answer would likely be yes.

Solutions: Academic research clearly shows that students have better learning experiences and achieve better outcomes when they are more active in the classroom. Simple ways in which you can make your teaching approach more student-focused include:

- **allowing students the opportunity to practise:** Alternating a teacher-fronted stage (e.g. grammar presentation) with a more student-centred stage (e.g. students working together in pairs on a grammar practice exercise).
- **decentralizing the learning:** Give students more responsibility through more group work, and also give students specific responsibilities with these groups, e.g. 'group captain' (responsible for getting agreement within the group), 'reporter' (summarizes the discussion to other groups / the teacher) and 'timekeeper' (ensures they do not spend too much or too little time on the activity). The people taking on these roles should change on a regular basis.
- **involving students in the 'mechanics' of the lesson:** You might find certain classroom tasks boring, e.g. handing out (or taking in) books, writing on the board, or doing the register. They are also time-consuming. You may be able to delegate these tasks to students, who often enjoy and feel privileged to help the teacher in this way. This can be a particularly effective way of involving older students, or students who may have behavioural issues.
- **using ▶ realia (real-life objects):** For example, when teaching words for vegetables and fruit, bring in actual oranges, apples, onions, potatoes – or whatever is available locally. Students can also do the same. Alternatively, they can bring in other objects which are important or relevant to their lives and do a ▶ 'show and tell' activity.
- **doing the student-centred tasks which are in the textbook:** Some teachers may ignore or skip over such tasks (e.g. project work, wider discussion, ▶ role play), concentrating instead on more traditional, controlled activities such as gap fill, comprehension or cloze.

Whichever strategies you use, you have to be 100% committed to them in the classroom. Students will know if you are not committed, and may be reluctant to do what you ask them. Making these sorts of changes represents a ▶ step change in many cases, and making a step change takes time.

Note

If you decide to implement some of these changes, try to get the support of other stakeholders. Explain why you are making these changes, and what impact these changes will have. If you do so, the chances of success will be higher.

4.2 Students as 'blank slates'

Challenge: In a teacher-centred classroom, students are rarely asked whether they already know information relevant to the lesson. It is assumed that they know nothing, but often this is not true. This is one of the advantages of large classes: the more students you have, the more likely it is that someone will have some relevant knowledge or experience. If you don't ask, you will never know…

Solution: It is extremely motivating for students if they have the opportunity to share things which they already know, or their life experiences. Personalizing and contextualizing what is learned will deepen the learning experience, meaning the student is more likely to remember what they have learned.

You might also consider asking your students ▶ **open questions** as well as ▶ **closed questions**. If their language level means that they will find this difficult to do in L2, let them do in L1 or a mixture of L1 and L2 (see ▶ **Chapter 8**). This will allow them to express themselves, and give their own opinions and views about a topic. You can sequence the questions so that you move from the simple (i.e. closed) to the more complex (i.e. open).

4.3 Ineffective group work

Challenge: In situations where teacher-centred methodology is dominant, group work is often done poorly. This is for a wide range of reasons:

- giving unclear instructions;
- not managing the group formation or seating well;
- not giving specific roles to students;
- poor ▶ **monitoring** and support;
- not providing a clear task outcome.

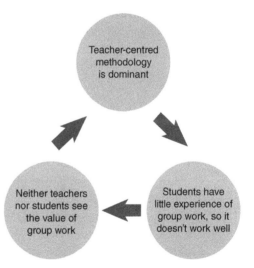

This can create a negative cycle, shown in the diagram.

Teachers sometimes complain that their students don't enjoy group work. The real situation, however, is that they are not enjoying the way in which group work is being done.

Solution: In addition to the language benefits and speaking opportunities which group work provides, it also helps students develop their team-working and collaboration skills. More information about ways to form smaller groups (and how to arrange the seating accordingly) can be found in ▶ **Chapter 9**. Whole-class activities are also a very effective way to make your teaching student-focused. When doing these, it's crucial to give clear instructions, otherwise there might be chaos! Read below three ideas for doing whole-class activities.

Mingle

A ▶ **mingle** activity is a way for students to talk to lots of different people, especially people who they might not normally work with.

Example:

Tell children they have to ask a question (e.g. *What's your favourite colour?*) to at least six people in the group (girls and boys). They go around the group and ask the question. You can then take feedback.

Share

A ▶ **share** activity is good for children to see what other groups have done. It is a bit more structured than a mingle activity.

Example:

Groups do work on a large piece of paper. When the activity is finished, one or two members of each group stay in their place, and hold their paper up. The other children then circulate and look at what all the other groups have done. They can ask questions, if they wish.

Doughnut / Onion ring

A ▶ **doughnut or onion ring** activity is useful for when you want children to repeat a communicative activity with different partners in a structured way. The steps are detailed in the activity below.

ACTIVITY: Doughnut / Onion ring

1. Half the group makes a small circle, facing outwards.
2. The other half of the group faces them in a bigger circle.
3. Each pair talks for a short time (e.g. one minute).
4. The outer circle then moves round one place, clockwise. They repeat the activity.
5. This can be repeated several times.

4.4 Different students in each lesson

Challenge: It can be difficult to make your teaching student-focused when the students you teach change every lesson. In challenging circumstances, students may miss lessons for lots of different reasons.
Solution: At the start of each lesson, recap or ask your students to recap what you learned in the previous lesson. There should also be constant ▶ **recycling** of material. When creating pairs or groups,

ensure that at least one person in each was present in the previous lesson. Don't do things which carry over between lessons – whilst there should be thematic links, there should not be direct links. This is also true for homework (in other words, even if the student didn't do the homework, they should still be able to participate in the lesson).

Variations

Another way to minimize this problem is to get students to keep a learning diary. Students make brief notes (in L1 or L2, or a mixture) about what they have learned in each lesson. You could even use the last two minutes of every lesson for this purpose. Students can then share this information with any of their classmates who missed the previous lesson.

4.5 *Difficulties outside the language class*

Challenges: It's important to see your students not just as a 'class', but as a group of individuals. This can be hard, especially if the class size is large, and you are stressed or overworked. There may be good reasons why a student is behaving badly, not concentrating or keeps answering incorrectly. Students may already have had a very difficult day by the time they come to your class. Five common issues which your students might be facing are outlined below, including some possible causes and the effect which this might have on them, as well as potential solutions, or ways to manage these challenges.

1 **Exhaustion:** e.g. students may have got up early to do chores or to work, or had a long and tiring journey to get to your institution.
   - Have low homework expectations.
   - Acknowledge what they are doing, and tell students this personally, or in front of the whole class (e.g. *I know how long it takes you to get to school, and I'm really impressed with how well you've been doing*).

2 **Depression:** e.g. students may have mental health issues, which they may not be receiving suitable treatment for, or which might have been triggered by a particular event.
   - Show understanding, talk to relevant people in their life (if appropriate), and help them get support (if possible).

3 **Stress** or **anxiety:** e.g. they were hit by a teacher; or something stressful is happening at home.
   - Present a friendly face. A kind word, and acknowledging that you recognize how they are feeling can have a big impact.
   - Refer the student to a specialist, if this option is available, who may be able to help them professionally.
   - Be a calming influence in their lives. Create a peaceful classroom atmosphere.
   - Avoid topics which may be triggers.
   - Don't ask personal questions which they may find it hard to answer.
   - Think about how you want to involve them in the class – e.g. in group work. There may be particular people they would work best with, when feeling as they do.

4 **Hunger:** e.g. students may not have eaten a proper breakfast or lunch. This may be particularly challenging if many or all of your students are fasting (e.g. during Ramadan or other religious or cultural festivals).
   - This is clearly a very sensitive area, and you may be limited in what you can do. For example, you may or may not be able to talk to the student's family about the issue.

- The kind of activities which the student can do may be determined by the time of day (e.g. they will have much less energy later in the day).

5 **Adverse weather**: e.g. it may be too cold or hot or wet or dusty, which affects the students and makes it difficult to learn.
   - Think about your seating plan (see ▶ **Chapter 9**).

Reflection

- How can you make your teaching more student-focused? What specific strategies could you use in your classroom?
- Are there different strategies which you would use for different students, or for different classes?
- If you made your teaching more student-focused, what would you be worried about? What could go wrong? What could you do to manage this?

Being effective in the classroom

5   Planning lessons

Where do you start? How do you choose a topic? Which order do you do the tasks in? What if you run out of time? What if you run out of materials? Ah! So many things to think about!

Jo Budden

The short version
1   The main question when planning lessons is: What will the students know (or be able to do) at the end of the lesson which they did not know (or could not do) at the beginning of the lesson?
2   A lesson plan doesn't need to be a long, detailed document. It doesn't even need to be written down. It can simply be a mental process.
3   Planning lessons carefully can help you minimize common challenges faced in the classroom, such as students feeling bored, confused, or that they're not learning anything.
4   Planning lessons can help you be flexible when unpredictable things happen, or when you realize you have too much or too little material for a lesson.
5   It can be useful for both students and teachers to follow a general lesson template, e.g. Introduction – Starter – Input – Development – Review.

Introduction
1   What do you understand by the phrase 'lesson planning'? How much do you plan your lessons at the moment?

2   Good lesson planning anticipates potential problems, and identifies how you would manage these situations. What plans would you make for the following common classroom situations?
   • Students often feel they aren't learning anything.
   • Students often feel confused.
   • Students often feel bored or cannot concentrate.
   • You might not cover what you planned.
   • You might not have enough material for the lesson – or you might have too much.

Lesson planning

Planning a lesson can be very beneficial for both students and teachers, especially when either group lacks educational experience. When talking about planning a lesson, people often think of a 'lesson plan', i.e. a long, complicated document which details the procedures for a single lesson. In general, this kind of lesson plan is usually only created when a teacher is being observed, or when an institution is being inspected. The rest of the time, such lesson plans are not created, and very often planning doesn't take place at all. As such, 'planning lessons' should be considered in wider, more general terms, and located within the real (rather than the ideal) world of teaching in challenging circumstances. Following these five key principles can help achieve this:

- Planning doesn't need to (and shouldn't) take a lot of time. Although a written lesson plan can be just a few notes on a piece of paper, planning is also something which can be done mentally.
- Planning means anticipating specific challenges in your classroom, and being prepared to respond appropriately should they occur.
- Planning should be collaborative. Share your planning decisions with a colleague, preferably one who is familiar with the class, textbook, or level. This can help you both with your own professional development (see ▶ Chapters 31–32).
- Planning is not a one-off event for a single lesson. Planning should also be done for a series of lessons, or a term, or an entire course.
- Planning should help you teach better. If there is no positive impact at the classroom level, it is a waste of time. Planning should not be done purely for the benefits of supervisors or head teachers.

When you start teaching it's 90% planning and 10% management. But for an experienced teacher, it's 10% planning and 90% management.

Scott Thornbury

The most important thing you need to do when planning a lesson is identify the main objective (see ▶ 5.1). Depending on your class and situation, you might also think about specific, relevant questions such as how you can make it student-focused (see ▶ Chapter 4), how you might want to arrange the seating (see ▶ Chapter 9), or how you can link this learning to the outside world (see ▶ Chapter 29). When planning a lesson, try and anticipate the most commonly faced challenges so you are as prepared as possible.

Note: Teacher's Guides
Some textbooks are accompanied by a ▶ teacher's guide, which contains instructions and ideas for how to teach the material. Whilst these can be helpful, they often adopt a 'one size fits all' approach. You need to do what you think would work best in your classroom. Other difficulties with teacher's guides is that they may follow a 'chalk and talk' methodology (see ▶ Chapter 4), ignore the presence and importance of multilingualism (see ▶ Chapter 8) and suffer from the same issues of bias as textbooks (see ▶ Chapter 21).

5.1   Lack of learning progress
Challenge: It's extremely demotivating for both you and your students if they feel they are not making any progress and aren't learning anything. Reasons why your students may feel this could be that they:
- have a generally negative mindset because of their economic, political or social marginalization;
- have low educational expectations – they feel that education is not for 'people like them';
- have repeatedly performed poorly in assessment;
- rarely or never received positive feedback from their teachers or parents.

Solution: Students' learning experiences and outcomes improve when they know the main objective of each lesson, and when they can evaluate their progress against this objective. When teachers don't plan their lessons, the 'lesson plan' is often just asking students to open their textbooks on a particular page, and to teach as much as possible until the bell rings. In such a system, it's very difficult for the students to measure how well they have done. Instead, when planning, you should ask yourself these two questions:

- *What will the students know at the end of the lesson which they didn't know at the start?* (e.g. how to form and use the present perfect for things which have just happened)
- *What will the students be able to do at the end of the lesson which they couldn't do at the start?* (e.g. conduct a basic interview)

At the start of each lesson, you should explain the main objective to the students. This is motivating and empowering for them and helps to develop trust (see ▶ Chapter 23).

You should also plan at which point in the lesson would be the best place to evaluate students' progress (see ▶ Chapter 24). Ideally, this is something which you would do briefly but regularly throughout the lesson, with perhaps a longer period of time for this at the end. One key point to remember throughout the lesson is: don't assume that the students have learned just because you have taught. Think of your lesson like a bus journey, in which you are the driver and your students are the passengers. As the driver, you obviously know the destination of the journey, but you should also tell your passengers as they get on. However, you don't need to tell them the exact route. Indeed, things may happen during the journey (e.g. bad weather, an accident, a closed road) which mean you have to take a different route than you had planned. This route may be more interesting (and more beautiful!) than the one you had initially planned.

5.2 Feeling confused

Challenge: Students can get confused when a lesson is not clearly staged, or when the contents are not presented in a logical order – e.g. if they read a text on a topic which they have no background knowledge of, or where they don't know much of the language or grammatical structures used. This might be because of the way the teacher has (or hasn't) organized the lesson, or the way in which the textbook has been written.

Solution: Every lesson is a unique event. The staging will depend on factors such as the level which you are teaching, or whether there are certain materials or textbooks that you have to use. A good lesson will move from the familiar to the unfamiliar, and from the simple to the more complex. In general, it will move from:

- **the known to the unknown:** Start with what the students already know and build on this. Realizing that they already have prior knowledge is motivating and empowering for students.
- **oral to written:** Students should become familiar with the spoken language before moving on to the written form. This is the natural way of acquiring language.
- **using receptive skills to using productive skills:** Don't ask students to use the ▶ target language until they have seen or heard it in meaningful context, otherwise mistakes may become fixed (see ▶ Chapters 13–14).
- **controlled practice to free practice:** Ensure students understand the meaning and form of the target language before they use it. They can manipulate the target language more effectively once they have ▶ secured it through ▶ controlled practice.

Using a lesson template is beneficial psychologically for both students and teachers. A general template which you can use or adapt is presented below:

Stage 1: Introduction (maximum 5% of lesson time)

Welcome students and ask how they are.

Ensure students are seated / grouped appropriately.

Explain the main objectives for the lesson.

Stage 2: Starter / Warmer (5–10%)

Do a short, fun activity which is related to the lesson's learning outcomes, or review what you did in the last lesson.

Stage 3: Input (40–50%)

Introduce the target language / main learning points.

Stage 4: Development (30–40%)

Do activities which allow the students to deepen and embed their knowledge of the new language. Initially this is through controlled practice.

Provide the opportunity for students to expand and use this new language in meaningful situations through free practice.

Stage 5: Review (5–10%)

Check whether students have acquired the target language.

Set homework (if appropriate).

Say goodbye.

Note

Stages 3 and 4 do not necessarily occur as 'blocks' (i.e. one after the other). Often, you may teach, say, ten minutes on some of the target language, then practise for five minutes, before going back and giving some more input, followed by further practice.

5.3 *Being bored or unable to concentrate*

Challenge: There are many reasons why students might feel this way, e.g. a) uninteresting textbooks, b) a teacher-centred approach, c) very hot weather conditions, or d) too much time spent doing one task. When students feel like this, their motivation will decrease, and the learning outcomes will be negatively affected.

Solution: When planning, think about which of these factors are more likely to affect each particular lesson. Each lesson is a unique event, and will be affected by specific factors – e.g. the weather on the day, whether this is the students' first or last class of the day, or the number of students in the class. Even if the objective is the same, your plan for a class of twenty students, in nice weather, in their first lesson of the day will be very different from your plan for a class of eighty students, in hot and wet weather, in their last lesson of the day.

Think about whether you can change or minimize any of the complicating factors which cause your students to feel like this. If not, think about how you can manage them positively in the lesson. Taking into account the factors described above, you could:

- look through the textbook before the lesson, and identify how you could teach the same content but in a more interesting or relevant way (see ▶ **Part VI**);
- make sure there is group work throughout the lesson so that you don't talk for too long at any point (see ▶ **Chapters 4** and **23**);
- plan regular, energetic activities to keep students active, so they don't feel sleepy in the heat;
- plan short activities, and keep changing the interaction patterns.

5.4 *Planning flexibly*

Challenge: When teaching in challenging circumstances, lessons are often affected by external events, which you don't have any control over. When these events happen, you may be unable to cover what you had planned.

Solution: When planning your lesson, identify which parts are 'core components', i.e. if you were unable to teach these parts, the rest of the lesson couldn't take place. For these parts, you need to make a 'Plan B' (that is, a backup plan). Since it's very difficult to improvise when external events happen, it is better to anticipate them in your planning.

For example, a core component of your initial plan may have been to play some audio material for listening comprehension using the school CD player, followed by students answering questions based on this listening. However, there may be a power cut, or perhaps the equipment doesn't work, or another teacher is already using it. Your Plan B might be that you read out the transcript of the recording, then continue as planned – which means, you'll have to take the transcript along into the lesson. However, if there is no transcript available, you might have to come up with Plan C (an emergency option), which is to get the students to read the comprehension questions. In groups (or as a whole class), they have to write a play or story about what they think the text would have been about. In a later lesson, they could then compare what they created with the actual text.

This flexibility is important even when something unpredictable does not happen. For example, if you give the students a particular task, and it becomes clear that it isn't working – stop the task. Ask the students why it's not working. They might say, 'we don't understand what we have to do', or 'it's boring', or 'I don't like working with him'. Try and manage these problems, but if this is not possible, move on to something else.

You should also be flexible for positive reasons, if a task goes much better than expected. Students might really enjoy a particular activity and be learning a lot from it. If so, keep it going. Your job is to teach language, and if this is what they are learning, let it continue.

5.5   *Under-planned and over-planned lessons*

Challenge: You might finish a lesson early for a variety of reasons, e.g. students completing a task quickly, or being unable to do a particular task. On the other hand, you might have over-planned, and have too much material.

Solution: You should always plan to have an emergency backup activity, which lasts for about five to ten minutes. It's important you don't just finish the lesson early. Look at these three types of backup activity you could include in your plan:

1   **a speaking task based on a recent text which the students have read:** Texts can be exploited in many different ways which provide extra practice. These are best if done as short oral activities:
    - performing the story (students create a role play based on what happens in the story);
    - extending the story (students talk about what happens after the 'end' of the story);
    - changing the story ending (students come up with an alternative ending);
    - creating a new story (students choose their favourite character and create a new story based around them).

2   **a short mingling task:** e.g. *Find someone who*: Give students thirty seconds to find as many students in their class as they can who:
    - can speak three or more languages;
    - have more than four siblings;
    - have brown hair;
    - travel at least an hour to school;
    - like football.

3   **a 'Socratic discussion':** Socrates was an ancient Greek philosopher, well-known for continually asking difficult questions. Divide the students into pairs. Students A plays Socrates, and has to ask Student B challenging questions about what they have learned in this lesson. For example, if the lesson objective was how to form and use the present perfect for things which have just happened, Student A could ask:
    - *How do you form the present perfect?*
    - *Can you give an example of the present perfect for something which has just happened?*
    - *Can you teach me how to use the present perfect?*

After one or two minutes, students can swap roles, and repeat.

Note

Students can use L1, L2 or a mixture when asking their Socratic questions (see ▶ **Chapter 8**). This activity could also be done using a doughnut / onion ring set-up (see ▶ **Chapter 4**).

As regards having too much material, try to be as realistic as possible when planning. Think about what you already know about the class, e.g. their level and how they work together, as well as the specific conditions of the class, how many students there will be and the time of day. However, if it quickly becomes clear in the class that you have prepared too much material for the lesson, you need to act quickly. If you carry on without making any changes, your lesson will be incomplete when the bell rings. In learning situations where there are large classes and irregular attendance, it is generally best that each lesson has a clear beginning, middle and end.

The ELT writer Jim Scrivener offers four ideas about what you can do to minimize timing challenges in the classroom:

1   Be aware of your timing throughout the lesson – whether you are over or under time for any particular stage. This will help you respond more effectively.

2   Don't start new activities late in a lesson. Generally speaking, it's better to extend a current activity rather than begin a new one which you have to finish too soon.

3   Give clear timings for activities, so students know how long they have. However, if you are running out of time, you can always say 'one minute left' to allow you to move on.

4   Involve the students in making decisions. For example, if you only have time to do one out of two possible activities, ask the students which they would prefer to do.

Two final points about lesson planning

• If you do write lesson plans, ensure you store them well, whether they are hard (paper) or soft (electronic) copies. You may well need them again, or a colleague may be able to use them.
• After each lesson, think about what you could have done differently – and what changes you would make next time. Make a note of these ideas in your plans. (See ▶ Chapter 31 for more details.)

Reflection
• What changes do you think you should make to planning your lessons? What impact will this have for your students?
• Do you face some of the challenges discussed in this chapter? How can you manage them more effectively?

6   Managing lessons

In the high school classroom, you are … a shoulder to cry on, a disciplinarian, a singer, a low-level scholar, a clerk, a referee, a clown, a counsellor … a philosopher, a collaborator … a politician, a therapist, a fool … a mother-father-brother-sister-uncle-aunt, a bookkeeper, a critic [and] a psychologist.

Frank McCourt

The short version

1   As a teacher, you have to play many different roles. These roles can be divided into four main categories: the Knower, the Organizer, the Coach and the Carer.
2   As the Knower, a teacher may be the students' main or only source of language information. However, teachers should still share this knowledge in a student-focused way, and use elicitation to build on students' knowledge.
3   As the Organizer, clarity of instructions is especially important for the success of classroom activities.
4   As the Coach, teachers should know how to ask students the right questions to enable them to work out answers by themselves, and the best ways to provide constructive feedback.
5   As the Carer, teachers should be kind and professional, but be wary of being too familial. Teachers should also have techniques for dealing with behavioural issues.

Introduction

1   What kind of teacher activities would you expect to see for each of the four roles listed above?

2   Which of the four roles do you take on most often? Which role do you take on least often?

3   Look at the teaching techniques and concepts connected to these four roles below. What do these terms mean?

> elicit   instructions   drilling   prompting   feedback   learned helplessness

The teacher's various roles in the classroom

As a teacher, you need to play a range of different roles in the classroom. These can be broadly divided into the Knower, the Organizer, the Coach and the Carer. In challenging circumstances, teachers often only play (or are expected to play) the role of the Knower. However, to maximize student learning experiences and outcomes, a teacher should play all the four roles when appropriate and necessary.

The Knower

6.1   Student-focused approaches

You know things which your students don't. In challenging circumstances, this role can be even more important as your students may have little or no access to other resources. As such, you may be their all-in-one dictionary, thesaurus, textbook and pronunciation source. It's important to remember that you may be the only person who can answer questions on these topics. However, as discussed in ▶ Chapter 4, the way in which you share this information is important. You should avoid the temptation to just 'dump' information on the students, and try to find opportunities to help them develop their knowledge in a more student-focused way.

For example, when presenting a new grammatical structure, rather than 'lecturing' the students and giving them lots of exercises from the textbook to complete, you might use some or all of the following techniques:

- ▶ **Elicit** information from the students, to discover what they already know. When doing this, ask weaker students first.
- Use ▶ **visual aids,** ▶ **gestures** and ▶ **mime** to make the presentation more engaging.
- Use as much L2 as you can, but don't be afraid to use the students' L1 where necessary (see ▶ Chapter 8).
- Use examples taken from the students' own lives, or the local culture in order to personalize and contextualize the language.
- Keep the initial explanation and presentation as short as possible. You can always explain more later in the lesson, as necessary.
- Check understanding throughout the lesson, and specifically at the end (see ▶ Chapter 24).

When teaching in resource-light environments, it's important to use all available resources. This includes your students. In such circumstances, elicitation is a very useful teaching technique. It is particularly effective before doing reading activities (see ▶ Chapter 15). For example, you might share with students:

- the **title** of the text, and ask them to predict the focus of the text, or what will happen in the text;
- the **topic or subject area** of the text, and ask whether anyone has any experience or knowledge of this;
- what the **type of text** is, and what kind of information or features it's likely to contain;
- some of the **potentially unfamiliar words** from the text, and ask whether anyone knows the meaning of these words.

The Organizer

Note
Other aspects of classroom management and being the Organizer can be found in ▶ Chapter 4 (forming and managing groups), ▶ Chapter 9 (managing the seating), ▶ Chapter 20 (using textbooks in class) and ▶ Chapter 24 (checking students' understanding).

6.2 Clear instructions
When doing any activity or task, students need clear instructions. This is especially important when students are working together in pairs or groups. As ▶ Chapter 4 showed, group work is very beneficial for language learning – but only if it is done well. When you introduce an activity, it may take a while for students to understand what they have to do. However, it is better to explain instructions thoroughly than to rush through them, as the latter will possibly lead to confusion. Also, if you repeat this activity at a later point, the process will be much quicker. You should therefore see giving instructions as a long-term investment.

When giving instructions, give the information in short sentences, and keep checking that the students understand what you are saying. If you give too much information all at once, students will be confused. The best way to give instructions is to model what the students have to do at the same time as you explain. This way, they are both listening and watching what they have to do. Use the flowchart below.

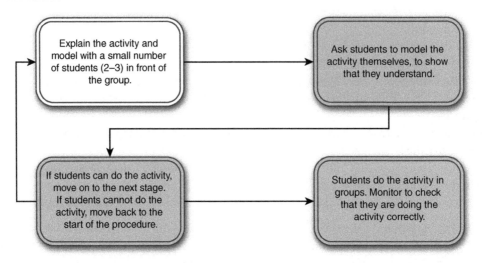

Note

If you are using materials for an activity, don't hand them out until the students are clear what they have to do. Otherwise, they may look at and use these materials rather than listen to you!

The Coach

Think about the qualities of a good sports coach – these can be transposed onto the language learning classroom in order to help students develop their confidence and abilities. These qualities include: 1. motivating players (i.e. students), 2. creating a team (class) dynamic, 3. maximizing training (practice) opportunities, 4. giving feedback, both during and after the training (lesson), and 5. relinquishing control, so the team can play without the coach (so students are empowered). The techniques below will help you achieve this.

6.3   Guided learning

As the Knower, students may expect you to just give them the answers. This may be the norm in their other classes. However, as their Coach, it can be very effective to guide them towards the answer rather than telling them directly. This process is known as **prompting**. Although this may take more classroom time, the learning will be deeper and more effective. Here are some useful phrases to prompt students:

- *Can you say any more?*
- *You're nearly there.*
- *Close, but not quite.*
- *Anything you can add?*

This prompting can also be non-linguistic, that is, using body language by, for example:

- using the size of your eyes to show how close a student is to the correct answer (i.e. closed eyes mean they are wrong, widening eyes show they are approaching the right answer);
- waving your hand behind you (to show a verb should be in the past);
- using the gap between your thumb and index finger to show how long a vowel sound should be (e.g. a wide gap to show the sound in *heat* or *sheep*, a small gap to show the sound in *hit* or *ship*);
- clapping your hands to show whether the syllable stress should be in a word (a louder clap shows which syllable should be emphasized).

6.4   Drilling

Drilling is a process in which students either repeat exactly what a teacher has just said, or else they change or manipulate it slightly to show more advanced understanding. In challenging circumstances, drilling can be especially useful because it can:

- be useful for getting the class to focus, and gaining their attention. However, be careful not to overuse the technique.
- provide students with a consistent model for pronunciation.
- be done at a whole class or group level. When students understand how to use drills, they can also do it by themselves in groups, with one of the students acting as the 'teacher'. Chain drills can be very useful in this situation – e.g. S1: *My name is Adil and I like watching TV*; S2: *My name is Maya and I like reading books*, etc.
- focus on grammar or language which students find especially difficult, such as those issues which are caused by ▶ L1 interference.
- also be used for fun, interactive activities which have a strong underlying structure – see an example below.

ACTIVITY: Disappearing words

1   Write out a short sentence, with each word on a separate piece of paper (ideally on A4, so all students can read them) – e.g. *Lupita went to the market yesterday.*
2   Give the words to six students and ask them to stand at the front, holding up their words for the class to see. (You could get the class to tell them what order they should stand in.)
3   Remove the last word (i.e. *yesterday*) by asking the person holding it to turn it over, and ask the class to say the full sentence.
4   Now remove the penultimate word (i.e. *market*) the same way and repeat. This continues until all the words have gone. The class say the full sentence each time.

6.5   How to be silent and 'disappear'

As mentioned before, and outlined in more detail in ▶ Chapter 23, teachers need to trust their students more. This will empower them, and help them develop ▶ agency and self-esteem. This is important not only in their academic lives, but also in their day-to-day lives and in the workplace. When students are working well together, let them get on with it. You do not need to get involved. It is also very motivating for students to have the opportunity to share their work with their classmates.

6.6 *Evaluation and feedback*

As noted in ▶ **Chapter 5**, it's important that students feel they are making progress. As the Coach, one of your roles is to evaluate what learning the students have been able to secure, or to enable students to do this for themselves. ▶ **Evaluation** does not have to be very detailed or time-consuming, as it's sometimes thought. It can be quite a simple, straightforward process (see ▶ **Part VII** for more details).

In challenging circumstances, how you give feedback can be as important as what you say. Feedback which is very negative (or which students perceive as being negative) can be upsetting for students who feel threatened, marginalized or anxious in their lives outside school. If this happens on a regular basis, students may develop feelings of **learned helplessness**. They might start to think that they have no control over their situation, and that anything they do (especially in terms of their education) will turn out badly. Furthermore, learned helplessness can be associated with a range of psychological disorders, including depression, anxiety, loneliness and phobias. On the other hand, overly positive feedback (especially when not justified) may give students a false sense of their progress. They may end up saying and doing things just to get praise, rather than actually focusing on their learning. Three key points for giving good feedback:

- **All feedback must be evidence-based:** Students need to know (a) how well they did; and (b) the reason they did well or poorly. Give examples. If not possible to do this on an individual basis, give a general indication at the whole class level – e.g. *A good answer included the following information....*
- **When giving feedback, be specific:** Feedback such as *Good job*, *Amazing*, *Wrong* or *Not really* is unhelpful if the students don't know what the feedback is referring to. Better feedback would be *Accurate pronunciation*, or *Good use of the past simple*, or *Wrong word choice*, or *Right verb, but change the form*.
- **Talk about processes as well as outcomes:** As noted above, in large classes you may not have time to give individual feedback or mark all students' work. In such situations, it can be motivating and empowering for students if you give positive feedback about how they are working. e.g. *I'm really impressed how well you all worked during that activity*, *You were very respectful when Habib read out his answer* and *I liked that so many of you worked with new people in that activity*. Noticing such things can help build a positive, trusting relationship in the class.

Note

If your students have a good and trusting relationship with each other, they may be able to give each other feedback. Although you may not need to direct this, you will need to facilitate and support peer feedback. If the feedback is on closed questions where there is only correct answer (e.g. ▶ **gap fill** or comprehension questions), ensure that students have these answers available. Otherwise, there could be disagreement. If they are evaluating students' work where there is no 'correct' answer (e.g. a piece of writing), they need to know how to give feedback responsibly and supportively. This strategy can be especially useful in large classes, where you might not have the time and resources to give detailed feedback to everyone.

The Carer

6.7 *Being supportive but not familial*

Everyday life can be extremely difficult for people living in challenging circumstances for a wide variety of reasons. In such situations, students often see school as a safe and secure space. When students have a difficult home life, they may see you as somebody they can trust, and develop a strong tie to you. Indeed, for some of these students, their teacher may be the most important adult in their life. This is especially true for younger students, and those who have lost important adults in their lives. These bonds can be hugely valuable for students and teachers alike.

In such situations, they may want (or indeed ask for) emotional support. However, it's important to remember that you are not their parent. It can become very difficult if this line is crossed. You cannot be their parent, and it's important that students do not get mixed messages, as this may be very confusing. There are a range of ways in which you can be kind and supportive and provide them with indirect emotional support, for example by:

- ensuring that they work with students who will respect how they are feeling;
- not asking them direct questions if this would make them anxious;
- giving them the option to not participate in speaking activities;
- ensuring that you give positive feedback where appropriate;
- saying hello / goodbye (i.e. a simple acknowledgement) to make the students feel more positive.

Note
If you feel that you are unable to provide the level of support needed for a particular student, you may need to refer them to expert ▶ **service providers**. Don't feel that you have to solve their problems if this is not possible. However, follow the suggestions given to create a more positive atmosphere in the class.

6.8   *Incorporating local customs*
Teachers and institutions should not ignore local customs and traditions, but welcome them into the classroom. The classroom should feel like a natural extension of society, not separate from it. If the culture enjoys songs or chants, or has particular ways of doing things, see how these can be incorporated into learning. This can make people feel that school is a place for 'people like them'. Otherwise, the classroom may feel like a dry, sterile and unfriendly place.

6.9   *Managing poor behaviour*
In challenging circumstances, instances of poor behaviour when learning are common. The reasons for this, and ways in which you can deal with this, are outlined in detail in ▶ **Chapter 30**. In short, there is always a reason why a student behaves poorly, and often it is not their fault, and when managing poor behaviour, focus on the action rather than the person. It's also important that students always have a way and an opportunity to fix the problem.

Reflection
- Do you play all of these four roles in your classroom? If not, should you?
- Which of the techniques discussed in this chapter should you use more?
- What impact would these changes have on your students' learning?

7 Teaching inexperienced students

Every child in every classroom brings a history to school.

Sarah Dryden-Peterson

The short version
1 Students living in challenging circumstances may have little or no experience of formal (or even informal or non-formal) education for a wide variety of reasons.
2 Inexperienced students may feel shy, nervous or even vulnerable when attending school. This may be caused in part by a lack of ability in their own L1.
3 These students may also lack basic classroom skills, which some of their peers have developed over time.
4 Bad behaviour and disruption in class may be caused by a wide range of underlying factors, such as confusion, frustration or embarrassment.
5 Despite the challenges faced by inexperienced students, there may also be some opportunities – e.g. a more positive, dynamic approach to education.

Introduction

1 How do you feel when you do something new? Think of a recent experience when you faced this situation.

2 What challenges do inexperienced students face when coming to school? Consider some of the ideas below.

> shy   nervous   poor behaviour   disruption   class norms   rules
> school protocols   using books   learning to learn   self-evaluation   assessment
> orthography   mother tongue   mental coding   formulaic language

Why some students may not have much experience of education

Students learning in challenging circumstances may have little or no experience of education, either within the home or in formal institutions, such as schools. Reasons for this may be that:
- they are from a low socio-economic background and are unable to afford the ▶ **direct costs** or ▶ **opportunity costs** of sending them to school;
- their parents may not be literate and may have had no formal education themselves; as a result, they may therefore be unable (or feel they are unable) to help their children in practical terms;
- because of their personal circumstances, their parents may lack the mental or emotional ability to support their children's education;
- they are ▶ **refugees** or have been ▶ **internally displaced**, and schools are generally found in a fixed location;
- even when children may have been to formal schools, the quality of education which they received may have been poor.

Depending on the situation, your students lack of formal education experience may actually have some advantages. For example, they may:

- have a very positive attitude to education, seeing it as a privilege and not something they have to do;
- have avoided some of the negative 'conditioning' aspects of formal education;
- be more willing to involve themselves in more community- / environment-based learning activities (see ▶ Chapters 18 and 28).

Note
Wherever possible, it's hugely beneficial to involve parents and guardians in their children's education. This is even more important if the students are inexperienced. One important point to note is that the parents don't have to have a high level of education themselves to support their children. A positive attitude is the crucial factor. (See ▶ Chapter 27 for more information about involving parents and guardians.)

Six challenges commonly faced by inexperienced students are outlined below. Potential solutions to these challenges are also given. Note that the success of these strategies in your classroom will depend on many factors, including the individual characteristics of the children involved.

7.1   *Being shy or nervous about being at school*
The classroom can be a scary place, even at the best of times. But for some students, it can be terrifying. As their teacher, you need to be conscious of this and respond accordingly. For example:

- Give praise and encouragement when they do something well or correctly, even it appears to be a simple task.
- Be careful about asking these students direct questions in front of everybody, or about bringing them up to the front of the room (e.g. to demonstrate an activity). This said, some students may want to participate in this way in order to 'fit in'. Try to identify and respond to each child as an individual to do what is best for them.
- Match them with a buddy – a responsible student who can help them with practical issues (like where to sit, where the toilets are, the playground rules, etc.).
- Ask key people in the school (e.g. head teacher, the cook or food server, playground monitors) to specifically look out for these students, and to offer support.

7.2   *Lack of basic classroom skills*
During the time students are at school, they develop an understanding of basic school skills and school norms. Sometimes these are taught explicitly, but often they are gained subconsciously (i.e. they notice and learn from what other students do). Inexperienced students, who have not had this kind of exposure, may therefore face difficulties such as:

a) Their ▶ orthographic skills may be poor, and they may not be able to use (or even hold) a pencil or pen.

Solution: When asking questions or setting work in class, give students the option about whether they want to answer the question orally or in writing. Don't put pressure on them to write things down. Where possible, provide them with handouts of materials.

b) They may be unfamiliar with classroom norms and protocols, such as how to borrow items from other students, and share materials. They may also be overprotective of some of their possessions.
Solution: When giving instructions for a task which may require this, be very clear about *what* you are asking the students to do, and *why* you are asking them to do this.

c) They may not know how to read, or even how to handle books.
Solution: Ensure the students are seated in a place where they can see other students, and copy what they are doing if necessary.

d) They may be confused when working in groups, and as a result they may try and dominate, or else stand outside of the group.
Solution: Think about how you organize groups, and who works with whom.

e) They may find it physically difficult to sit in the same place for an extended period of time.
Solution: Ensure that your lessons include movement and not sitting around for too long.

How you deal with these issues will depend on how many students it relates to. If it is just a few, you may need to provide individual or small group support to them. If it is a majority of the class, you will probably need to work on these issues together as a whole group.

7.3   Lack of learning skills

For the reasons stated above, the general academic skills of inexperienced students may also be quite weak, e.g. note taking, revising and doing exams. Exams are of particular concern, since in most education systems exams play a very important role. These exams are often ▶ **high stakes.** This means that if they perform poorly, there may be a negative impact not only on their own educational achievement, but on how education is perceived by their family and their community.

Developing these skills may require you to provide additional classes for inexperienced students, or else to include some of the following techniques in your regular classes:

- Show them previous exam papers so that they can see what to expect. It can be stressful to do an exam when you have no idea what it's going to look like.
- Give them the opportunity to do practice exam papers. There is a big difference between *reading* an exam paper, and *doing* it.
- Share examples of good exam answers from the past, so that they know what is expected in terms of style and content.

7.4   Underdeveloped L1 skills

Some inexperienced students may find themselves in a difficult situation where they are learning a second language but their L1 skills are relatively weak. This is cognitively difficult to do. In the process of doing this, they may also feel that their own language lacks value. They might think that it is more crucial to learn a second, 'more important' language before they have developed basic skills in their first language (see ▶ **Chapter 8**):

a) Writing may be very hard as students may lack basic orthographic skills. They may use a different script, or write in a different direction, or the ▶ **mental coding** may be different (e.g. the phonological representation of English as opposed to the visual / conceptual representation in Chinese or Japanese).

Solution: Initially, focus only on lower-case letters (ignoring upper-case letters, as they are used far less frequently and only add to the confusion). Don't teach the letters in alphabetical sequence, since there is no underlying reason for the 'abc' order of English. Rather, teach them in order of frequency: *e a r i o t n s l c u d p m h g b f y w k v x z j q*.

b) Students' lack of vocabulary may be a barrier to acquiring new words in the L2. They may also lack some of the specific skills to quickly and easily memorize and recall new words.

Solution: Teach ▶ **formulaic language**, i.e. fixed phrases and patterns, so-called ▶ **'lexical bundles'** or ▶ **'lexical chunks'**, which students may be better able to remember and link together, such as *for example*, *a lot of*, *in order to*, *as a matter of fact*, etc. This will also help them use the language more quickly, which will be motivating and encouraging.

c) They may have limited understanding of general grammatical ideas and principles.

Solution: Remember that 'learning a language' is not the same thing as 'learning about a language' – students do not necessarily need to be taught grammar in a formal, sequential way. They may be able to recognize grammatical patterns in L2 (without 'understanding' the grammar), or they can acquire the grammar in a lexical way through using formulaic language (as discussed above).

d) Their overall confidence in using language may be low, resulting in them often remaining silent, and not wanting to participate in discussions.

Solution: Don't overwhelm the students with too much information at once. Keep the pace of the lesson moving. Use a range of activities.

As a general point, your teaching should also focus on the non-linguistic features involved in developing language skills, such as body language, visual clues, gestures and eye movement. Finally, it should be noted that this problem may be compounded if the student's L1 is different from the predominant language of the classroom (see ▶ **Chapter 8**).

7.5 Poor behaviour and disruption

For some or all of the reasons outlined above, inexperienced students may behave poorly in class. The reason for this may be frustration, loneliness, confusion, disappointment or embarrassment. As such, if a student is disruptive, you should try and understand the underlying reasons for this. Don't assume they are a 'bad' or 'naughty' student. Try to understand and correct the behaviour rather than punish the individual. (See ▶ **Chapter 30** for more on this challenge.)

7.6 Difficulty in self-evaluation

Such students will have had very little exposure to feedback, especially ▶ **formative feedback**. Where they have done assessment, they are likely to have only received a mark rather than any actual comments. As a result, they may find it hard to evaluate their own strengths and weaknesses. This kind of feedback does not help them identify their problem areas, and where they need to improve. As noted in ▶ **Chapter 6**, it would be extremely beneficial to these students to identify specific areas for them to work on. When you give this feedback, make sure that you (a) say something positive, (b) be specific about the problem, and (c) suggest how they can address this problem. Example feedback you might give them is given below:

'Although your listening skills are quite strong, you need to do more practice with your reading.'

'When you write, your vocabulary range is good, but your sentence is weak. Think about word order more (i.e. subject-verb-object).'

'Your writing fluency is strong, but the accuracy is sometimes not. For example, your use of the definite article is often wrong. Look again at some of the key rules for using the *in English.'*

Note
Some students may find the idea of getting feedback scary as they may feel they are being judged. If giving feedback in students' books, consider only focusing on a few key points (rather than identifying all the problems). The colour of pen may also be important – e.g. they might associate the colour red with feelings such as anger, embarrassment and warning. If so, use a different colour pen.

Reflection
- Do you have any inexperienced students in your class? If so, what could you do to help them more effectively?
- Is there anything your school, more generally, could do to help these students?

8   Using different languages

The punishments [for speaking local languages] include washing dining-hall plates, weeding, scrubbing, writing lines and wearing labels that say 'I will not speak vernacular in school again'.

Beth Erling, Lina Adinolfi and Anna Kristina Hultgreen

The short version

1   Students' mother tongues need to be seen as a resource and opportunity rather than as a problem. This is especially important as national and international languages become increasingly dominant.
2   There should be greater tolerance towards using L1 in the classroom, acknowledging the benefits which it can have for acquiring L2.
3   Three potential ways to promote different languages in your classroom are code switching, translanguaging and using bilingual teaching assistants.
4   Creating materials and resources, both for classroom and wider use, is another important way of promoting minority languages in schools.
5   Having a more open and welcoming approach to different languages in the classroom also presents challenges, but these challenges can be managed.

Introduction

1   What language, or languages, are used in your school in:
   - the classroom?
   - the playground?
   - staff meetings?

2   Are these the same languages which are spoken in the wider community where the students live?

3   Do you think the language policy in your school is fair and equitable? If you could change it, would you? How?

4   Below is a list of strategies which can be used to encourage students' use of local languages in the classroom. What do you think they mean? Have you ever used these strategies?

> code switching   translanguaging   learning materials   extensive reading
> bilingual teaching assistants   advocacy

Multilingual classrooms

In challenging circumstances, especially in conflict and post-conflict areas, language can be both a threat and an opportunity. It can be a threat because it is commonly used as a tool of division and 'othering', and to prioritize a particular ethnic, social or cultural group over others who live in the same community. Languages can also be an opportunity as they can give people life chances, and promote communication between disparate groups.

As such, a school's policy towards language, perhaps more than any other single factor, can affect students' learning outcomes. When students are forced to use a language which is unfamiliar or which they are not proficient in, their educational progress and experiences are negatively affected. These policies may be both formal (e.g. the language of instruction, the language in assessments, or the language in official documents) or informal (e.g. the language of the playground, or language used by the children themselves in the classroom).

Teachers as well as students need to feel comfortable with the school language policy. This is a common problem in schools which use EMI (English as a Medium of Instruction), a rapidly growing phenomenon across the world. Teachers who do not have the necessary skills to teach in the target language are nonetheless being asked to do so. The result of this is a poorer education for the students involved.

Finally, promoting minority languages in the classroom and the school gives minority groups recognition and influence. It has an importance beyond the classroom. Because it is such a sensitive issue, decisions about language policy in schools needs to involve a wide range of stakeholders, including the head teacher, teachers, parents, students and governors.

Note

Research by the British Council (2019) shows that when teachers use languages they are more comfortable with, it results in several benefits including:

- more confidence in own subject knowledge and linguistic ability;
- less reliance on traditional classroom practices and 'safe talk';
- deeper engagement with the language (not just 'doing the lesson');
- greater use of appropriate and effective teaching strategies (not just drilling and memorization).

Making your classroom a language-friendly space

The strategies below could help make your classroom (and school) more language-friendly. Depending on your situation, some of these strategies may be very difficult, or indeed impossible, to implement. Therefore, focus on those strategies which you think will work in your school, and introduce them at a speed which you think has the greatest chance of success.

8.1   *Code switching*

▶ Code switching refers to the practice of changing between languages within and across sentences. Historically, this practice has been seen negatively in the language learning classroom. The reason given for this, generally, is that the most effective way of learning an L2 is by using only the target language. However, most research now shows that moderate and targeted use of L1 can be effective in acquiring L2. This process is known as ▶ scaffolding, and it enables students to work more effectively in the ▶ zone of proximal development. This is because:

- using L1 allows students to work at a higher cognitive level;
- students are more interested in the tasks;
- students are better able to manage tasks;
- students can better check and clarify their understanding with each other. This kind of learner cooperation is especially useful in large classes;

- it respects students' individual identities, which in challenging circumstances is important. Students can express themselves how they want. Making the classroom a safe space can be more important than the tangible learning outcomes.

For you as the teacher, you should use L1 appropriately and purposefully. This could be for a range of purposes, e.g. to translate, paraphrase, clarify, explain and give examples in order to help students understand more effectively. However, if you overuse L1, it may actually hinder L2 learning. Ensuring a balance between the two is crucial. Specific instances where L1 may be useful include:
- giving instructions;
- checking comprehension at the sentence level;
- explaining difficult grammatical points;
- giving an example from your own life or experience;
- managing or organizing the class;
- managing sensitive and difficult topics.

> *Research that shows that judicious and strategic use of code switching can enable students to understand concepts in both languages and to participate actively during lessons.*

Beth Erling, Lina Adinolfi and Anna Kristina Hultgreen

8.2 Translanguaging

▶ **Translanguaging** is a similar communicative practice to code switching. Indeed, the two are often confused. Translanguaging is a related but deeper process. The process is one where people use the resources they have from different languages together, using elements of each language to communicate more effectively. As García and Kleifgen explain, 'Translanguaging includes code switching – the shift between two languages in context – but differs from it in significant ways, for it includes other bilingual practices that go beyond a simple switch of code, such as when bilingual students read in one language and then take notes, write, or discuss in another.'

Here are two examples of activities which encourage translanguaging:

ACTIVITY: Reconstructing a L2 text from L1 notes
1. Give students a reading or listening task in L2.
2. Students read or listen, and take notes about the main points in their L1.
3. Students work in pairs. They should reconstruct what they just read or heard together in L2, using their L1 notes.

ACTIVITY: Labelling images in multiple languages
1. Draw a picture on a poster or the board (e.g. your classroom; the human body; an urban scene).
2. Ask students to label the picture in as many languages as they can. There can be multiple labels for the same object. For example, in Lebanon, it might be labelled *eyes* (English); عيون (Arabic); *les yeux* (French).
3. Encourage students to ask questions to each other about any of the words they do not know.

8.3 Five-minute language takeovers

Your classroom should celebrate all the languages which are represented. To allow this, and to show the importance and value of all these languages, you can periodically allow students to teach their friends some of their L1. This is empowering for the students. The focus should just be on a few words (e.g. family, classroom objects, animals) or set phrases (e.g. *my name is*, *I am … years old*, *I live in …*).

Alternatively, if the students work in an open pair or small open group, one could tell a story, or do a 'show and tell' in their L1 while the others translate into the classroom language.

8.4 L1 materials for extensive reading

In places where people speak minority languages, it may be extremely difficult to find books which are published in those languages. This presents a serious challenge for students to develop both (a) basic reading skills and (b) a love of reading in those languages. In such situations, the only way of creating reading materials may be to do this yourselves. There are two ways you could do this – one in the old-fashioned way, using pen and paper, and the other using new digital tools, like online platforms.

Using pen and paper

This simple activity below enables students to celebrate and create stories in their own language, whilst not ▶ **ghettoizing** them. Through the activity, they work with students who have the same and different mother tongues.

ACTIVITY: Storytime

1. Tell the whole class that you are going to create a story. Ask students to come up with a title for the story. Alternatively, you could give a title (e.g. *The naughty monkey*, *Two sisters*, *The longest journey*).
2. Students (whose L1s are different) work in groups and brainstorm ideas for the story.
3. Take ideas from different groups, and together create the story in the dominant language of the class.
4. Students (whose L1s are the same) now write this story in their own L1.
5. Students read the story to the rest of the class in their L1.

Using an online platform

Online platforms like The Bloom Library (bloomlibrary.org) offer a wide range of tools to create your own books in whatever language you like. This particular site contains a wide range of books in a number of languages, which users can translate and then print by themselves. There are also templates for other types of written products such as picture dictionaries, comic books and calendars.

8.5 Bilingual teaching assistants

As explained further in ▶ Chapter 20, classroom teaching assistants can be valuable in supporting your teaching. One of the main ways in which they can help is to work as translators with students who are struggling to understand the language used in the classroom.

Whilst teachers can, perhaps, control the language their students speak, they cannot force them to think in the target language … like it or not, translating won't go away. It makes more sense for a teacher to use translation in a principled, overt way than to pretend that the students are not using it covertly.

Philip Kerr

Language diversity at the policy level

As a teacher, you may feel that you do not have much influence on educational policy. However, for education systems to be as successful and effective as they can be, they need to draw on the skills, knowledge and experience of those working at the classroom level. As such, it can be useful if you can share examples of how managing multiple languages in your classroom and school can work positively. Doing this can potentially influence educational language policy locally, nationally or internationally.

As the world converges, many schools are rushing to adopt EMI (English as a Medium of Instruction) in the belief that doing so will prepare their students more effectively for the future. The research, however, suggests this is not the case. Although some research shows that using only English to teach English is effective, there is very little research which shows that students learn academic subjects as effectively in English as in their L1. The view is strongly held, however, and this is what many parents want. The rise of low-cost private schooling in many parts of the global South has made this even worse. In fact, it seems that using EMI is a direct way of increasing the gaps in society between the haves and the have-nots. It is important not to confuse EMI with CLIL (Content and Language Integrated Learning), which is when subjects, or parts of subjects, are taught in another language (often English), and where the focus is on the simultaneous learning of the content and the language.

Some of the challenges associated with promoting language diversity are described below, alongside suggestions about how to manage them.

a) If your class is extremely diverse (▶ 'superdiverse') and many different L1s are present, allowing the space for all these languages may be difficult. However, if you adopt a more open and welcoming approach to minority languages, you cannot omit or ignore some of these languages. If you do, then these students (and perhaps the communities which they come from) will feel marginalized.

- Whilst there will be a dominant classroom language, you can still provide a platform for speakers of minority languages in your class – e.g. in group discussions, or through some of the activities suggested above.

b) There is a risk that language groups may form their own cliques, resulting in this group talking mostly to themselves and not engaging more widely with the whole class. Although there can be benefits to this (e.g. as a form of protection and feeling safe), it could also lead to wider feelings of alienation, stereotyping and misperceptions.

- Discuss with students the reasons why, and the times when, they should use their L1. You could draw up a class list of rules or norms which explain this in detail, and which everybody should agree to.

c) There may be no learning resources available in some of the languages.
  - Turn this problem into an opportunity, and set the creation of some materials as a group project. You can use pen and paper, or online library platforms (see ▶ 8.4) to do this.

d) Students may be negatively affected in assessment since exams are often conducted in a ▶ **dominant language.** It may be difficult for them to even understand the questions, let alone answer them.
  - Support students with additional sessions or information regarding exams (see ▶ **Chapter 7**) and perhaps focus on developing their skills in key words commonly found in exam task instructions, so that they are clear what they are being asked (e.g. *Compare...*, *Contrast...*, *To what extent...* etc.)

e) Because language is such a sensitive issue, it's important to manage relations well with the wider community – other educational stakeholders, groups within the community, official government agencies, and so on.
  - Hold meetings, events or forums with these groups to honestly discuss the issues. Explain your school or classroom language policy that you follow with your students, so that they can be advocates for the issue.

Reflection
- Which of the strategies discussed in this chapter would be useful in your teaching environment? What conversations would you need to have with other educational stakeholders before making any changes?
- How could you address some of the challenges in your classroom? How could you manage these effectively?

III Teaching large classes

9 Managing the seating arrangements

A good seating arrangement is one which facilitates specific learning tasks and activities and communicates a teacher's beliefs about learning and teaching.

Hue Ming-Tak and Li Wai-Shing

The short version
1 Classroom seating arrangement has a big impact on how you teach, and therefore on how learning takes place.
2 Many of the assumptions about the advantages of fixed-desk classrooms are untrue.
3 In situations where the desks and seating are fixed and cannot be moved, there are still many things which you can do to improve learning experiences and outcomes.
4 If you are able to change the seating layout, there are many advantages to doing so. What you can do depends on the size of your class, and the existing infrastructure.
5 Remember: even if the desks and benches are not mobile, your students are!

Introduction
1 What are the seating arrangements in the classroom(s) which you teach in? Are you satisfied with the arrangements? Why / why not?

2 Do you have a seating plan for your students, or can they sit where they want?

3 The names of six possible classrom layouts are given below. Draw a diagram of what you think each would look like.

| Double U | Mirror | Inside out | Islands | Family table | Circle |

The link between seating arrangement and teaching approach

The seating plan in a classroom says a lot about the pedagogy and methodology which is used. Typically, in a classroom without any furniture (e.g. just mats on the floor), the learning includes more activities and is more learner-centred, and students interact more effectively and with more of their classmates. In fixed-desk classrooms, a 'chalk and talk' or 'sit and listen' approach is commonly used. This leads to students working more by themselves, being less active, and talking to the same people much of the time.

Robert Sommer said that we should not talk about a single 'classroom environment', but rather several 'classroom environments'. Within one room, there can be huge differences in terms of comfort, atmosphere, temperature, lighting and sightlines (i.e. the view of the board). Just one of these factors could negatively impact the students. A combination of these factors would likely be very significant.

Why does the seating arrangement matter?

To maximize the learning experiences and outcomes, children need a comfortable, safe workspace. They should also feel some ownership of that space. This is not the same thing as simply having a desk, or sitting in the same place on the same bench every lesson. Across the world, the most common classroom seating arrangement is one containing fixed desks in rows. Four reasons why fixed-desk classrooms are so common, especially in challenging circumstances, is because they:

1 maximize the space which is available;

2 enable the teacher to control the students more effectively;

3 make it easier for students to write;

4 provide an easy mechanism for dividing the class into boys and girls.

These assumptions can, however, be challenged. A lot of research suggests that other seating layouts are better for language learning:

1 Whilst true that fixed-desk classrooms are an efficient use of space, most of the alternative layouts (see below) use a similar amount of space.

2 This is also a very negative way to look at education – learning should be much more than simply the avoidance of bad behaviour. In any case, students generally behave badly when they are either not interested or not included in the lesson. Therefore, the best way to 'control' a class is to make lessons interesting and involve everyone.

3 Students would benefit from developing L2 speaking and listening skills, rather than just writing. Writing, however, is often prioritized – with students commonly doing writing tasks without any real understanding of what they are writing. Alternatively, they may be given writing tasks, but are unable to do them because they don't have a pencil or paper.

4 Other layouts can also separate boys and girls, if desired. These other layouts can also provide more opportunities for 'safe' interaction (e.g. mingle or doughnut / onion, see ▶ 4.3), which can help normalize the relationships between boys and girls.

Based on these arguments, one option might be to remove all the classroom furniture and have an 'empty' classroom (see ▶ Chapter 12). Even if desired, this may be difficult to implement for a variety of reasons. As such, let us consider how you can make the most of a fixed-desk classroom. Although you might not have a choice about which room(s) you teach in, and what furniture is inside, you can choose how you manage this situation. The next part of this chapter looks at some of the specific challenges of fixed-desk classrooms, and how these challenges can be solved.

9.1 *Preferred seats next to friends*

Challenge: Students often run into the classroom to get their preferred seat, or so they can sit next to their friends. As they rush into the classroom to avoid the broken window, the uncomfortable bench, or the dark corner, the start to your lesson can be chaotic. This can lead to delays and disorder. Also, knowing that this is what happens can also cause anxiety, leading to the student's affective filter (see ▶ Chapter 23) being high, which has a negative effect on the language learning process.

Solution: Allocate students specific places to sit. This can be for a fixed length of time (e.g. a week, a month, a term). At the primary level, you can mark each student's place with an picture they can easily recognize (e.g. an animal).

9.2 Same partners in pair or group work

Challenge: Students often only want to sit next to their friends, and therefore always work with the same people in pair or group activities. This is not an authentic way to develop L2. Much of the time, people use L2 with strangers. Also, when working with friends, students are more risk-averse. This means they are likely to use only language they are already comfortable with, and not push themselves.

Solution: Once a week you can have a 'working with a new friend' session. Here, you ask (or plan) for students to sit next to others they know less well. For this to have the biggest impact, explain to your students why you are doing this.

9.3 Partners at a similar language level

Challenge: Students tend to work with people at a similar language level, and consequently won't develop useful and necessary language skills such as ▶ accommodating, ▶ paraphrasing, asking for clarification, etc. These skills are all crucial when students use L2 in a real-life situation.

Solution: Create a seating plan in which students sit in heterogeneous rows where there is a range of different abilities side by side (but don't tell them this). As they work together, these language skills will develop naturally.

9.4 The back and the front of the class

Challenge: In many classrooms, weaker students generally sit at the back of the class, and strong ones at the front. Stronger students participate actively but weaker students don't. This lack of equal participation leads to an increase in the gap between their levels. Weaker students may experience frustration and boredom, which results in poor behaviour.

Solution: Use a 'one day front, one day back' system. If students sit in the back half of the class on one day, they must sit in the front half the following day (and vice versa). You will need to monitor this to ensure it is happening. Eventually, this will become natural, and you shouldn't need to manage the process.

9.5 Difficulty accessing seats

Challenge: If students have to climb over other students in order to reach their seats, this causes time delays, and can also lead to discipline and behavioural problems.

Solution: Tell students that when they enter the room, they must fill the rows up from the inside. This stops students having to climb over other students' legs.

9.6 The teacher is static

Challenge: When the teacher stays mainly at the front of the classroom (near the board or their desk), students at the back find it harder to understand what they are saying. As a result they can feel less involved in the lesson, which may lead to poor behaviour.

Solution: Teachers need to be more active, and ensure that they move about the whole room. It's something teachers must be conscious of. Teachers should only use the board when necessary.

Why do teachers need to manage seating?

It can be argued that a 'first come, first served' seating system disadvantages students who need the most support. This would include students who are shy or who are weak in the L2, as they can hide away at the back of the room. Students who have long or complicated journeys to school (who are unable to arrive early or indeed on time) may also often have to sit in the worst parts of the classroom, and are thus doubly disadvantaged.

The decisions which you make about seating will depend on your own context. There is no reason why your seating plan system has to remain the same throughout the academic year. Indeed, at the start of the academic year, there are good reasons for allowing students to decide themselves where they want to sit. For example, a student might decide to sit with students they share a first language with, or students they already know or who are in the same family / ethnic / community group as them. This can build their confidence, which is especially important for inexperienced or vulnerable students. However, you may wish to change this as students develop relationships with both you and with other members of the class. When you make this transition, doing a series of mingle or doughnut / onion activities (see ▶ 4.3) can be a useful bridge.

What different seating layouts are possible?

In situations where it is possible to move the classroom furniture, there are several ways you can arrange the classroom seating. Particular layouts which could work well in challenging circumstances are outlined below. Ultimately, whatever layout you choose, it is important to explain your reasons to your students (and also to colleagues) your reasons why, and to consider the issue from the students' perspective. In his book, *Classroom Management Techniques*, Jim Scrivener makes this suggestion:

> *After the students have all gone home, take a few minutes to view your classroom from their viewpoint. Choose three or four random student desks at different places round the class, and sit in them for a minute or so. Imagine watching yourself up front at the board. Is the view clear? What might cause problems? What makes each place pleasant or uncomfortable? Based on what you experience, reflect on what changes you could make to the room to improve it.*

U, or double U-shape
A U-shaped layout allows students to easily work together with many different students. The teacher can also move around, and be close to every student. Nobody can hide at the back of the class. The double U can be used with larger classes.

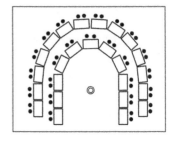

Mirror

Students are seated opposite each other. This encourages discussion, and emphasizes speaking and listening rather than just copying information from the board. It's also easy for the teacher to walk up and down the room.

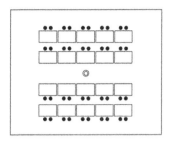

Inside out

Speaking and listening becomes the primary focus with this arrangement. There is no barrier between the teacher and students. The option to write on a desk is there. Students can turn around and do this when necessary.

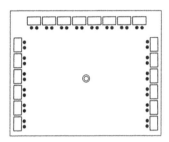

Islands

Students are arranged in groups, making communication easier. They can also work together effectively, reflecting the collaborative nature of language learning. Note how students are not seated at the end of the island – so that they can still see the teacher clearly. When doing tasks together, however, they can work round the whole table.

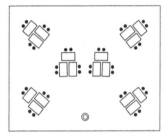

Family table

The whole class works as one. This is a very useful layout if you don't have a large class (e.g. fewer than twenty students). It can also be useful for group project work.

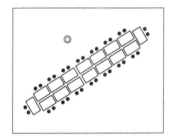

Circle

Remove all the furniture, have students (and you) sit on the floor in a circle. (See ▶ **Chapter 12** for more details.)

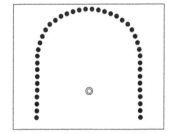

Many of these changes might be easier at the primary level with younger children. As children get older, their bodies and mindset change. It's therefore crucial that if you want to make these changes, you must be committed and passionate. If you don't have this enthusiasm, your students definitely won't.

Reflection
- What are the advantages and disadvantages of each of the layouts discussed?
- What do you think would be the best seating arrangement for your class(es)? Remember that the best arrangement may differ from class to class.
- Can you implement these changes in your classroom? If this would be difficult, is there anyone you could talk to in order to make this happen?
- What impact do you think changing seating arrangements would have on your teaching, and your students' learning?

10 Managing mixed-ability classes

All classes are mixed-ability classes.

Jim Rose

The short version

1 All students have different abilities, which should be recognized and celebrated within the classroom.
2 You should adapt your key classroom skills (e.g. eliciting, correcting, giving feedback) according to the language ability and knowledge of your students.
3 It's possible to use the same materials and resources but differentiate the task, so that all students can participate equally in the lesson.
4 An important consideration when forming groups is whether they should be homogeneous (same ability) or heterogeneous (different ability).
5 A more radical alternative to mixed-ability classes is to mix grade levels, so classes consist of mixed-age students of similar ability.

Introduction

1 Think of a class you teach. What different skills and abilities do the students in that class have? What impact does this have on your teaching?

2 Look at the list of teaching skills below. How would you do them differently for weaker and stronger students?

> eliciting ideas   correcting mistakes   giving feedback   giving instructions   setting tasks

What is a mixed-ability class?

There is no such thing as an 'average student'. Students have different skills and abilities in different areas, both linguistic and non-linguistic. However, when teaching large classes, it can be difficult to find out what these different skills are. Generally speaking, you don't have the time to know the students well on an individual basis. In challenging circumstances, you may be teaching students who have had very difficult educational and life experiences. This is likely to affect the way you teach.

Classes with mixed-ability students offer several advantages. However, you should be aware of some of the potential negative outcomes, and take steps to avoid them. Not only may stronger students feel bored and lack interest, weaker students may also feel lost and confused. There is also the risk of ▶ **stereotyping** students according to their sex, ethnic ▶ **identity** or language which they speak (e.g. *'girls are good at X', 'boys are bad at Y'*).

Note

Keep a notebook so you can make notes about individual students' different skills and knowledge. Recording this information can help you recall key facts about them (e.g. Student A likes flying kites, or Student B knows a lot about animals), which you can use and refer to at appropriate times. This is a powerful way of showing students you think about them as individuals and not just as 'students'. Caution: keep this notebook private, and in a secure place!

Managing mixed-ability classes

It is important to adapt how you teach (▶ **differentiate**) in order to support your students as effectively as possible, whether they are weaker, average or stronger. The better you can get to know your students on an individual basis, the more effective you can be. Here are some ideas for how you can adapt the way you teach:

- **Eliciting ideas:** Asking students to share what they know is an effective and empowering teaching strategy (see ▶ **Chapter 4**). When doing this, take contributions from weaker students first. Stronger students can then add their ideas later on. For example, if you are brainstorming a list of animals, weaker students might suggest more basic words like *dog, cow* or *cat*. Stronger students will then be able to add more challenging words, e.g. *giraffe, gorilla* or *rhino*. When asking questions in class, you should also think carefully about ▶ **nomination**. If students are allowed to shout out answers, it is likely that strong students will answer most of the time. If you nominate specific students to answer, weaker students can be given an opportunity to answer. However, only ask students if you think there is a reasonable chance they know the answer, otherwise they may lose confidence.
- **Correcting mistakes:** Think carefully about *what* and *when* you correct, as this should be different according to the students' level. If you heavily and frequently correct weaker students, they may feel embarrassed, lose confidence and not contribute again in the future. However, if you don't correct stronger students, you are not giving them the best opportunity to develop their own language skills. When learning new language, for example, you might focus on correcting weaker students' understanding of the words' meaning and form, whereas for stronger students, you might also focus on pronunciation and intonation.
- **Giving feedback:** When giving feedback to weaker students, you should be clear and direct. It is important that they have the correct answer, and understand why it is correct. With stronger students, you can be more ambiguous – e.g. identify where there is a problem, but don't tell them explicitly why it is wrong. When giving feedback on a piece of writing, you can use a marking code (e.g. write *V* if they need to change the verb form, or *SP* for a spelling mistake) so they can correct it by themselves, or in pairs. Doing this will also free up some of your time that you can allocate to helping weaker students.
- **Giving instructions:** Your instructions should be clear for all students, and you should always check with the class before doing an activity that they have understood what they have to do. This is especially important with large classes. If you check instructions with weaker students, and they understand what they have to do, it is likely that the rest of the class also will. When the activity begins, you should initially monitor weaker groups to double-check they know what to do.

- **Setting tasks:** One option for differentiating learning in large, mixed-ability classes is to create and use different sets of materials. However, this is not only a very time-consuming process, you also need the equipment to do this. In challenging circumstances, therefore, this is not really a viable option. Instead, you can create a range of tasks using the same materials which steadily become more challenging. The activity can have 'must', 'should' and 'could' components. This staged approach means that 'every student can leave the room feeling that they have been challenged and that they have achieved something' (Jim Rose). Here is an example of a writing task which uses such an approach.

> You **must** write a short description of an interesting local geographical feature (e.g. river, mountain, valley, desert).
>
> You **should** swap your description with a partner, and give / receive feedback.
>
> You **could** rewrite your description based on this feedback.

Similarly, there may be ways of adapting the task within the class for students who are at different levels. One straightforward way to do this is to give students' different time limits for activities. For example, using the same reading text you could give students different options about what they do. They can either: (a) read the text for two minutes and then rewrite it from memory (in eight minutes) – individually or in pairs; or (b) read the text and answer the comprehension questions (in ten minutes).

Another option is to either advise weaker students how they should do the task, and let stronger students decide for themselves.

Speaking / writing activities

Weaker students	Stronger students
• Students should use as many L2 words as they can, but can use L1 when necessary. • The task is more structured or better supported (e.g. step-by-step guidance is provided, or a list of key words or phrases is provided).	• Students are only allowed to use L2. • The task is free, or less scaffolded, so students need to use language at their own disposal.

Reading / listening activities

Weaker students	Stronger students
• Students use dictionaries whenever they want. • Students answer questions together in pairs or small groups. • Students read / listen to a text in shorter segments (e.g. in short paragraphs or audio clips).	• Students are not allowed to use dictionaries at all. • Students answer questions individually. • Students must read / listen to whole text without pause.

Forming groups in mixed-ability classes

When creating groups, consider these questions: 1. What size of group do you want? 2. Will the groups contain similar or different levels? An important general factor is that you should vary the ways in which students work together.

1   What size of group do you want?

As discussed in ▶ **Chapter 4**, there are many advantages to doing group work in your class. Although working in pairs maximizes how much time students are given to speak, when teaching in challenging circumstances it may be better to have a minimum of three in a group. This is because some students may be less confident or have weaker language ability, meaning that they don't say anything. If working in a pair, neither student gets any practice. If working in a three, this student can at least listen to the other two students speaking, and all students benefit. There is also a practical benefit to this in a large class, as larger groups means fewer groups, which is easier to monitor. Also, when there are three or four students in a group, they may self-monitor.

Note

The more you know about your students (e.g. their level, their strengths and weakness), the better you can divide them into groups.

2   Will the groups contain similar or different levels?

Groups consisting of students of similar abilities are known as ▶ **homogeneous** whilst groups with students of different abilities are ▶ **heterogeneous**. In heterogeneous groups, stronger students may be able to help the weaker ones, and thus develop leadership skills and ▶ **autonomy**. However, there is also a chance that they will get bored and/or frustrated. Whilst homogeneous groups can develop students' confidence and focus, it is not a natural learning situation. Be careful not to overuse homogeneous groups, or always have the same students in these groups, as weaker groups may feel they are not making any progress. They may feel that their level is fixed.

The table below identifies particular situations where there is a clear advantage to using either a homogeneous or heterogeneous group.

Advantages of homogeneous groups	Advantages of heterogeneous groups
Securing new language: students can work at the appropriate speed, through restricted practice, to fully acquire new words, grammatical structures, etc.; *Reading / listening comprehensions*: otherwise stronger students in a group may dominate and answer all the questions.	*Brainstorming / mind mapping*: encourages rich, diverse content; *General 'open' discussion*: weaker students can notice how stronger students perform the task; *Speaking sub-skills*: students have to use skills like asking for clarification, paraphrasing, or accommodating.

In some longer activities (across the entire, or at least a large part, of a lesson), it is a good strategy to mix groups. Students might start in homogeneous groups (in order to develop their confidence and establish a knowledge base) before they work in groups which are more heterogeneous. A good way of doing this is the 'snowball' approach, in which the initial number of groups must be a multiple of two (4, 8, 16, etc.), and the size of the groups doubles each time.

Imagine you have a class of 45 students, and you have asked them to do a spoken ranking activity, for example: *Rank these foods from 1–6 (favourite to least favourite).*

1 sixteen groups (3 of 2 students, and 13 of 3 students); then

2 eight groups (3 of 5 students, and 5 of 6 students); then

3 four groups (3 of 11 students, and 1 of 12 students); then

4 two groups (1 of 22 students, and 1 of 23 students).

The initial sixteen groups should be as homogeneous as possible. Each time the groups are enlarged, they become more heterogeneous. During each new discussion, the students share what they talked about in their previous group. They must then agree on an order which all the group is happy with. Depending on your situation, it may become difficult to do as groups grow larger – in which case, just stop when it is too difficult to manage, and take feedback from the remaining groups.

Another quick and easy way to reorder groups is to give each student a number (e.g. 1, 2, 3, 4, 5, 6).
- Begin by saying: *Form groups with six people in. Each person should be a different number.*
- For the next stage, give the instruction: *All 1s over here, all 2s there, all 3s over there…, etc.*
- If you want to create heterogeneous pairs for the follow-up, say: *Work in pairs. Together you must add up to 7.* (In other words, student 1 can pair up with 6, student 2 with 5, student 3 with 4.)

This process allows students to benefit from working with a wide range of students, and to share and compare their different ideas.

What if none of this works?

In some situations, you might find that the gap between students within a class is so wide that it is impossible to teach them as a single group. In such cases, you might need a more radical option. Otherwise, the stronger students will get bored, and the weaker students will still find it difficult to make progress.

You might also find that some of your colleagues are facing the same situation in their classes. If this is the case, one potential solution is to organize classes by ability rather than age. Throughout the world, most schools arrange classes by age: e.g. primary class 4 contains 8–9 year olds, class 5 contains 9–10 year olds and class 6 contains 10–11 year olds. An alternative is to group students by ability, regardless of their age.

Making this change may be controversial. Therefore, if you did decide to do this, it would need to be clearly communicated to all stakeholders. You could experiment with this system at first – e.g. for 1–2 sessions / days a week – to see if it works in your context. One aspect which might complicate this (at some levels) is whether students have to do government exams at a certain grade (e.g. end of primary).

Reflection
- Do you need to make changes to the way you teach in order to help students of different abilities?
- Which of the strategies described in this chapter do you think would work well in your situation?
- Do you like the idea of dividing students by ability rather than age? Why / why not? Would it work in your school?

11   Managing mixed-age classes

In mixed-age classrooms, children are more likely to cooperate than compete … They generate a family of learners who support and care for one another.

Vine Academy

The short version

1   Mixed-age classes are common, but they can be particularly challenging when teachers don't have specific training or support in how to manage such classes.

2   Within a single class, you can have students at very different stages of their emotional, mental and physical development – this has a massive impact on how they are in the classroom.

3   There are practical classroom implications for students who have already covered material in previous years.

4   Be sensitive in giving homework since older students may have significant home or work duties to perform.

5   Present mixed-age classrooms to all your students as an opportunity to be celebrated, rather than a problem to be minimized.

Introduction

1   What is the age range in your class?

2   How do the different ages of the students influence the way you teach?

3   What issues do the students face (both younger and older) because of their age differences?

Why do some classes have such a wide range of ages?

Sometimes, creating mixed-age classes is a deliberate pedagogical strategy. In such cases, teachers are usually given specific training and are well supported by school management. In challenging circumstances, however, there may be no such training, no such support, and no pedagogical reason for having a wide range of ages in a class. Three common reasons why classes may have such a wide range of ages are: 1. There are not enough teachers for each grade level, so classes have to be combined. 2. Students may have missed a lot of schooling (e.g. for economic reasons or due to migration) and come to schooling late. 3. Students fail exams and have to repeat school years. Your institution may also have taken a deliberate decision to arrange classes by ability rather than age (see ▶ Chapter 10).

When the age range is not that wide (e.g. 1–2 years), there may be little noticeable difference between students. However, when the age range is wider, the children may be at very different stages of development. There are huge differences between a 10- and 16-year-old, whereas the difference between a 20- and a 26-year-old is not that significant. Whilst having students of a wide range of ages can have many benefits, it also presents a number of challenges.

11.1   Attitudes towards mixed-age classrooms

Challenge: In challenging circumstances, the symbolic value of the school is often very important. It can represent hope and opportunity. Therefore, educational stakeholders want their institution to appear 'proper' and look and feel like a 'good school'. There is a strong perception that a 'good school' has classes in which the students are approximately the same age. When this is not the case, educational stakeholders may develop a more negative attitude towards the institution.

Solution: Firstly, this is not true. In many 'high-quality' education systems around the world, such as Australia, Finland and New Zealand, mixed-age classrooms are common. It can be helpful to talk to educational stakeholders about the advantages of mixed-age classrooms. For example, this kind of classroom resembles a family, and so can feel more normal for many students. This is especially valuable if they do not have a lot of experience of education, and it can make schooling feel more natural. A mixed-age class also resembles the majority of workplaces, and so prepare students for the world of work.

11.2   Choosing appropriate topics

Challenge: The interests of a 10- and 16-year-old are likely to be very different. As such, older students may not be interested in the contents of the textbook, or it may be difficult for you to create materials and resources which interest the whole class.

Solution: When doing speaking activities, try to focus on topics which students may have in common – discover what this is by asking them and having them vote on topics. Doing this is an interesting and valuable activity in itself.

11.3   Different life experiences

Challenge: Older students may have life experiences, or opinions, which are not appropriate for younger students.

Solution: Talk to older students about this situation, and ask them to think about managing or editing some of the things which they might say to each other.

11.4   Repetition of material

Challenge: This is a practical concern: if older students are repeating a year, they may have already done (and can remember) some of the same material. If they have the textbooks, they may have already completed some of the activities.

Solution: Talk to older students, and explain how they should take responsibility to be a teacher / mentor for the younger students. They should also realize that they are repeating these materials because they did not learn them well enough before.

11.5   Losing face

Challenge: Older students don't want to risk ▶ **losing face** with younger classmates. For this reason, older students may be more risk-averse, and not push themselves as much. The best language learning, however, occurs when students are slightly out of their ▶ **comfort zone**.

Solution: When making groups, whether homogeneous or heterogeneous (see ▶ **Chapter 10**), try to ensure that older students are in the same group, and can work with each other. This is especially important if the group size is small. Another option is to give them specific roles within the group, for example being the 'group captain' (see ▶ 4.1), and responsible for getting the others to reach a consensus.

Note
A more difficult situation may be when there are a small number of older students in the class, or when the students are much older. In such cases, you could make them unofficial teaching assistants, and give them specific roles in class to help you.

11.6   *Different rates of physical and sexual development*
Challenge: In addition to significant differences in cognitive development, mixed-age students will be at very different stages in terms of their physical and sexual development. This may mean that it is difficult for some students to sit near each other or work together. Additionally, there may be considerable parental / community concern if, for example, older boys are interacting on a regular basis with younger girls.
Solution: Think carefully about group organization and dynamics, and also seating arrangements (see ▶ Chapters 9–10). Also, be understanding of the different sanitary / bathroom requirements of some students (e.g. girls who already menstruate) and also how bodily changes, like hormones, can affect certain students, especially teenagers, in the classroom.

11.7   *Homework conflicts with other duties*
Challenge: Older students are likely to have more significant, or more stressful, responsibilities outside of school. This might include looking after younger siblings or other members of their family, doing housework, or working for income.
Solution: Think carefully about what homework you set: it should not be too time-consuming. It should not be directly tied into the next lesson – that is, if a student is unable to do the homework, they should not be disadvantaged in participating.

Reflection
• What changes do you think you could / should make for the classes you are teaching where there is a wide range of different ages?
• What conversations could / should you have with students and parents about how to see the mixed-age classroom as an opportunity? How could you minimize any concerns which they have?

12   Learning outside the classroom

A tremendous imbalance of power exists in the classroom … The instructor has freedom of space, the students do not.

Robert Sommer

The short version

1   The space outside a classroom can be just as good for learning as inside a classroom (if not better!)
2   Some outdoor language learning activities are based on existing games known by the students (e.g. tag, running), making students feel they are playing rather than learning.
3   An empty classroom is a room full of possibilities.
4   One of the main advantages of removing classroom furniture is that the process of learning language is closer to real life.
5   If you decide to go 'furniture free' in your classroom, you need an implementation / transition plan, and to involve as many people in the decision as possible.

Introduction

1   Does your existing classroom furniture (desks, benches, chairs, etc.) help or prevent learning? Why?

2   How much do you use outdoor space for learning? Why / why not?

3   Look at the list of language learning activities below, all of which can be done outside. What do you think happens in each?

> Running dictation   Vocabulary tag   Conversation basket   Reading in interesting places
> Treasure hunt   I spy   Total Physical Response

Taking the learning outside

In ▶ **Chapter 9** we discussed ways in which you can manage a fixed-desk classroom. We looked at different ways in which this situation could maximize language learning opportunities. One additional option is to forget about the classroom and take the learning outside. This is not something you have to do all the time. However, if you do it on a regular, periodic basis, it can be fun, interesting and motivating both for students and for yourself.

Part VI of this book looks more widely at language learning opportunities when not using textbooks – in your local community and beyond. The focus of the current chapter is on activities which you could do within the school grounds, but away from your classroom (e.g. in the playground, or sports area if there is one). Please note that the space required does *not* need to be large. Whilst some of these activities could be done inside the classroom, they are much more effective in an outdoor space.

Taking learning outside can also have important health benefits. This is especially important if your classroom is badly lit, poorly ventilated and too small for the number of students. Students cannot be properly mentally focused on learning if they are physically uncomfortable.

ACTIVITY: Running dictation

1   Put a short text on a wall in the playground (or place it on the ground). If you have a larger class, the activity works better if you can make three or four copies, and space them about a metre apart.

2   Divide the class into groups (a maximum of ten groups). They should be standing about ten metres from the texts, and be widely spaced out.

3   In each group, one participant is the 'runner' (or you can have two runners per group if your class is very large). Runners should sprint to the texts, remember as much as they can, and then run back to their group. They dictate what they can remember. The 'writers' write it in their notebooks, and ask for clarification and repetition as necessary.

4   The runner then goes again, remembers more text, and returns. This process is repeated until the text is complete.

5   The winning team is the one which writes down all the text first. Finally, the runner should bring the text to their group. They then check to see how accurate the dictation was.

Note

The activity should be quick – around 5 minutes. You can repeat this activity multiple times with the same groups, but using different texts. The short texts could all form a longer story. The runner should change each time.

ACTIVITY: Vocabulary tag

1   Tell the students to think of words in a particular category (e.g. animals, colours, jobs, adjectives). Allow 5–10 seconds for this.

2   Tag about 20–25% of the students (so in a class of forty, tag eight to ten students). These students now try to chase and tag their classmates when they catch them. Unlike normal 'tag', when a student is about to be tagged, they can go down on one knee and say a word in the category. If the word is correct, they cannot be tagged. If they cannot think of a word, or it is incorrect, they are tagged. You may need to be the referee if there is disagreement about whether a word is acceptable.

3   When a student gets tagged again, they cannot repeat a word they have already said. They must always say a new word.

4   After a few minutes, change the category and continue the game. You can also change the 'taggers', so that students play different roles.

Variations

If you have a large class, play simultaneous games of tag at the same time in the same space (e.g. if you have 105 students, play three games with 35 students in each – each game would have eight or nine taggers).

An alternative version of this game is that when a student gets tagged and cannot say a word, they also become a 'tagger'. The last student not to be tagged is the winner. This is a quicker version of the game.

You can also play this game at higher levels, with more complex language and grammar (e.g. intransitive verbs, adjective + noun combinations, sentences in the past simple).

ACTIVITY: Conversation basket

1 Tell the students to think of interesting topics for conversations. They write these ideas on small bits of paper, and put them into a basket.
2 Students sit in groups of around six. Each group picks out a topic, and discusses it. You should circulate between groups, and help or advise as necessary.
3 After a few minutes, groups take out a different topic, and have another conversation. This can be repeated several times.

Note

It may be useful to appoint a group captain for each discussion. Their role is to ensure that all students get a chance to speak, and that they are focused on the topic.

ACTIVITY: Reading in interesting places

1 Tell the students to take a book or piece of text they want to read. They should find an interesting (but safe) place to read (e.g. in a tree, under a bush, in some grass).
2 You should walk around and monitor students' reading, and be a resource as necessary.

Variations

If your students have smartphones (or similar devices), they can take selfies where they are reading (or ask a friend to take the photo). There could be a class competition for who has found the most interesting place to read. You can also do the activity with writing instead of reading.

ACTIVITY: Treasure hunt

1 Divide the class into groups of four or five students. Give each group a list of items to find (which are available nearby) – e.g. pen, pencil, twig, leaf, bottle. This is a good way of practising general vocabulary items.
2 First team to find all the items wins.

ACTIVITY: I spy

1 Do an example with the whole class. Say: *I spy with my little eye something beginning with… P.* The students then guess objects they can see which begin this letter – e.g. *pen, paper, pencil.* The actual answer should be a word which they know but may be unfamiliar (e.g. *page, paint* or *parent*). You can give them clues to get to the correct answer.
2 Divide students into groups of three, where they play this game.

Variations

'I spy' can be made more challenging for higher levels. Examples include:

- I spy … something ending with *e / s / t*
- I spy … something rhyming with *hen / ball / plate*
- I spy … something containing a ▶ **schwa** sound

ACTIVITY: Total Physical Response (TPR)

1   Say a verb and do the action at the same time. They can either do the activity 'on the spot' (i.e. where they are) or use the whole open space. Choose fun, interesting, active verbs such as *walk, stretch, run, jump* and *clap*. It's important that students say the word at the same time as they are doing the action. This will help them learn the word, by linking it to the action.

2   Once students understand the game, they can work together in groups of five or six. They take it in turns to be the leader, and give instructions to the other students.

Note

Not only is ▶ **Total Physical Response** good for language learning, it is good for physical fitness.

Variations

Make the activity more complex by telling students that they should only do what you say if you begin the instruction with *Simon says…* (or a more locally appropriate name). This helps them develop their listening accuracy. e.g. *Simon says clap your hands.* → All students should clap their hands and say the sentence. *Clap your hands.* → Students should remain still and say nothing.

Creating space indoors

A more radical idea is that if you do have a fixed-desk classroom, you remove all the furniture. As discussed in ▶ **Chapter 9,** a classroom without desks and benches can be seen as an opportunity rather than a problem. The empty space of a classroom can encourage more interesting, creative and learner-focused lessons.

Advantages of removing the fixed desks

- The emphasis changes from 'schooling' to 'learning'. The learning becomes more focused on the end user (the learner) rather than the facilitator (the teacher). Education should be about what the students can do and know, rather than on sitting nicely, listening to the teacher, behaving well, etc.
- Desks can atomize learning. The focus is on the individual, and education is seen as a competition. Using language, however, is a social activity, and almost always involves more than one person.
- There is a lot of room for students to move, which opens up many different possibilities for activities.
- It enables students to work with a much wider range of people. This mirrors how language is used in a real-life situation, and so is more authentic. This interaction is more like real life, and students will also develop their soft skills more effectively.

Disadvantages of removing the fixed desks

- Making such a big change can be disruptive to learning – especially since it is so unfamiliar for students.
- This kind of fundamental change could be seen as a challenge to the school management – taken to imply that what has been happening before was not good enough.
- Resources have already been spent on buying the furniture, and so people feel that they should be used.
- It needs all teachers and other staff to fully support the idea – teachers will need to change their methodological and pedagogical approach.
- For communities with little experience of education, having a school with classrooms that have furniture makes it feel like a proper school. This can have a powerful psychological impact.

If you decide you want to remove the classroom furniture, follow these steps. This will help to make the implementation and transition as easy as possible:

1 Involve other educational stakeholders in the decision. It's important to explain what impact this will have. In some cases, you may need to obtain permission (e.g. from the head teacher or colleagues).

2 Have a plan for what to do with the furniture which you remove – e.g. are you storing it, selling it, dumping it?

3 Put mats down on the floor for both comfort and so that students can keep their clothes clean.

4 Talk to your students about the change, as this will be different and new to them. Emphasize the benefits which it will have on their learning experiences.

5 Think about what seating plan would be most appropriate, considering the available space, the shape of the room, and the number of students you have. They can be laid out as a circle, a double circle, around three sides of a square, or as islands. (See ▶ **Chapter 9** for further details.)

Note

Removing classroom furniture is a big decision. As such, it could initially be done on a trial basis – e.g. for a month, or for a term, to see whether students and teachers like this arrangement. It does not have to be done in all classrooms at once, but just one or two as an experiment.

Reflection

- What outside space do you have where you teach? How and where could you do some of the activities listed?
- If you wanted to teach outside (or remove your fixed desks inside), who would you need to speak to, and include in the process?
- What impact do you think this would have on your students and your teaching situation?

Teaching language skills and systems

13 Teaching receptive skills

There's a lot of difference between listening and hearing.

GK Chesterton

The short version

1 Make reading and listening texts as interesting as possible for students – they will be more motivated to learn.

2 Focusing on high-frequency words is a quick and effective way to help students develop reading competency and confidence.

3 Listening lessons can be difficult due to the resources required and the classroom environment. However, there are ways of managing these challenges.

4 You should do reading and listening tasks which help students develop skills and strategies. Be explicit about what skills and strategies you are aiming to develop.

5 Create opportunities for students to do extensive reading and listening, both inside and outside of your institution.

Introduction

1 What challenges do your students face in developing their reading and listening skills? What do you do to try and overcome these challenges?

2 The following words about teaching / learning reading and listening are used in this chapter. What do you think they mean? (They are all explained in the ▶ **Glossary**.)

> script   sound–letter correspondence   corpus   ambient noise   metalanguage   mind map

Teaching reading and listening

In challenging circumstances, teachers often don't have a choice about what written or audio texts they have to teach, especially if they work in formal education. Many of the challenges and suggestions in this chapter recognize this limitation (see ▶ **Part VI** for further information). If students are bored by the texts you have to teach, it's crucial that you adapt your pedagogical approach so that they do find it interesting. If you don't adapt, students will be confused and demotivated, and their ▶ **receptive skills** will not improve.

If you do have flexibility in which texts you can use, ask your students what interests them and find or create texts accordingly. If you involve them in the process, they will be more focused. If it's difficult to do this in L2, ask students to bring in L1 texts they enjoy. You can work with them to translate these texts into English. They will be motivated to do this because they already like the content, and this activity also creates written texts in English which you could potentially use with other students.

13.1 Lack of books

Challenge: In challenging circumstances, many of the students may not have books. Managing this issue is crucial, otherwise many students will be unable to fully participate in the lesson.

Solutions:

1 Divide the class into groups, and ensure that each group has a book.

2 Read the text aloud to the whole class so that everybody can hear. Ask lots of checking questions so that they have more opportunity to remember the information.

3 If you read the text aloud, get students to also act the story. If a group of students does this at the front of the class, this will help students understand what is happening. It is also fun. Encourage students to use different voices, actions, props, etc. to make it as authentic as possible.

4 Get students to copy out the text for homework so that there are more copies.

13.2 Poor reading skills

Challenge: There is often a significant gap between students' reading level, and the level of the reading and listening texts which you have to use. As discussed in more detail in ▶ Chapter 20, textbooks often do not reflect the daily reality of being a teacher in challenging circumstances. As a result, you may feel as if you are always 'swimming against the tide' when trying to teach your students to read in English.

Solutions:

1 Where possible, build on the students' reading skills in L1. Many core reading skills, such as focusing on key words, or predicting the meaning of unfamiliar words, are similar in different languages. However, when students haven't already secured L1 reading skills, it can be very difficult to develop the same skills in L2. This problem can be particularly acute when students learn English from a young age. With regards to reading in English, particular areas which they may find difficult include when:
   • L1 uses a different alphabet from English (e.g. Malayalam, Thai, Chinese);
   • the script is read in a different direction (e.g. Arabic, Farsi, Urdu);
   • L1 has sound–letter correspondence, i.e. a letter or a group of letters is always pronounced the same way (e.g. Spanish, Swahili, Mongolian), whilst in English this relationship between sounds and letters is not as straightforward.

2 To help build students' reading confidence and ability to get through a text, focus on teaching them how to read common, high-frequency words. The Oxford English Corpus estimates that one-third of all written English is composed of the 25 most common words, and that half of written English is composed of the top 100.

The top 100 words of written English: *the, of, and, a, to, in, is, you, that, it, was, he, for, on, are, as, with, his, they, I, at, be, this, have, from, or, one, had, by, word, but, not, what, all, were, we, when, your, can, said, there, use, an, each, which, she, do, how, their, if, will, up, other, about, out, many, then, them, these, so, some, her, would, make, like, him, into, time, has, look, two, more, write, go, see, number, no, way, could, people, my, than, first, water, been, call, who, oil, its, now, find, long, down, day, did, get, come, made, may, part.*

As learners become more familiar with the different sounds of English, they will be able to guess how to read new words. For example, when they know *cat*, they can predict *bat, hat, mat, sat*, etc. In addition to teaching the top 100 words, the majority of which are structure words, you should also focus on high-frequency nouns – especially concrete nouns which are easy to visualize (e.g. *house, book, car, tree*). It can also be very effective to focus on cognate words, i.e. words which are similar in the students' L1 and English, e.g. *television* and *televisión* (Spanish), *fridge* and *friji* (Kiswahili), *bicycle* and *bisiklet* (Turkish). ▶ **Flashcards** can be a very effective way to teach these, especially if they contain both words and pictures. If you don't have any, you can make your own – or get your class to make some.

13.3 *Difficulties in teaching listening*

Challenge: It's crucial that students do listening activities so that they are exposed to spoken English. This is especially important if the language classroom is the only place where they have this opportunity. In challenging circumstances, however, teachers often avoid doing listening for a range of reasons, including:

- the audio tape or CD, or the equipment is damaged, missing or being used by another teacher;
- students complain that they can't hear the audio clearly, e.g. because of the large size of the class or room, or ▶ ambient noise;
- the audio is too long, and students can't follow what is happening;
- students complain that they don't understand the accents (having had no exposure to them before).

Solutions:

1 When planning a listening lesson, think about what preparation (Plan A, Plan B, Plan C etc.) is required in order to make the lesson a success. For example, ensuring you have the audio transcript in case it is needed (see ▶ Chapter 5).

2 In large classrooms and/or where there is ambient noise, it might simply be impossible for all students to hear the audio properly. If you try and do the listening comprehension in these conditions, students are likely to complain and there may be disruption. It is also unfair on those students who sit further away. One solution is to stand in the middle of the room and read the text out in a loud voice. Another is to record the audio on your phone (either direct from the tape or CD, or using your own voice), which gives you two 'audio centres' which you can play simultaneously.

3 Break the audio into smaller chunks. You could first play for thirty seconds and then ask two questions, then play for another thirty seconds and ask two more questions. This 'in and out' approach can usually help students follow better.

4 It's important that students are exposed to different accents, so that when they talk to other speakers of English, they have a better chance of understanding them. You can support and scaffold your students' understanding by first reading out the text yourself, and then playing the audio. Alternatively, you could even let them read the transcript before (or while) listening. This will familiarize them with the content, so they have a 'way in' when they listen to the unfamiliar accent.

13.4 Lack of receptive skills and strategies

Challenge: Teachers often do not explain to students the reading and listening sub-skills which they are developing. As such, they may be unaware of the progress they are making – or which they need to make.

Solution: Be explicit when a particular activity is developing a particular skill. You should not be afraid to use ▶ **metalanguage** when doing this, but make sure that students understand what you are saying (or use L1 if appropriate). Some of the specific sub-skills which you might focus on in the lesson (and which you can share with your students) include:

Reading-specific	Common to reading and listening	Listening-specific
• scanning to find key words • reading for detail • reading for main ideas • identifying text purpose • identifying text audience • working out meaning from context	• making predictions (e.g. based on visuals, title) • activating prior knowledge • making inferences • summarizing • paraphrasing	• listening for main ideas • listening for details • identifying opinion • identifying reasons • identifying signposts

13.5 Formulaic approaches to teaching reading and listening

Challenge: Reading aloud (▶ 13.6) is the default reading strategy used by many teachers, partly because it's a way controlling large (and possibly noisy) classes. However, reading aloud can't really be considered a reading 'skill' since apart from parents reading to their children, or newsreaders, people rarely do this in real life. It's important to use a range of techniques and activities to keep the learning interesting for students. Developing reading and listening skills is much more effective when students have a clear focus.

Solution: Give students specific tasks to do before, while and after the reading. Many of these tasks develop the sub-skills described in ▶ 13.4. Pre-reading / Pre-listening tasks get students ready. While-reading / While-listening tasks help students understand and extract information. After-reading / After-listening tasks show what they have understood, and develop this understanding further. Examples of tasks which you can use, and the positive impact they can have, are outlined below:

Pre-reading / Pre-listening tasks:
- Explain the meaning of key words. ➜ Students can read / listen more fluently.
- Elicit from students what they already know about the topic. ➜ Students are motivated and empowered, and are better able to understand the text. ▶ **Mind maps** can be very useful for this purpose.
- Get students to predict what will happen, based on the title or a picture. ➜ Students think more about the text, and are motivated to discover if they are right.
- Ask students to skim read the whole text very quickly, and share (in pairs / groups / whole class) what they can remember. ➜ Students focus on the main ideas, and every learner has a better opportunity to understand the content.

While-reading / While-listening tasks
- Get students to check their predictions to see if they were correct. ➜ Students are active, and learning from their mistakes.
- Ask students to extract information from the text, e.g. by filling in gaps or putting pictures in order. ➜ When students 'transform' information in this way, they have to understand it at a deeper level.
- Ask students to make notes. ➜ Students can make notes about specific things which you ask them to identify, or they can write down information they think is useful. They can also identify things which they don't understand or are confused by, in order to get clarification later on.

After-reading / After-listening tasks
- Ask your own questions (or get students to write their own). ➜ You (or they) can personalize the learning.
- Ask students to say what they think happens next (i.e. after the end of the story) and why. ➜ Students show whether they have understood the text, and it also gets them to use their imagination.
- Get students to say / write a short summary of the story. ➜ Students have to identify and recall key information.
- Get students to draw pictures based on the text. ➜ Students enjoy this activity, and it is also a good way of evaluating whether they have understood the main points.
- Get students to create a role play, where they play characters from the story. ➜ Students engage with the text, and mix their own ideas with what they have read.
- Ask students to say whether they liked the story, and to give their reasons. If they didn't, how would they have written it differently? ➜ Students are empowered, and must give a personal reaction to what they have read.

Note
These suggestions may be very different from how you have taught reading and listening before. Therefore, it might take some time for you and your students to become familiar with these methods. Make sure that you give clear instructions for each task. It's important to not worry if it doesn't go well. Try to understand why it didn't go well – so that you can do it better next time.

13.6 Reading aloud individually

Challenge: Although a common strategy in many classrooms, getting students to read aloud individually is a poor strategy in general for developing reading skills. This is because:

- it only gives speaking practice to one student at a time, and so is not an efficient use of limited classroom time;
- often, the learners asked to read aloud are already good readers;
- some learners may feel stressed if asked to read in public;
- often it's difficult or impossible to hear people's voices;
- it can be very boring! This is especially true when students don't have a deep understanding of the text. If they are just 'saying the words' rather than 'reading the text', none of the rhythms of the language will be there (e.g. emphasis, pauses, intonation).

Solution: Students can read aloud to each other in small groups, with people taking turns to read. In large classes, these groups can be heterogeneous, so that stronger readers can help the weaker ones. You can also encourage students to use Michael West's 'Read and Look Up' technique:

> *You read a little silently and then look up and say it to someone. Gradually you are able to take in larger and larger units, at first only a line, later two or three lines… as you become better, you paraphrase more and more, until eventually you are gathering the ideas from the book and expressing them in your own words.*

This slight change can make reading aloud a much more effective reading strategy. West continues as follows:

> *The pupil should be made to look up when they read aloud. The teacher says, 'Don't read to the book! Read to me. Look up at me.' He makes them read a phrase or short sentence silently then, looking up, say it to someone – to the teacher, or to another pupil, or to the class. In doing this the reader must look up during the speaking of the whole sentence; he must not just look up for a second and then look down again.*

Students therefore have to process the meaning of what they have just read, and then recall it meaningfully. Furthermore, because there is an audience, *meaningless reading* is transformed into *meaningful speaking*:

> *The pupil is speaking to someone – not to the book or the empty air; and the more realistic recall is, the more vivid and effective is the learning.*

13.7 Lack of extensive reading or listening

Challenge: Students can improve their receptive skills by reading and listening to L2 texts for pleasure, without any particular plan. This contrasts with the intensive reading or listening which is done in class, which usually has specific learning aims. However, often students don't do any extensive reading or listening outside class.

Solutions: Different strategies which you could implement for improving students' extensive reading include:

- **being a role model** for your students: Share with them what you are reading or listening to, or even put a poster up in the classroom which contains this information. You can encourage students to add to this list.
- creating a **reading record box**: Learners write their name and a book which they read, and put it in a box on your desk. You can read out these names in public, or else congratulate students in private, about the books they have read.
- creating (or helping students set up) a **reading group**: Students meet up on a regular basis (e.g. once a month), and the members talk about the same book, which they have all read during the previous month.
- checking that learners are actually able to borrow books from the **school library** – if you have one: Books are often locked away, and students have very limited access to them, which prevents extensive reading. If the school doesn't have a library, could you and your students establish one? Even a small handful of books can be a great starting point.
- create a **reading corner** in your classroom: This can be a specific space which students can go to and read without disturbance. If possible, put some books, pictures, cushions, chairs, etc. there to make it a more appealing and desirable space.
- talking to your **students' families** about this as they can support and motivate them: This is especially important if students are not learning for an extended period of time (e.g. holidays, closure). For example, students could be encouraged to read to parents, grandparents, young sisters and brothers – of even to any animals which the family own! It doesn't matter, so long as they are getting practice.

A Chinese teacher said this about the benefits of involving parents and the wider family in helping children develop reading skills:

> *Parents joined in the reading class. Chinese parents want their children to learn English. They push them a lot! I want them [to] stop pushing, but start conversation. Thus parents were invited to the class. They joined in the conversations. They continued the conversation at home. The more they know, the more they are relaxed. No more push, everyone is a learner!*

Sometimes these changes can take a long time, and it's important that families understand change cannot happen overnight, and that reading is a process, not just an outcome:

> *She [the grandmother] agreed to be patient. Understanding doesn't come from translation. It came from getting familiar with the language and understanding the contexts. It was slow, however, soon it became fast. Niu Niu understood the language, not by others do[ing] translation for him. His understanding came from himself.*

It may be more difficult for students to do extensive listening in L2. If students do have access to television, the radio, or the internet, the more input they can get (even if they only understand a small proportion of what is said) will be beneficial. Podcasts represent another huge opportunity for extensive listening, and are often accompanied by learning materials. Several organizations provide excellent English language specific podcasts, for example the BBC World Service (bbc.co.uk), the British Council (learningenglish.britishcouncil.org) and Voice of America (learningenglish.voanews. com). There are also useful websites offering podcasts, like podcastsinenglish.com or eslpod.com. Online video-sharing platforms can also be very useful because of their huge range of videos, and also because it's often possible to watch videos with subtitles.

Reflection
- What changes to the way you teach reading and listening could and should you make? What challenges would you face in trying to make these changes?
- How can you make your class more interested in extensive reading and listening?

14 Teaching productive skills

Language is a thing which is learnt by practice.

Michael West

The short version

1 Students often find writing boring and difficult. It's the teacher's job to try and make it more interesting and less frightening.

2 Flexibility, positivity and collaboration can help build students' confidence in both speaking and writing.

3 Before they can do meaningful production, students may require support in developing basic L2 orthographic skills and understanding the structure of the language.

4 Stories (particular folk tales) are an effective way of engaging students and encouraging them to speak and write in L2.

5 Task repetition, and focusing on quantity rather than quality, can help students become more confident L2 users.

Introduction

1 How do your students feel about speaking and writing? Do they enjoy it? Why / why not?

2 What are the main barriers to your students being able to develop speaking and writing skills?

Teaching speaking and writing

Students may have good grammar, a wide vocabulary, and strong ▶ receptive skills in the L2. The main goal of language learning, however, is to be able to say and write what they want to. In challenging circumstances, there are many factors which may obstruct or prevent students from being able to do this. This chapter looks at some of these issues, and provides a range of solutions and activities to address the situation.

In a blog post, Jack C. Richards identifies two particular challenges related to speaking and writing: '1. While learners' receptive competence continues to develop, their productive competence remains relatively static. 2. Language items that learners recognize and understand in the input they hear do not pass into their productive competence.'

When teaching ▶ productive skills, there may be a gap between what you want to teach and what you are able to teach, in terms of textbook or curriculum content (see ▶ Chapter 1). Even if you recognize that it's vital that your students can speak and write in the L2, many factors may prevent you from doing this: e.g. class size, seating plan, a grammar-based ▶ syllabus, the fear of creating too much noise, the amount of time it takes, and the fact that productive skills are often sidelined in exams. This is nothing new. In 1956, Peter Strevens wrote (in a book for teachers in Africa), that 'One of the commonest complaints about language teaching in schools today is that nearly all the language is that of the teacher and hardly any is spoken by the children.' More than six decades later, in many language learning situations, nothing has changed. By applying some of the suggestions below, however, it may be possible to make a ▶ step change in terms of productive skills.

14.1 Feeling bored about writing

Challenge: When students are asked to write about topics they have no interest in, or little knowledge about, it's not surprising they find it boring. Furthermore, some of the classroom techniques traditionally used to teach writing, e.g. copying and dictation, are demotivating. As students are frequently asked to do writing as homework, it becomes a very solitary activity where they get little support or formative feedback.

Solution: Where possible, get students to write about things which they are interested in. Or, if it's a piece of writing from the textbook, ensure that they have enough background information / knowledge to complete the task. One way to do this is to create a mind map with the whole class on the board before they start the writing. Writing to somebody also makes the process more interesting and motivating, as there is an audience. Students writing to each other (e.g. short questions and answers) is one way of doing this.

Four other activities which could make teaching and learning writing more interesting are suggested below. All these activities use minimal resources, and also integrate other skills.

ACTIVITY: Running dictation

See ▶ 12.1 for more details on this fantastic, energetic activity which focuses on writing, but uses all four skills. The activity works well either outdoors or indoors.

ACTIVITY: Dictogloss

1   Give students a topic to discuss in groups. The purpose of doing this is to brainstorm relevant ideas and words.
2   The teacher then reads out a short (below 100 words in length) pre-prepared text on this topic (from a book, newspaper, the internet, or written by themselves). Reading should be done at a natural pace, without pauses.
3   In groups, the students try to reconstruct the text together as accurately as they can.
4   If several groups are finding reconstructing the text too difficult, read the text again (possibly at a faster speed).

Note

Dictogloss uses some of the principles of dictation (and so it will be familiar for students and teachers alike), but it is much more active and interesting. It requires a deeper degree of processing because learners have to reconstruct a complete text, not just isolated words or sentences. This requires them to use their overall L2 knowledge, not just their short-term memory. The collaborative nature of the activity also provides opportunities for students to 'teach each other'.

ACTIVITY: Simultaneous translation

1 The teacher reads out a text in the students' L1. The students just listen.
2 The teacher reads out the text again, sentence-by-sentence. In groups of four or five, students write down their translation of the text. Allow the students time to discuss this.
3 The teacher reads the text out a final time. Groups check their translations, and make any necessary changes.
4 Ask different groups to share their translations. Groups can feed back to each other, and compare to their own versions.

Note

There is no 'correct' answer to this, as translations can be interpreted in different ways.

ACTIVITY: Double translation

1 Write a short text on the board in the L2, or provide on paper if possible.
2 Working in groups, students must translate the L2 text into L1.
3 Remove the L2 text (or hide it). Students now have to reconstruct the original L2 text using their translation.
4 When finished, students compare their translation to the original text.

14.2   Lack of confidence in communication

Challenge: Two related reasons for students lacking confidence when speaking or writing is: (a) students' lack of opportunity to use L2 inside the classroom; (b) students' lack of opportunity to use L2 outside the classroom. This is true for both speaking and writing in English. Teachers often feel negative or pessimistic about their students' ability to produce language, feeling that their level is so low that there is no point even doing these activities. In many challenging circumstances, therefore, a negative cycle exists: teachers believe that their students cannot speak / write the L2 ➔ so they don't do any speaking / writing tasks ➔ which means the students can never improve their L2 speaking or writing. Instead, teachers tend to focus on receptive skills, or vocabulary and grammar activities, since these are easier to manage.

Solution: Teachers must break this negative cycle. Just as every human makes mistakes when developing their L1, unless your students practise (and make mistakes with) their L2, they will never improve. Suggestions about how you can do this include:

• **creating a positive, friendly atmosphere:** Many students may be worried about ▶ **losing face** when producing L2, or may feel overwhelmed, nervous, shy or scared when asked to speak. Given this, it's crucial that you create an atmosphere in which mistakes are tolerated, and accepted as a normal part of the language learning process. When students speak, think carefully about error correction. With inexperienced or nervous learners, focus on communication rather than accuracy.

- **making productive tasks flexible:** When setting the level of a task, try to make it slightly beyond their current level. For the reasons described above, students may be risk-averse, and prefer to stay in their comfort zone. This will not help them develop L2 competence. In this way they will be stretching themselves, but only within limits. Be prepared to change the task if needed, for example if it becomes clear that it's too difficult – e.g. you could allow them to do it first in L1, or in a mixture of L1 and L2. And if students are finding it too easy, give them an additional task to do which practises the same language but in a more complex way (e.g. make up a story using the target language, or create a role play).

- **not being afraid of silence or 'thinking time':** Busy teachers needing to 'get through the textbook' often feel pressure to move on quickly, and hurry students. But when speaking, students need time to think of what they want to say. Speaking with others can be a very difficult thing. Silence is actually the sound of thinking. Similarly with writing, asking students to write in a foreign language about a difficult topic can be very scary. It is linguistically and conceptually difficult. Allow students time to think about what they want to write. If you force them to jump straight in, the quality is likely to be poor.

- **emphasizing that students should not worry about their pronunciation or accent:** One reason why students are reluctant to speak is that they think their pronunciation / accent is 'bad', and they are embarrassed by it. In your classroom, try to create an atmosphere where the emphasis is on comprehensibility – i.e. that students can understand each other, rather than that they sound British or American. Remind students that the majority of English interactions is between L2 speakers (in which case a British or American accent might actually be a disadvantage)! Nevertheless, helping students differentiate the sounds of English can be very useful. Using ▶ **minimal pairs** is one way to do this (e.g. *bit* vs *pit*, *ship* vs *sheep*). Telling students what part of their tongue and mouth should be used for certain sounds is also useful (e.g. to make *v*, bite your bottom lip with your top teeth). You can also give them tips about how to form (and practise) sounds which are particularly difficult (e.g. for the *th* in *teeth*, they can put their index finger over their lips, and their tongue should lick it).

- **doing collaborative tasks in writing as well as speaking:** Whilst speaking is clearly collaborative (you can't speak to yourself), writing is usually not seen in the same way. However, there is no reason why writing can't also be collaborative. Students can work together in pairs or groups to create one piece of writing. Through this process, they will be sharing their knowledge and ideas, and is a good way of building confidence. Key benefits of an activity like **Collective story writing** below are that students can remain anonymous, and that it doesn't matter whether some students write a lot, and some very little. It's also a good way of developing students' reading skills (as well as speaking and listening, if they need to clarify anything which their classmates have written). Whilst students may be slightly confused by this activity at first, it will soon become clear what they have to do.

ACTIVITY: Collective story writing

1   Give students a blank piece of A4 or foolscap size paper. They should fold it in half, so that it looks like a book. Tell the class that they are going to write a story – but that they are going to do this collectively, not by themselves.

2   Tell students to write the name of their story at the top of their 'book'. Encourage them to be creative. Give a specific time limit (e.g. thirty seconds).

3   Tell students to give their 'book' to the person sitting next to them. They should now draw a picture (like on the front cover of the book) based on the title.

4   Now students should pass the 'book' on again. They should now write the first sentence or first short paragraph (depending on their level) of the story.

5   This can continue several more times, depending on how much time you have for the activity. By the end, you will have one story per student, but each story will have been written by many different students. These stories can then be read out. The best ones (or all of them) could be put into a class library.

Note

Collective writing can also be done with essays: e.g. an introduction, three body paragraphs, and a conclusion.

14.3   *Lack of basic writing skills*

Challenge: Students in challenging circumstances may lack the fundamental skills needed for writing, such as orthography and understanding the basic structure of sentence construction. Without these skills, they won't be able to do any writing whatsoever effectively. This is particularly difficult when the level of the textbook and assessment is far higher than the level of the students.

Whilst students are more likely to face challenges using the English alphabet at the primary level, students of all ages may also face such problems. There are many possible reasons for this – they may not have been taught how to do it at school, had little or no support from home to do it, or their L1 may use a different writing system (see ▶ **Chapter 1**). Furthermore, the English alphabet is often taught in a very confusing way. Problems with the ABC order of English are outlined in ▶ **Chapter 7**. More to the point, students are often taught upper-case (capital) and lower-case letters simultaneously, and as if they have equal value. As such, students who may not have secured the script in their L1, are being asked to learn fifty-two new characters.

Solution: It would be far better to adopt a more focused approach by: (a) disregarding upper-case letters entirely, and (b) focusing on high-frequency lower-case letters. In an average piece of written English text, only 3% of the letters used are upper-case. It therefore doesn't make sense to spend an equal amount of time learning them. Furthermore, if a student is still learning how to write capital letters, they will definitely not have the necessary grammatical knowledge about when to use them. Focusing attention (in the first instance) on high-frequency letters such as *e, a, r, i, o, t, n* and *s* is a much more effective strategy. Hundreds of common words can be made from these letters for students to learn from, such as *an, no, on, to, so, ear, tea, ten, toe, sat, rat, late, near, last* and so on. In terms of the structure of English sentences, the activity below is a fun, interesting and interactive way of talking about word order.

ACTIVITY: Who what why where when

1. On the board, write a very simple sentence (just subject + verb), for example: *I visited*. Ask the class whether this makes sense (= no). Elicit from them a question based on the sentence. The complexity of the question will depend on their level. Lower-level students might just ask: *Who?* Higher-level students might ask: *Who did you visit?*

2. Answer the question by adding information on the board: *I visited my sister*.

3. Get the class to ask another question based on the new sentence, e.g. *When did you visit your sister?* Add to the sentence on the board: *I visited my sister last Saturday*.

4. This continues with more questions being asked, and the sentence becoming more complex. Note: you may sometimes need to rub out the sentence and rewrite the whole thing (for example, if the information has to go in the middle of the sentence). When the students can no longer understand or expand the sentence, stop the activity.

5. Students repeat this activity in groups.

Note

This activity can also be done orally.

14.4   Lack of creativity

Challenge: When asked to do productive tasks, students often just repeat what the teacher has said, or copy down what they have read in their textbooks. They are not creative. The production is 'robotic', and students do not use the language as if they are in a real-life situation. There is also a lack of joy and fun in this process.

Solution: As noted elsewhere, students often don't have the opportunity, support or direction about how to be creative. Although it's a huge jump to move from ▶ controlled practice to ▶ free practice, it is nonetheless crucial. Stories are found in every human culture, and they can also have an important role to play in the language learning classroom. They are fun, authentic, creative, and they introduce language in a comprehensible and meaningful way. They have a clear value in developing listening and reading skills, but as the two activities below show, storytelling can also be used to effectively develop productive skills.

> *Children learn and create their mother tongue not by sitting at their desks doing pencil and paper tasks in isolation from their peers, or drilling structures out of context, but by interacting in a community of language learners.*
>
> Mauro Dujmović

ACTIVITY: Multi-voice storytelling

1   Stand at the front of the class. Ask four students to come and stand next to you, two on either side. You should all face the class.

2   Begin telling a story. This can be a story from the textbook, or another story you know, for example: *Once upon a time, on a mountain a long way from here, there lived the most amazing …* [pause] *I can't remember*! [turning to the four students] *Can you help me? What was it?*

3   Students suggest who or what lived on the mountain. The teacher then carries on telling the story, pausing every two or three sentences to do the same thing. Allow students to use L1 to make suggestions. You can then provide the L2 equivalent for them.

4   When you get to the end of the story, ask the whole class to predict what happens next.

Whilst textbooks often contain stories, these stories may not necessarily mean much to your students. As noted later in ▶ **Part VI**, they might not engage or motivate the students, or be geographically or culturally relevant. Folk tales, however, are likely to interest the students much more, and therefore be better for language learning. Such stories were shaped by location or regional traditions, and are rich, detailed and full of interesting characters. Whether in the L1 or L2, oral or written, they can be an excellent basis for language learning.

> *Folk tales have many special characteristics that make them exceptionally good for language teaching. Their frequent repetitions make them excellent for reinforcing new vocabulary and grammar. Many have natural rhythmic qualities that are useful for working on stress, rhythm, and intonation in pronunciation. And the cultural elements of folk tales help both bridge common ground between cultures and bring out cultural differences – developing cultural awareness that is essential if we are to learn to think in another language and understand the people who speak it.*

> Eric Taylor

14.5   *Lack of progress in writing skills*

Challenge: In challenging circumstances, due to lack of time and the pressure to make rapid progress, students are often not given the space and time to properly develop their productive skills. As a result, students' language use is often risk-averse, and they are not encouraged to experiment with new language – their writing doesn't improve. Furthermore, students seldom receive any feedback about their spoken or written work except in ▶ **summative assessment**. Even then, the feedback may just consist of: 'correct' or 'incorrect'.

Solution: Students should do less production, but in more detail, and with greater focus. ▶ **Task repetition** is a very important technique for this. When students repeat a task, they can learn from the mistakes which they realize they have made, and they can also apply any feedback which they have received. When students don't have to think as much about the content (because they are already familiar with it), they can concentrate more on the language. This means they are likely to take more risks. This is another reason why using stories, especially folk tales, is so useful – they may already be very familiar with what happens. For example, if students have to do a dialogue about a particular topic, they should do it once, and then do it again (and then again, if necessary, either with the same partner or a different partner). The doughnut mechanism of arranging the class (see ▶ 4.3) can work very effectively for doing this.

In terms of written feedback, if you have time to give individualized feedback, use a ▶ **marking code**. In this way, students have the opportunity to try and correct their mistakes by themselves – e.g. underlining an incorrect verb form and writing *V*, or *?* next to a section which is difficult to follow, is very useful ▶ **formative feedback**. They can then identify their mistakes, and rewrite their answer accordingly. An alternative mechanism is to provide students with a model answer to a writing task which they did. In pairs or groups, they can then compare what they wrote to this model, and note any differences.

Reflection

- What are some of the specific speaking or writing problems which you face in your class? What ideas in this chapter could help you overcome these problems?
- What additional difficulties might you face in trying to implement these changes? How could you overcome them?

15   Teaching grammar

If she asked me to speak in English, I would be silent … our head is heavy of grammar.

anonymous student, Jordan

The short version
1   Grammar is something to be used, not simply understood.
2   When using the traditional PPP (Presentation Practice Production) method for teaching grammar, teachers often omit the final, crucial phase of production, meaning students don't secure the knowledge.
3   Textbook grammar is often presented (and therefore taught) in a boring, repetitive way, which is demotivating for both students and teachers.
4   There's no reason why textbook grammar can't be taught using fun, interactive activities.
5   Since students are often reluctant to use new grammatical structures, the teacher needs to create a classroom atmosphere where they feel they can try.

Introduction

1   Is it important to teach grammar in challenging circumstances? Why / why not? Is your view the same as those of other educational stakeholders?

2   How do you currently teach grammar in your classes? How do your students feel about this?

3   The following 'grammar' words are used in this chapter. Do you know what they mean (see ▶ **Glossary**)?

> deductive approach   inductive approach   gap fill activity
> PPP approach   model sentence   metalanguage

Why do we teach grammar?

What is grammar? Grammar is not just rules, and it is not just accuracy. Rather, grammar is the way we sequence and modify words in order to achieve greater clarity and precision. It is a toolbox for making meaning. As Tanya Cotter says:

> *Without grammar, words hang together without any real meaning or sense. In order to be able to speak a language to some degree of proficiency and to be able to say what we really want to say, we need to have some grammatical knowledge.*

In many educational contexts and institutions, 'teaching language' means 'teaching grammar'. Furthermore, 'knowledge about' grammar is often prized more than 'the ability to use' grammar. Grammatical knowledge is often the basis of many language exams, whether assessment within your institution, national exams, or college and university entrance tests.

Grammar is traditionally taught using a ▶ **PPP (Presentation Practice Production) method.** This is how many teachers were trained to teach, and how they were taught themselves at school. The main problem with this approach is that the final stage is often either forgotten or not done properly. Teachers first explain the new grammatical construction (e.g. how it is used, the rules, examples) (**presentation**), then provide opportunities for **practice** (e.g. gap fill exercises or ▶ **substitution drills**), but then omit the final, crucial P (**production**). Without the opportunity to produce the grammar in meaningful context, the students will not ▶ **secure** the knowledge.

Note: Grammar in L1 and L2
'Translating' grammar between languages is problematic because different language (and cultures) think about notions such as time, person and countability in different ways. Grammatical differences between languages can cause problems for students – e.g. articles (*a, an, the*) are used very differently in Arabic and English – meaning that Arabic students are more likely to make mistakes in this area. Multilingual students may face additional challenges, as they are managing the grammars of a number of different languages.

Since grammar is such a dominant aspect of language learning (and takes up so much classroom time), it's important to continuously reflect on the methodology you use. Questions you might think about include:
- Am I teaching this grammar because I *have to*, and because it's useful for my students, or because I find it easy and comfortable to do so?
- Can I flip the learning, and ask students to learn about the grammar for homework, or in their home time? If this is possible, classroom time can be spent on practice rather than explanation.
- Would it be helpful (and time-efficient) to explain the grammar point in L1?
- Before doing a grammar activity, consider: a) Is it easy to set up and manage? b) Does it focus on or produce lots of examples of the targeted item? c) Does it allow all students to participate (whatever level they are at)?

15.1 *Unclear and complicated grammar explanations in books*
Challenge: As discussed later in ▶ **Part VI**, textbooks may be written by people who have little understanding of your context. In their mind, grammar rules are simple and easy to follow. They might not appreciate the difficulties faced by your students in trying to understand grammar – e.g. that their general understanding of grammar (including of their own language) may be poor, and they might not understand the ▶ **metalanguage** used. They often find the explanations unclear and complicated.
Solution: The transmissive, teacher-fronted approach to teaching grammar described in the introduction to this section tends to be ▶ **deductive.** This means that the teacher presents the rule, and the students must then apply this rule, through controlled practice, to a series of tasks or contexts. You could consider changing – or at least varying – the approach which you use to teach grammar. An ▶ **inductive approach** is data-driven rather than rule-driven. The teacher presents model sentences which contain the target language / grammar, and the students try to ▶ **notice** these patterns and work out / discover the rule for themselves ('rule discovery'). In a purely inductive approach, the teacher would provide no support to the students; however, it is best to provide some indirect guidance to your students, e.g. through asking questions, or highlighting particular features which you want them to focus on.

For example, imagine you are introducing the past simple to your class. Using a **deductive approach**, your procedure might be:

1 Explain to students that the past simple is used to talk about completed events / situations. You form it by adding *-ed* to the end of the ▶ **root form** of regular verbs, and use different forms for irregular verbs. Present several model sentences to show this (e.g. *help, helped / walk, walked* and *go, went / say, said*).

2 Give students a practice exercise where they fill in the gap with the correct form of the past simple.

However, an **inductive (i.e. 'discovery') approach** might have the following procedure:

1 Students are given model sentences (e.g. on a handout, or written on the board). In groups, they have to work out what the sentences have in common, and what the rule is. Add clues to help them do this (e.g. here, you might add time words like *yesterday* or *last week*).

2 Take feedback. Get the students to teach you what they have discovered. Clarify as needed.

3 In groups, students identify more examples by themselves (e.g. *clean, cleaned*). They then try and use these verbs in sentences.

Depending on your class and your context, it might also be possible to move away from the traditional way in which the word 'grammar' is actually understood. In many situations, grammar is imagined as a set of rules which have to be followed in order to accurately use a language. Grammar is composed of a set of abstract ideas called things like 'the present perfect' and 'adverbs of frequency' and 'subject pronouns'. But if we think of language in this way, it's difficult to see the links between all the different ideas.

Note: Lexical grammar

Some scholars have argued that the distinction between grammar and vocabulary is a false one, since corpus research shows that many high-frequency words attract their own highly productive patterns that are just as common as the traditional grammar you find in textbooks (e.g. the past continuous or the zero conditional). For example, the pattern [*go*] + *and* + verb produces *go and ask, go and look, went and asked*, etc. The pattern [verb] + [possessive] + *way* + preposition produces *they made their way down the road*, or *she elbowed her way to the front* and so on. (See *Lexical Grammar* by Leo Selivan (Cambridge University Press, 2018) for ideas of how to teach and practise this kind of grammar.)

15.2 *Grammar-focused language exams*

Challenge: For the reasons discussed above, and also because marking true or false grammar questions is easy (see ▶ **Part VII**), grammar questions are frequently a key component of language exams. This may not be something you can change directly – although there may be ways in which you can advocate for change.

Solution: Even if you can't change the exams, you can change the way you teach grammar in the classroom. Indeed, students will develop their grammatical knowledge, and secure it more effectively, if there is a focus on production and usage, and if grammar is taught inductively (or through a mixture of inductive and deductive approaches). This should mean that not only will students' learning outcomes increase, but also their learning experiences.

15.3 *Textbooks dominated by grammar*

Challenge: In many challenging circumstances, where a transmissive, teacher-fronted pedagogy is the norm, textbooks and materials are grammar-heavy. Formulaic, repetitive exercises dominate. This is boring not only for students, but also for teachers. Moreover, these exercises rarely provide opportunities for students to actually *use* the target grammar.

Solution: Gap fill or cloze exercises are the most common type found in English language textbooks. As noted above, it may be important (for assessment purposes, and also because of the expectations of educational stakeholders) that textbook content is taught in the class. It is possible to do this whilst also making the learning more student-centred and interactive. Imagine the following review exercise of different verb forms:

Complete the following sentences with the correct form of the verb.

1 Thomas *visits / visited / has visited* his friends in Cairo last year.

2 My sister *talk / talks / talked* to my mother on the phone every day.

3 My father *works / worked / is working* in Kinshasa at the moment.

A common situation would be for the teacher to ask students to just complete this task individually, and then go through the answers. Not only is this boring, the answer may already be in the book (from previous years), and the students are not actually using the language. Instead, you could:

- nominate different areas of the classroom for each word (e.g. for sentence 1: the far end of the classroom = *visits*; middle = *visited*; front = has *visited*). Students have to stand in the correct area. You can then take feedback, asking each group to explain their answer. They have to convince their classmates to join their group, or they can consider moving to a different group.
- read the question aloud, and ask the students to hold up their fingers to show what they think is the answer (e.g. for sentence 2: one finger = *talk*; two fingers = *talks*; three fingers = *talked*). You can then ask particular students to explain their answer.
- ask students to use the same sentence structure, but change the content words to make it true for people they know (e.g. *my father is working in Delhi at the moment … my brother is working in Qatar at the moment*).

Using actions at the same time as using the grammar can help students secure the language. This physical connection, that is the ▶ **Total Physical Response (TPR)** technique (see ▶ 12.7) deepens the learning. The activity below is an example of how this can be done simply and effectively.

ACTIVITY: Get in line

1 Tell the students the grammar item which you want them to practise. This should be grammar which you have recently worked on in class, such as talking about their age (e.g. *How old are you? / I am … years old. When is your birthday? / My birthday is in …*)

2 Tell students that they must line up in order, from oldest to youngest. They must only communicate in the L2, using the target language. This activity is particularly empowering if you leave the room and let them do it by themselves (you could appoint two or three students to be 'English monitors' to check they are using the target language).

15.4 Reluctance to experiment with new grammar

Challenge: Students commonly only use grammatical structures they have already secured, and which they are confident about using. They may be worried about losing face if they make grammatical mistakes. As a result, they are reluctant to experiment with new grammatical structures.

Solution: Unless you create a positive atmosphere and a safe space in the classroom (see ▶ Chapter 2), many students will not take risks. There needs to be a greater tolerance for mistakes (see ▶ Chapter 24). Making grammar learning real and interactive can encourage students to be creative. One way in which you can do this is to use a substitution table (from the textbook, or written on the board) as a platform for creating funny, interesting (but also grammatically correct) sentences. An example substitution table is given below. Students are likely to begin with real sentences (e.g. *I like cooking food; I like helping my parents*), but they can then move on to funnier sentences. These can be the basis for a very communicative activity (*I like chasing animals. / Really, which ones?; I like cleaning my friends. / How do you do that?*)

I like	kicking cooking chasing helping cleaning building surprising frightening	food. a football. my friends. houses. rooms. people. my parents. animals.

15.5 Irrelevant and demotivating grammar contexts

Challenge: Students may feel bored or uninterested by the context in which the textbook grammar is presented (see ▶ 15.1). The situations may not feel real, appropriate or authentic to them. If so, they will not be motivated to use the different grammatical structures.

Solution: When presenting model sentences, or when practising and producing the grammar, students should focus on content which they find interesting. Identify what are topics and subjects they are interested in, for example talking about their personal desires, goals and dreams. The activity described below could be used to teach the future perfect.

ACTIVITY: Pictures of the future

1 Ask students to draw a picture of all the things they'd like to happen in their lives over the next decade. You should also draw a picture about yourself.

2 Students share their pictures in small groups. They can discuss them briefly in L1, or a mixture or L1 and L2.

3 On the board, write *Within the next decade…*, then present your picture to the class. Elicit their ideas using the future perfect form (e.g. *you will have bought your own house / you will have visited another country / you will have had children*).

4 Students repeat step 2, but using the target language.

Developing students' grammar with minimal resources

Three other activities for teaching grammar, requiring zero or minimal resources, are presented below. Specific grammar items are given as examples, but these activities are extremely flexible, and you could adapt them to teach a wide range of different structures.

ACTIVITY: Changing places

1 All the students stand in a circle, except for one, who stands in the middle. If you have a large class, you can do this outside (or in several smaller groups in the classroom).

2 The student in the middle says *Change places if…* and then adds the target languages. e.g. … *you are taller than me.* (comparatives) … *have visited the capital city.* (present perfect) … *can swim.* (modal verb of ability). If the statement is true for a student, they swap places with another student. If it is not true for them, they must remain in their place.

3 Change the student in the middle every three turns. If necessary, you can be in the middle and give the instructions.

ACTIVITY: Ask me anything

1 Draw a mind map on the board (or share as a handout) which contains personal information about you.

2 Students must identify the questions which relate to the information (e.g. *How old are you? Where do you live? What is your favourite food?*).

3 Students then work in pairs or small groups and follow the same procedure. As well as practising question forms, the students also get to know each other better.

ACTIVITY: One of us

1 Write the following sentence starters on the board: *One of us can…*; *Two of us can…*; *Three of us can …*; *All of us can…*; *None of us can…*

2 Put students into groups of four. Ask them to create as many true sentences about their group in a set time limit (e.g. five minutes). Depending on their level, these could also be written down.

3 Take feedback from the groups. You could ask other groups to guess the person. (For example: *One of us can swim. Who do you think this is? / Carlos. / Why? / He lives near a river, so I'm sure he can swim.*)

Variations
One of us could also be used for: the present perfect (*One of us has…*), likes and dislikes (*One of us likes/hates…*), ambitions and desires (*One of us would like to…*), and so on.

Reflection
• Which of the approaches or activities do you think would work in your classroom?
• What changes should you make to the way you teach grammar?

16 Teaching vocabulary

Learning is not a spectator sport ... Students do not learn much just sitting in classes listening to teachers ... They must make what they learn part of themselves.

Arthur Chickering and Stephen Ehrmann

The short version

1 Developing students' vocabulary is very motivating and empowering, as they feel they are making progress.

2 Vocabulary is often taught as a series of words to be remembered rather than used. This is why students' active vocabulary is often much smaller than their passive vocabulary. Students need as many opportunities as possible to use language.

3 There are many ways in which new language can be presented, including mime, drawing or using real objects.

4 To secure understanding of a word, students need to not only know its meaning, but also its form, pronunciation and spelling.

5 Students need to develop their vocabulary *skills* as well as their actual *knowledge* of words, for example recognizing patterns across the language.

Introduction

1 How do you currently teach new vocabulary to your students? Is it successful? Why / why not?

2 What are the main challenges you face when teaching students new vocabulary?

3 The following words about teaching and learning vocabulary are used in this chapter. What do you think they mean?

> realia   secure   synonym   antonym   gradeable word   collocation
> prefix   suffix   connotation   lexical set   class gallery
> lexical chunk   content word   cline   word class

Teaching words

Without words, students cannot communicate in the target language. The ability to use or understand just a few words is empowering for students. It can give them confidence in their language learning ability and feel like they are making progress – even if/when they find things like grammar or reading difficult. A crucial issue when teaching new language is: how can students develop their active vocabulary (i.e. the words they can use) and not just their passive vocabulary (i.e. the words that they know, or can understand)?

Internalize, retain and retrieve

Learners need to first learn the new language, then feel confident using the new structure, expression or word. They have to be exposed to the new term multiple times, with different examples and in different contexts. After some time, the word becomes familiar and therefore usable.

Cristina Cabal

16.1 Encountering and recycling new words

Challenge: To secure a word, students need to 'meet' it (and use it) several times. Just learning it from a list or using it in a gap fill might suggest a student knows a word, but their understanding will be very shallow.

Solutions: To deepen students' understanding of new language items, try to:

- recycle words within a lesson, and between lessons, in order to 'top up' students' understanding of the new language;
- use all available resources to develop vocabulary: the natural world, magazines, newspapers, etc. Your students, however, are your biggest resource (see ▶ **Chapter 17**), and the bigger the class, the bigger the resource. Ask them to share words which they know, or have heard from the television, radio or internet;
- encourage students to keep a vocabulary book, in which they record new words;
- create a class 'word box', in which words can be stored for recycling and review;
- use activities to develop the students' ability to recall words. For example, show students a picture which contains several different objects or items (ideally words which you have recently been learning). Then remove the picture, and ask students to say (or write down) all the items they can remember. This can also be done with real objects (if available).

16.2 Translation for presenting new language

Challenge: Often the only way that new words in L2 are introduced is by direct translation from L1. This approach makes it hard for students to secure the language.

Solutions: The translation method is the most economical and efficient way of introducing new words. It is particularly useful for concrete nouns (where there is a clear 1:1 relationship between the languages). A range of other techniques can also be used to present new words in order to provide students with a wide range of input, such as:

- **miming:** acting out the word (this is especially good for verbs);
- **pictures / illustrations:** drawing on the board (or using images from newspapers or magazines) – even quick and simple drawings can be very effective (you don't have to be an artist!);
- **real objects (realia):** bringing in actual objects (e.g. fruit, vegetables, household objects, classroom objects), or asking students to;
- **synonyms / antonyms / gradeable words:** for example, the word *freezing* can be presented as a ▶ synonym of *very cold*; the ▶ antonym is *boiling*; these words can also be placed on a ▶ cline: *freezing / cold / chilly / mild / warm / hot / boiling*;
- **descriptions:** using the L2 to define the word, or to describe the relevant context for the word (e.g. for *market* you might say it's the place where you buy fruit and vegetables).

Using a variety of approaches also makes it more interesting for students. Combining these techniques can be especially effective – e.g. for *hammer*, you might mime hitting a nail, and explain to the class that you are building a house.

Note
Back to the board (see ▶ 24.6) is another good activity for developing students' vocabulary.

16.3   Focus only on meaning
Challenge: Textbooks may not provide that many details about words (beyond a basic definition), and teachers may feel pressure to move on quickly to other things. The result of this is that students only understand the general meaning of the word, and nothing else, which may negatively impact their confidence in using it.
Solution: When presenting new words, it's important to not only teach the word's *meaning*, but also its *form* (its word class) and its *pronunciation* and *spelling* (in English these can be difficult to predict). With particular groups, you might also discuss the particular *context* in which the word is used (e.g. formal / informal or speaking / writing), any *connotations* (e.g. positive / negative), its *grammar* (e.g. if it's always followed by a preposition) and whether it has any high-frequency *collocations*.

16.4   Random choice of vocabulary
Challenge: Textbooks often introduce new language in a random way, determined by the contents of the reading and listening texts. The words on these lists often have no relationship to each other, and they may just have L1 translations, or complicated L2 explanations about what they mean.
Solution: Present language in a more structured way, e.g. in ▶ lexical sets (words which are all in the same category, e.g. jobs, animals, transport). Although this may take more class time, the learning will be deeper and more effective. For example, if the text contains the word *north*, you could also teach *east*, *south* and *west*.

16.5   Retaining new words
Challenge: Students often don't retain the new words they learn. There is a simple reason why this happens: students don't use the language. Students are generally only tested on whether they can remember the general meaning of the word, usually through repetitive gap fill or cloze activities as with grammar (see ▶ Chapter 15), rather than whether they can use it in a realistic situation.
Solution: It's crucial to provide opportunities for students to retrieve and use the new language. A list of suggested vocabulary activities is provided at the end of this chapter. Furthermore, as noted in
▶ Part I, decorating your classroom with student and teacher-generated content can create a positive learning atmosphere. Putting up words and phrases around the room will familiarize students with this new language, and give them many opportunities during the day to 'meet' these words, e.g. when they come into the class, when waiting for the lesson to start, when looking around during the lesson. These words must have some sort of context (e.g. illustrated with a picture, example in a sentence, a translation) otherwise the word will be meaningless.

ACTIVITY: Class gallery

1 Choose a category of words (e.g. buildings, jobs, parts of the body, classroom objects, animals).

2 Divide the class into groups, giving each a blank piece of paper.

3 Each group must draw and label as many items in the selected category as possible. They can use any resources which are available (e.g. mobile phone, dictionary, teachers) to help them do the task.

4 The pictures are then displayed in a class gallery. One representative from each group should stand by their picture. The rest of the class then move about and look at all the pictures.

5 If students see a word they don't know, they should ask the representative to explain it. These pictures (with words) then remain on the wall.

16.6 Recognizing patterns

Challenge: In many challenging circumstances, the textbook content and the dominant teaching style is focused only on the instant learning of new language and grammar. Students also need to develop their ▶ autonomy in how they use the language – by recognizing and applying patterns across the language. This is why a student-centred approach is so crucial, in order to genuinely empower them (see ▶ Chapters 4 and 23).

Solution: Students need to take responsibility for their own vocabulary learning. One of the teacher's main roles is to support students in developing their autonomy, which includes strategies for recording and reviewing words, and using clues (e.g. context and word formation) to work out the meaning of unfamiliar words.

Prefixes and suffixes

One way to achieve this in English is to build students' understanding of prefixes and suffixes – that is, the groups of letters at the beginning and end of words which can tell you something about it. This knowledge can help students guess the meaning of new words, and it can also help to build their active vocabulary.

Common prefixes in English, and what they refer to, include: *anti~* (against); *auto~* (self); *bi~* (two); *co~* (with, joint); *ex~* (former); *extra/hyper/out/super~* (more than usual); *inter~* (between); *multi/poly~* (many); *pre~* (before); *post~* (after); *re~* (again); *semi~* (half); *sub/under~* (under); *trans~* (across); *uni~* (one, same). Many prefixes in English refer to opposites, e.g. *dis~*, *in~*, *mal~*, *mis~* and *un~*. Many are also scientific or numerical, e.g. *dec~* (ten); *kilo~* (thousand); *mega~* (million).

Recognizable suffixes in English often relate to which word class they are found in. High-frequency examples include:

Nouns: *~age* (marriage); *~ance/ence* (importance, science); *~dom* (freedom); *~er/or* (teenager, actor); *~ist* (artist); *~ment* (equipment); *~ness* (happiness); *~ship* (friendship); *~sion/tion* (television, reaction)

Verbs: *~ate* (indicate); *~en* (strengthen); *~fy* (clarify); *~ise/ize* (recognize)

Adjectives: *~al* (usual); *~ent* (excellent); *~ful* (beautiful); *~ic* (historic); *~ive* (active); *~less* (helpless); *~ous* (famous)

Adverbs: *~ly* (quickly)

In class, you should make specific, explicit reference to prefixes and suffixes, as a way of developing this skill. This is a quick and effective way of building students' vocabulary as well – e.g. if the word *use* is found in a reading text, you can also teach the students additional words such as *user, useful, useless, usual, usually* and *reuse*.

Note
It's important that students realize this is just a guide, not a foolproof system! There are many words with *re-* which are not related to 'again' (e.g. *realize*).

Lexical chunks
Adopting a different understanding of the idea of vocabulary might also help students develop greater competency. As noted above, vocabulary is often taught in an atomized way – a series of individual words which students must try and remember. Michael Lewis argues that a lexical approach, where language is divided into 'lexical bundles' (which include ▶ collocations), is a more effective way of acquiring a language. A ▶ lexical chunk or bundle is a pair or group of words which are often found together, or close to each other, for example: *a bit, a couple of, as a matter of fact, by the way, come on, don't mention it, do your best, if I were you, kind of, nice to see you, there's a lot of, What's the time?*

It's much easier for students to remember these chunks as single vocabulary items (rather than analysing their grammatical construction). If they understand the context in which they are used, they are more likely to be able to use them. Once students understand this is how the language is constructed, they can play around and manipulate it, and increase their active vocabulary. For example, for the chunk *What's the time?*, the content word (*time*) can be replaced with: *difference, point, problem, score, temperature* and so on.

Activities for retrieving and using new language

The following activities can be used to help students retrieve and use new language. It's important to use a wide variety of different activities and ask students to do different things with the words. By recalling, categorizing, linking, or personalizing the words, students are developing a much deeper understanding of them. These activities are particularly effective for challenging circumstances in that they:
- require students to retrieve words from their memory;
- require zero, or very minimal (i.e. paper and pencil) materials;
- are student-focused and participative;
- can easily be replicated by the students in groups, with one of the students acting as the teacher (and students could also do the activities by themselves at home).

This last point is particularly important. When doing these activities, you want the students to have as much practice as possible. To achieve this, follow the three-step procedure below:
1 Demonstrate the activity with the whole class, so they have a clear model.

2 Organize groups, and check they understand what to do.

3 Groups repeat the activity in step 1, with one student acting as the 'teacher'.

ACTIVITY: Word Bingo

1   Write twelve words on the board which you have recently been studying. Tell students (individually or in groups) to write down eight of these words, and to keep them secret.

2   Explain that you will read out these words in a random order. If you read a word which the student has written down, they should cross it out. When they have crossed out all the words, the individual or group should shout: *Bingo!*

3   The first person or group to cross out all their words is the winner.

Note

Students can also do it with more words (e.g. they choose ten out of fifteen, or fifteen out of twenty).

ACTIVITY: Snowman

1   Tell students you are thinking of a word (e.g. *camel*). The class must guess letters to identify this word. On the board, write one short line for each of the letters:

_ _ _ _ _

2   Ask the students to guess a letter which is in the word. If the letter is in the word, add it. So, if they suggested *e*, the board will look like this:

_ _ _ *e* _

If the guess is wrong, you write the letter with a cross through it below the lines, and you draw one part of a snowman each time (a circle for its body; another circle for its head; two dots for eyes; a line for its mouth; lines for its two arms; dots for its buttons; finally a shape to represent its hat).

3   The game continues, with students guessing letters. They can only make nine mistakes before the snowman is completed. If you draw the snowman before they guess the word, you win.

Note

Snowman is a good activity for developing spelling. Encourage them to think of the most common letters in English (e.g. vowels, *s, t, r, d*). Also, the drawing doesn't need to be a snowman; it could be something more locally relevant (e.g. a giraffe, a train or a building) – but it should ideally have eight or nine components.

ACTIVITY: Categories

1 Ask two students to come up to the front to demonstrate the game. Give them a category (e.g. colours) and tell them that they have to alternately say words which are found in this category (e.g. Student A: *red*; Student B: *green*; A: *yellow*; B: *blue*, etc.). When a student can't think of another word, or repeats a word, they lose.
2 Students play the game in closed pairs. If Student A hears a word they don't know (or don't think is correct), they can make a challenge. Student B must explain what this word means. This game can be repeated several times.
3 At the end, ask students to share any new words which they have learned with the whole class.

ACTIVITY: Head word

1 Tell students to write down a word which you have learned recently in class. They should attach a piece of tape to it.
2 They should keep this word secret, and attach it to a classmate's head (or their classmate should attach it themselves).
3 Every student should walk around the class, asking questions about their word (e.g. *Is it an adjective? Is it a person?*). Other students can only answer yes or no. Students have to guess the word that's on their head.

ACTIVITY: Chain reaction

1 Ask five or six students to come to the front. Ask Student A to say any word which you have recently learned (e.g. *camel*).
2 Elicit from the class what the final letter is (= *l*). Write it on the board. Point to the letter, say the sound and ask Student B to say a word beginning with *l* (e.g. *like, light, leaf*). This continues for the other students. When a student can't say a word after three seconds, they are out. The last student left is the winner.
3 The students now play this in their groups. You can make it more challenging according to the level (e.g. only using nouns, only using words with two syllables or more).
4 After the activity, take class feedback. Ask students to share any new words they learned.

ACTIVITY: Wordsearch

1 Identify ten to twelve words which you have recently taught and write them down. On the same piece of paper, draw a 10 by 10 grid. There should be 100 boxes. You can also make larger grids, but the activity then takes longer.
2 Write the selected words in the grid. The words should be in a straight line, and can go in any direction (e.g. left-to-right or right-to-left; top-to-bottom or bottom-to-top; diagonal in any direction). It's fine for words to share letters (e.g. *cook* could run left-to-right, and *carpenter* could use the same *C*, and go diagonally). When you have added all the words, randomly fill in the empty boxes with other letters.
3 Make copies and give to students (individually or in groups). When they find the words, they should circle them in the grid, and cross it off the list. First team to find all the words wins.
4 Students can then make their own wordsearch grids and give these to their classmates to complete.

Note

You can also create crosswords using a similar method. Whilst very effective, this is more time consuming. If you have access to the internet and a printer, there are many websites which help you create wordsearches and crosswords for free.

Reflection

- How can you help your students turn their passive vocabulary into active vocabulary?
- What changes should you make to your classroom teaching with regards to vocabulary?

V Teaching language without textbooks

17 Creating your own resources

In my 12 years of teaching in Senekal, there has not been a year in which learners had all the textbooks they needed. This is why the system continues to produce learners who can't read and write.

anonymous teacher, Senekal, South Africa

The short version
1 The term 'teaching resources' is often understood as only meaning 'written' or 'printed' materials. However, our classrooms, our environment and our community are full of teaching resources.
2 If you do create your own written resources, manage your time well, ensure they are inclusive, and make them interesting and relevant for your students.
3 The one resource available in every lesson is your students. Use them. Other non-written resources include the local environment, local community and 'found objects' (i.e. items which people have discarded).
4 Empower students by asking them to bring in their own resources to class, e.g. newspapers, photos or real objects.
5 Whilst technology provides opportunities for accessing resources, it's important that they are 'AAA' (accessible, appropriate, accurate).

Introduction
1 What are the challenges in creating your own written resources?

2 How could the following be used as language learning resources? Do you use any of these resources in your current teaching?
   • your students
   • your local area
   • people in your local community
   • found objects

3 What kind of learning resources could your students bring to lessons?

Learning resources in challenging circumstances

When learning languages in challenging circumstances, no written resources may be available, or else they may not be completely fit for the purpose. In such situations, you will need to develop / use your own resources. Although this may initially feel quite challenging, it may be easier than you think. Key to this is rethinking what we understand by the term 'resources'. This term if often interpreted as meaning 'written materials created by an expert'. But learning resources can, and should be, understood in much wider and more democratic terms than this. Four general categories of resources are therefore explored in this chapter: 1. written resources created by the teacher; 2. non-written resources identified by the teacher; 3. resources found or created by the students; 4. online resources used in the classroom.

Written resources created by the teacher

Details on how you can supplement existing textbook materials, for example to make them more locally or individually appropriate, are outlined in ▶ **Chapter 22**. However, there is a wide range of original materials which you could potentially write yourself, if you follow the advice below about how to do this successfully.

1   **Use your time well:** Don't spend hours on making something look beautiful as it's unlikely that most students will notice. Use your limited time efficiently.

2   **Extract the maximum value:** Considering the time it takes to create resources, ensure they can be used and reused in different ways. For example, if you write a story, add a simple question at the end like: *Create an alternative ending*. This is an interesting and valuable activity which could easily take 15–20 minutes.

3   **Be inclusive and avoid bias:** Ensure that all the students in your class (and the wider community) are fairly and equally represented in the materials which you create. (See ▶ **Chapters 3 and 21**).

4   **Share the workload with your colleagues,** if possible: If you all create resources, they can be used in your different classes. If doing this, print the materials on the best quality paper you can, and keep them in a safe place (e.g. a file or folder) so that they can last for longer. Depending on your context, you might even be able to share these materials digitally with colleagues in other institutions.

Reading texts
When creating reading texts for your students, ensure that the text:
* is interesting;
* is an appropriate level (i.e. at, or just above, the students' current level);
* is an appropriate length (e.g. based on student level, time available, complexity of language);
* provides opportunities for interesting questions.

Listening texts / audio
Follow the same advice as for reading texts. If recording the audio, ensure that an appropriate model of pronunciation is used. A variety of voices and accents is useful and interesting for students. Ask colleagues to help you in doing this.

Grammar and vocabulary activities
Further information about how to teach grammar and vocabulary effectively, including tasks which require zero or minimal resources, can be found in ▶ **Chapters 15–16**. You might want to create written resources in order to provide students with a written record of what they have learned in class,

or as a way of checking their understanding. When creating a written record of what was learned in the classroom, follow the principles below:

- Be clear and concise (i.e. don't use long sentences / paragraphs).
- Focus on usage, not just knowledge.
- Use a 'question and answer' format.
- Give examples.
- Use images or diagrams where appropriate.
- Provide space for students to add their own notes / comments.

THE PASSIVE

Examples of the passive

1 *Arabic, French and English are spoken in Lebanon.*

2 *My car has been stolen.*

3 *Olga discovered she was being paid less than her colleagues.*

When should I use the passive voice?

You should use the passive when:

1 the speaker wants to emphasize the object (i.e. the three languages);

2 the subject is unknown or unimportant (i.e. 'someone', 'a person');

3 the subject is obvious (i.e. 'her company').

How do I make the passive?

The usual word order in English is subject–verb–object. In the passive, the logical object becomes the subject of the sentence:

Someone has stolen my car. → *My car has been stolen.*

To make the passive, use *be* as an auxiliary verb, and the past participle of the main verb (e.g. *are spoken, has been stolen, was being paid*).

Notes

Only transitive verbs (verbs which take a direct object) can be put into the passive. Intransitive verbs (which don't take a direct object) cannot – e.g. *stand, sleep, arrive.*

Non-written resources identified by the teacher

Teachers may not feel confident creating their own materials. Alternatively, teachers may not have the ability to produce (either by printing or photocopying) or to distribute (digitally) these materials to their students. In such cases, non-written resources can be used to teach language. Here are four techniques for doing this:

17.1 *Students as a resource*

Students know things. They are not a ▶ **blank slate**. Although this may sound obvious, it frequently gets forgotten in the classroom. We need to move away from the outdated idea of language teaching, where teachers are the holders of knowledge filling up their students with information. We need to see our students as resources. Whatever the teaching and learning situation, wherever in the world you are, there is one thing which is always present: students. Two particular areas of student knowledge which teachers can use are their language experiences and their life experiences.

Everyone has experience of learning at least one language, i.e. their L1. In addition, even if they aren't aware of it, they will also know some of the main features of their L1, e.g. pronunciation, grammar, sentence structure. When teaching L2, ask students to think about the similarities and differences between the two languages. For example, L1 Arabic speakers when learning English might be able to recognize that:

- 'I find it difficult to say the *p* and *v* sounds.' (because they don't exist in Arabic – students usually substitute *b* and *f* sounds instead);
- 'I often put the adjective after, rather than before, the noun.' (because this is the order in Arabic);
- 'My written sentences are often too long.' (because punctuation rules are different between the two languages).

However old a student is, they have life experience which they can use in the classroom. Teachers can draw on this experience to help teach language. For example, imagine that the L2 reading text is about a journey. All students will have experienced a journey before, even if only a short one in their local areas (e.g. from home to school). Asking students to think about and share their experiences of journeys they have made (in L1 or in L2) can help them better understand the L2 text. Questions you could ask include:

- *Has anyone been on a journey before? Where did you go? Who did you go with? What happened during the journey? How did you feel?*
- *Why do people go on journeys?*
- *What kind of language would you use to describe your journey* (e.g. past simple, adjectives, ▶ sequence words)?

One of the opportunities a large class offers you is that you have many different experiences which you can use. Eighty students means eighty unique experiences.

17.2 Local environment as a resource

Too often, we think that education can only take place within the four walls of the classroom. Good institutions, however, know and appreciate their local environment. There is a good relationship between the two. Understanding your local environment can positively influence how students learn language.

For example, a common issue when teaching vocabulary and grammar is that they are too abstract. Phrases like *past simple* or *prepositions*, frequently used in textbooks, don't mean very much to most students. However, if we can link these ideas to students' real lives, particularly to physical objects in their local environment, they are more likely to remember them. Teachers already often do this with physical objects which are immediately visible (e.g. chair, table, window, ruler, door). So when we teach prepositions, students could draw a map of the local area, and then describe it. You can then guide them towards the target language (e.g. *Monica lives <u>next to</u> the river; there are goats <u>in</u> the field; there is a mosque / church / temple <u>on</u> the hill*).

Here are some further examples about other aspects of language and grammar, and how they could be taught using the local environment:

- **directions:** *How do you get from X to Y?*
- **used to:** *How has the local area changed in the last 5 years / 50 years?* (this could be in the students' own experiences, or asking their parents / grandparents)
- **adverbs of frequency:** *Describe the climate in our local area.* (e.g. *it never rains in December*; *in February it is often dusty*).
- **language of description:** *My village is* + adjective; *There is / there are … ; It's got …*

See ▶ Chapter 18 for further ideas about specific language learning activities where students are in their local environment.

17.3 Community as a resource

The local community represents a huge opportunity for language learning. There are people from many different backgrounds, doing many different jobs, with many different opinions. The local community is a rich resource. Good institutions understand the community where they are located. Engaging with the local community also offers an opportunity for your students to learn more about who they are, and where they come from. (See ▶ Chapter 28 for ideas for specific language learning activities involving the local community.)

17.4 Found objects as a resource

There are 'found objects' in every community in the world. And although waste is generally considered a negative thing, we can use items which people have discarded positively for language learning. This is a real opportunity in environments where there are no other learning resources.

ACTIVITY: Upcycling

1 Collect found objects in or near your school (e.g. paper, leaves, plastic bottles). Ensure that none of the found objects are dangerous (e.g. sharp metal, broken glass). Note: you could also get students to collect the found objects for you.

2 Divide the class into groups. Give each group a pile of the found objects.

3 Ask each group to make something using the found objects. Let them use their imagination and creativity. If they find this difficult, give each group a specific thing to make (e.g. mountain; truck; market; television).

4 When complete, everyone looks at what the other groups have created, and tries to guess what it is. They can ask yes / no questions to the group which created it.

Note
In addition to lots of language practice during the creation of each piece of art, and afterwards during feedback, this activity also develops ▶ **soft skills** such as confidence, teamwork and critical analysis.

Resources found or created by the students

Depending on the context in which you teach, it may be possible for students to bring in materials themselves for use in class for language learning purposes. This process is empowering, and gives ▶ agency to the students. The resources, and how they might be used, include:

Newspapers: Available in most communities, newspapers are usually relatively inexpensive. They contain huge opportunities for language learning, and can be exploited in many different ways. Find some examples below of how they can be used in the classroom:

- If the newspaper is not in the target language, students can work in groups and translate parts of it (either orally or in writing). Different groups can then compare their translations and create a combined version (e.g. using the snowball approach, see ▶ Chapter 10).
- If the newspaper is in the target language, students can work in groups to act out the stories. This is a good test of their reading comprehension.
- If the newspaper is in the target language, it can be used as a platform for analysing text features (e.g. word order; sentence structure; paragraph structure; language and grammatical choice).
- Whatever language the newspaper is in, students can work in groups and retell the story from the viewpoint of a different person in the story (in the target language).
- Any pictures in the newspaper can be used together with the text, or on their own.

Photographs: Pictures are very rich sources of information, and are excellent source material for speaking and writing activities. Here are three activity ideas:

- As part of a **show and tell** activity, ask students to present a photo in groups / to the whole class and explain what is happening, and why the photo is important. Classmates can then ask follow-up questions.
- In groups, students **describe** what is happening in the photos. They can also discuss what they think happened immediately before and after the photo was taken.
- Groups are randomly given several photos, and have to **create a story** which uses them all.

Real objects (realia): When students are interested in something, they are motivated to learn the specific language needed to talk about it. Given this, ask them to bring objects from their homes, and to discuss in L2 what they are and why they are important. In class, this can be done in different ways. One way is to have it as a regular class activity which takes place once a week, at a fixed time – e.g. five different students do it every Friday morning. Another way is to do it as a regular whole-class activity – e.g. once a month every student brings in an object, and they talk about it in small groups. As students become more familiar with the activity, you can add more complexity to it, for example:

- A student describes the object (without showing it). The rest of the class / group have to draw it. The student then reveals the object, and explains why it's important.
- Students write a life history of the object (e.g. where it's been, where it might go in the future).

Student-created texts: An in-class procedure for creating and using student-generated texts is described below. Note that the first stage could also be done at home by students as a piece of ▶ flipped learning.

> **ACTIVITY: Students' own reading worksheet**
>
> 1 Students work in groups and write their own texts. Give a specific amount of time for this activity (e.g. twenty minutes). Give regular time reminders to ensure that they complete the text within time. Don't worry that the texts will not be 100% grammatically or structurally accurate. Their focus will be on things the students are interested in.
> 2 Once groups have finished writing their texts, they swap them with another group. They should then read the new text, and write comprehension questions based on this text. They should write them directly underneath the text.
> 3 A third group is then given the text and questions, and must answer them.
> 4 The text, questions and answers are returned to the original group, who then mark the answers.

Online resources used in the classroom

In your situation, you may have access to 3G/4G/Wi-Fi but not to printed materials or textbooks. Clearly, the World Wide Web contains a huge number of materials which could be used for language learning. The challenge is the extent to which these materials can actually be used in the classroom. For example, do you have facilities to print and photocopy materials so you can use them in class? Can you display the materials to the whole class, e.g. using a projector? Does your class have enough electronic devices so that all the students can look at them?

If everybody (or nobody) has an electronic device, it's easier to decide what resources to use in a class. When some students have a device, it can become more challenging. Some students may be happy to share their device with others, but others might not. Even if they are happy to share 'viewing', it's unlikely that many would be happy to share 'using'. It's important to consider the principle of ▶ **digital equity**.

If you are able to share online materials with your class, think carefully about what materials you use with your students. It can be tempting to assume that all online materials are good quality, but this isn't true. You must be critical of these materials. Before deciding to use them, ask yourself whether the materials are 'AAA', which means:

- Are they **accessible**? Has the information been created in a user-friendly way which your students will be able to understand?
- Are they **appropriate**? Are the contents relevant to your students' language learning needs, and also their social, economic and cultural context?
- Are they **accurate**? Is the source of the information reliable, e.g. a well-known organization working in the language learning field?

Note
See ▶ Chapter 19 for more details about using technology for language learning.

Reflection
- What resources are available in your local area which you could use for language learning?
- What language and life experiences do your students have which you could use?
- How could you use the ideas in this chapter in your own teaching?

18   Using the local environment

Using the local environment enables children to develop a sense of belonging to the local community.
It helps them to develop a sense of place which in turn will develop their feelings of security.

The British Association for Early Childhood Education

The short version

1   In our busy, day-to-day lives, we often don't see the language opportunities which are right in front of us.
2   When using the local environment, learning can be deepened as students not only see and hear, but touch, taste and smell.
3   Learning walks are one type of activity which enables students to engage with where they live, and to learn.
4   Community mapping is another activity, through which students can learn more about where they live (and each other).
5   Any activities you do should be adapted to the specific characteristics of the local area.

Introduction

1   How can the local environment be used for language learning? (If you haven't looked at ▶ Chapter 17 already, you might benefit from reading it before moving on to this chapter.)

2   Look at the photos below. How might you use these environments to teach language?

Learning and the local environment

In *Teaching Without Textbooks*, Edward John Wade describes how, as a volunteer teacher in 1963 he was recruited to start up, alone, an Australian government primary school deep in the rainforests of New Guinea. Having lost the few materials he had in an accident, he describes how, impelled by the children's needs and interests, he covered the primary school curriculum by working from what was immediately available. 'I asked the children to show me what they wanted to know about, and gradually introduced English through their responses. …We did our math and science in the bush by estimating how many kernels we could get from an ear of corn. We checked with the villagers where and how far apart we should plant them, and how big an area we would need to clear …' and so on.

When he finally saw a copy of the primary school syllabus, he was gratified to find that he had 'covered' just about every item listed. 'So I put the syllabus away and continued as I had been doing.' Out of this experience, Wade evolved a textbook-free pedagogy that, he maintains, 'not only empowers your learners, it also makes the teacher's job in the classroom a lot more fun and much easier'. In a sense, Wade had replaced *teaching* material with *learning* material.

The importance of using the local environment for language learning has already been outlined in ▶ Chapter 17. This chapter looks specifically at four activity ideas which use the local environment to promote language learning.

Clearly, your location plays a significant role in how you use the local environment in your teaching. As such, some of the activities may be inappropriate, or else you may need to adapt them for your circumstances.

Note

If and when you go outside of the classroom, make sure students are safe. Take all necessary precautions. You may need to get the permission of parents, and you should tell colleagues at your school what you are doing, so they know where you are, and when you should return.

18.1 *Learning walk (general)*

When we know an area very well, often we don't see what is really there. Everything is so familiar that we don't notice the small things. Taking students on a learning walk, therefore, is a way of connecting them with their local environment. It also provides many language learning opportunities. Walking has been described as 'the most fundamental pedagogy known to humans' (Jickling et al., 2018).

When going on learning walks, look for 'objects of interest' which could be used for language learning. Depending on where you live, these 'objects of interest' will be very different. You should be responsive to the situation, reacting to whatever the students show an interest in.

An example condensed transcript of a learning walk is given below, between a teacher (T) and her students (S1, S2, S3, etc.). Wherever possible, you should use the target language – but move into L1 as and when necessary. Interesting and relevant pedagogical choices by the teacher are labelled and explored after the transcript.

T: What is this called in English?

S1:   A tree.

T: Good. Everyone say 'tree'.

T drills the word 'tree'. (1)

T: (pointing at a tree) What's this?

SS: Tree.

T: (holding up three fingers) What's this?

SS: Three.

The teacher points at the tree then her three fingers a few times.

T: Ok, you have one minute to touch as many trees as you can. (2) Every time you touch one, shout 'tree'.

The students do this activity.

T: How many did you touch? (3)

The students shout out various numbers.

T: Ok, what words can we use to describe a tree? (4)

S2:   Brown.

S3:   Green.

S4:   (says words for 'hard' in L1)

T: Does anyone know this word in English? (waits) 'Hard'.

SS: Hard.

S5:   Tall.

S3:   No, not tall. (5)

T: Why not?

S3:   Some trees are tall.

T: That's right, they can be tall, but when they are young they might be quite short. Okay, now draw a tree in your book and label it. (6) If you don't know some of the words, ask a friend. If they don't know, ask me.

The students complete the activity.

T: Ok, so why are trees useful? What do we use them for? (7)

(1) **Pronunciation skills development:** After teaching *tree*, she contrasts its pronunciation with its minimal pair *three*.

(2) **Physical activity:** She gets the students to touch the trees and say the word – an example of Total Physical Response (see ▶ **Chapter 12**). This will deepen the students' ability to remember the word, and also energizes them.

(3) **Student feedback on activity:** She asks the students how many trees they touched, but note that she doesn't declare a winner. Doing so might lead to an argument, cheating and disruption. It would also be time-consuming. Instead, she moves on quickly to the next activity.

(4) **Eliciting what students already know:** She asks students to say words they know which can describe a tree, getting them to think critically. Note that she also encourages students to use their L1 (for *hard*) when they don't know the word in English.

(5) **Peer feedback:** One student challenges the use of *tall*. The teacher encourages this discussion, but also acts as the referee.

(6) **Recording the learning:** Students write down what they want to remember, bringing together what has been discussed.

(7) **Linking to other subjects:** At the end, she opens up the discussion, and could link to areas such as geography, science, the environment, etc.

18.2 Learning walk (specific)

Building on the same idea, you can also give students specific tasks to do on a learning walk.

ACTIVITY: Learning walk

1 Divide the class into groups of about four students. Present a random list of ten adjectives (e.g. *small, narrow, oval*).

2 Check students understand the meaning of these words.

3 In groups of four, students must go outside and find objects which can be described using these adjectives (e.g. *small* = stone; *narrow* = river; *oval* = egg). If they can, they should bring them back to the classroom (or a photo, if they have mobile phones). Give a specific time limit (e.g. 10 minutes).

4 Groups share their combinations with each other (i.e. small stone, narrow river, oval egg). Note that there may be disagreement, especially related to opinion adjectives.

5 Take class feedback.

Variations
Useful categories / adjectives which you could use include:
- **colours:** red, green, orange, red, black, white, bright, dark, pale;
- **shape:** square, rectangular, circular, triangular, oval;
- **size:** big, small, huge, tiny;

- **general description:** beautiful, young, old;
- **physical attributes:** long, short, tall, narrow, straight, wide, high, fat, thin;
- **opinion:** good, bad, important, interesting.

18.3 Community mapping

Most maps use a specific set of categories, and record information in a uniform way. In so doing, they often ignore local knowledge, experience and priorities. A map created informally by a community can look very different from the 'official' version. Whilst the final creation can be an important object, the process of creating the map can also be extremely valuable and empowering.

Throughout this activity, students should try and use as much target language as possible. Your role is to monitor, and provide additional language as needed.

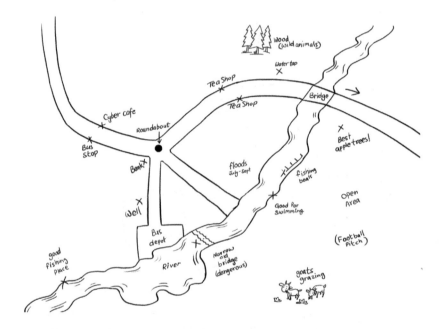

ACTIVITY: Community map

1   Explain to students what a community map is.
2   Students work in groups of two or three. They discuss (and write down) what they think should be in a map of their community.
3   Combine two groups together. This larger group of four or six share their ideas, and agree on what they should include on their community map. They then draw this map.
4   Each group shares or displays their map with the rest of the class. Students should look, in particular, at the different things which each focuses on. If possible, also compare it to an official map of the area.

The community map which you create can be a useful tool for organizing field trips. Field trips offer many language learning opportunities, especially when students find the places interesting. Particular places in your local area which might be good places for a field trip include: artist studios, carpentry workshops, factories, galleries, garages, government buildings, museums, parks, religious buildings, shops, sporting venues, or universities.

Note

This kind of map may have other practical benefits, for example regarding natural disasters – e.g. noting high points, safe spaces, medical professionals, communication sites.

18.4   Listen to the world

This listening and speaking activity is another way students can engage with their local environment.

ACTIVITY: Listen to the world

1   All the students get up and go outside. They should take a pencil and some paper. They walk around wherever they like for five minutes.

2   As they are walking, they should write down all the sounds they hear (e.g. *I heard a dog barking*). They should do this in English if they can, or in their L1 if not.

3   Students return to the class. In pairs / small groups, they discuss these questions:
What was the sound you heard the most?
What was the most interesting sound?
What was the most unusual sound?
What sound is easiest to make with your own voice? Can you do it?

4   Take feedback from the whole class.

Reflection

- Which of the activities suggested in this chapter would work best in your environment?
- What practical steps would you need to take in order to do these activities?

19   Using technology effectively

Technological solution[s] might mitigate some of the ill-effects of poverty and isolation experienced by many students in Kenya and elsewhere in the world.

Seymour Papert

The short version

1   Technology is a core component of our everyday lives. We cannot and should not ignore its value in education.

2   However, it's also important to note that technology is not a magic solution. It has to be used responsibly and appropriately to be fully effective.

3   Since young people like to use their mobile phones (and technology, in general), we should use them positively and constructively in education.

4   Remote teaching can play an especially important role in education when face-to-face teaching is difficult or impossible, e.g. following disasters or during disruptions or crises.

5   There are many different ways for students to participate in learning online – we should choose those which are most appropriate for their needs.

Introduction

1   Do you use technology effectively in your teaching? Does it add value to the learning? How?

2   Do you allow students to use mobile phones (or other electronic devices) within lessons? Do your students use them for learning outside lessons? Why / why not?

3   Are there any specific websites which you use in your classroom or to prepare for your lessons?

4   What experience, if any, do you have of online learning and teaching? How do you think it could be useful in your situation?

Technology in teaching

Teachers sometimes think that just using technology means that learning will automatically follow. While it is true that showing a video or sharing a slideshow presentation can provide educational benefit, this is not enough by itself. If not used well, technology can have zero, or even a negative, effect on learning. Technology helps learning, but it is not a magic solution. Technology supports, rather than replaces, good teaching. Consider, for example, the situations outlined below.

> Zubeda teaches English to Syrian refugees at a primary school in Lebanon. She wants to show her class (50 students) a video of a nursery rhyme. She stands up at the front of the class, holds up her phone and plays the video from an online streaming service.

> John teaches French, but he does not have enough books in his school for the class. He finds a useful slideshow presentation online. He plugs in the projector and laptop, but the equipment doesn't work at first. He spends ten minutes trying to fix it, but realizes he can't.

Although Zubeda is trying to do something positive with technology, it is highly unlikely to be successful. Most of the children will not be able to see the video, and many of them won't be able to hear the audio either. It's important to work within the constrains which you have, and adapt how you use technology. Zubeda could have divided the class into three groups and played the video to each group separately (whilst giving the other groups another task to do at the same time). Alternatively, she could have borrowed a phone from another teacher, and played the same video simultaneously.

As for John, he has shown initiative by going online and finding materials which can help his students. However, when using technology it's important to have an alternative plan (a Plan B, see ▶ Chapter 5) – in case the technology doesn't work, or there is no electricity. When it became clear that he couldn't show the presentation, John should have done something else. As teachers, we need to constantly think how we can maximize the learning in a class.

Note
When deciding whether, or how, to use online resources, remember AIR. Ask yourselves these three questions: 1. Are they **appropriate** (A)? 2. Are they **inclusive** (I)? 3. Are they **relevant** (R)?

Students and mobile phones within the lesson

Even though mobile phone use is widespread around the world, teachers are often reluctant to let their students use them in the classroom. To simply ban phones from the classroom is to ignore the positive impact they can have.

Of course, it's important to manage how mobiles are used – to make sure that students are using them properly. Some students or groups will inevitably use their mobiles for other reasons – just as when you do a speaking activity, some students will not be discussing the specific question you gave them. Don't worry too much about this. Realize that your job is to maximize the amount of learning that takes place in the whole class. Although we should not use mobiles all the time, where they are appropriate, relevant and add value to learning, it seems like a wasted opportunity to not use them, considering the advantages:

- Young people like using mobile phones in their everyday lives. We should take the opportunity to build on anything which students like doing, so we can maximize motivation.
- Allowing students to use their mobiles responsibly within class can be a way of showing that you trust them. Trust is a crucial component in learning.
- In large classes, using mobiles can be an effective way of involving all students in the learning. In many places, it is easier, quicker and cheaper to get materials online rather than waiting for printed books to be distributed.
- Information found online is likely to be more relevant and up to date than information found in many books.

Smartphones contain basic application (apps) which can be very useful for language learning, e.g. voice recording apps for speaking tasks and to check pronunciation, note-taking apps for recording information and practising reading, music / audio apps for listening to songs in the target language, social media apps for reading text and communicating with others in the target language.

Students and technology outside the lesson

If students have access to mobile phones or computers at home, this can be a real opportunity for students to consolidate their learning from the classroom. They can check or add to the knowledge which they have learned. It also provides an opportunity to flip the learning, where students can prepare at home – by looking at a list of vocabulary, or reading about a grammar point. You can then maximize the classroom time for aspects of language learning which can only occur in the classroom, such as spoken communication.

ACTIVITY: Flipped homework (present perfect)
1 For homework, ask students to find five song titles with the present perfect in their title (e.g. U2's *I Still Haven't Found What I'm Looking For*).
2 Students share them in class – check their examples are correct.
3 Elicit the rules about the form. You could also get the students to play, or even sing, the songs.

Variations
The activity can be adapted for any other language point, as necessary.

Using websites in the classroom
There are a lot of useful websites which can be used in the classroom. Many sites have a 'freemium' model, meaning that you can use it for free at a basic level, but have to pay if you want a more advanced version. Other sites offer full functionality for free, but only for a limited period of time. Before you use any website, you should have a look around them to make sure they would be useful in your context. Here are a few examples of websites used in language teaching:
* Quizlet (quizlet.com) and Kahoot (kahoot.com) can be used to create flashcards and a range of different quizzes to check your students' understanding, or to make progress tests.
* Mentimeter (mentimeter.com) offers quick and easy ways for students to share their ideas in a class. Padlet (padlet.com) is similar but simpler, with less flexibility to do what you want, as is Answer Garden (answergarden.ch). These websites are particularly useful if you are able to display the results on a screen in a classroom, and if your students feel nervous or worried about saying what they think (since the comments can be made anonymous).
* Web services like Fake Chat App (fakechatapp.com) and Fake Meme Generator (imgflip.com/memegenerator) can be used to create realistic-looking social media content (like instant messaging or memes) which can be used for language learning.

Online learning and teaching in challenging circumstances

The world has become increasingly connected, with more people than ever having access to an electronic device. Following discussion about how ▶ **face-to-face teaching** can integrate technology, we now turn to online learning and teaching which is done entirely remotely, where there is no face-to-face component. For most teachers, 'online only' teaching is a very new concept, but one which can be extremely valuable. It is also likely to increase considerably in the future.

As outlined in ▶ **Chapter 2**, institutions in challenging circumstances are particularly at risk from natural disasters (e.g. earthquakes, hurricanes) and epidemics or pandemics (e.g. Ebola, Covid-19). Whilst institutions might be able implement classroom teaching after such disasters (e.g. using teaching outside, placing desks further apart, placing more emphasis on ▶ **peer-to-peer learning**), it would undoubtedly be extremely difficult. In such circumstances, online learning can play a very significant role, not only to ensure that there is the smallest possible gap in students' education, but also as a means of social and psychological support during those traumatic times.

> *The primary objective in [emergency] circumstances is not to recreate a robust educational ecosystem but rather to provide temporary access to instruction and instructional supports in a manner that is quick to set up and is reliably available during an emergency or crisis.*

> Charles Hodges et al.

Online learning also has an important role to play during 'normal' times when face-to-face teaching is impossible, or very restricted. For example, in countries which have wet seasons, heavy rainfall may make it very difficult for some students to get to school because of landslides and the lack of transportation. Similarly, during exam periods, schools sometimes shut down completely except for those who are taking the exams. In both these instances, online learning could play a significant role in providing learning opportunities.

Instinctively, many teachers don't like remote teaching, and may even fear it. They believe that face-to-face teaching is 'real' teaching, and therefore superior. Whilst there are clear benefits in learning face to face (e.g. students working together, the social benefits), there are many advantages to online learning, such as its flexibility and the 'one to many' approach. Of course, online learning is not without its challenges (e.g. the potential online dangers, as well as connectivity and/or device problems). However, as with anything, the more experience which teachers and students have of doing it, the more comfortable people feel with it, and the bigger the impact.

Different types of remote learning

Online teaching, like face-to-face teaching, comes in many shapes and forms. One of the main divisions is between synchronous and asynchronous learning. **Synchronous learning** happens in real time (e.g. a 'live' online class with a teacher and students) whereas **asynchronous learning** can be done by students at any time (e.g. the teacher uploads activities which students either complete online, or download and then upload when complete). What you are able to do in your particular circumstances depends on two key factors, namely **bandwidth** (how much 3G/4G/Wi-Fi connectivity do students have) and **immediacy** (when does the learning take place). The educational technologist Daniel Stanford has created the very useful diagram below to categorize different activities according to these two parameters.

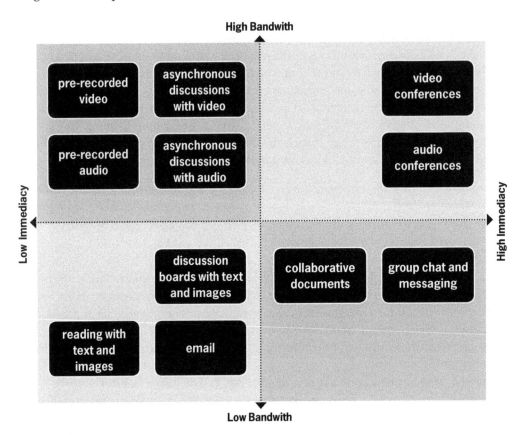

high bandwidth / high immediacy
There are an increasing number of platforms which allow you to teach 'live' through video or audio conferencing, like Zoom, Skype or Microsoft Teams.

high bandwidth / low immediacy
Some teachers prefer to record themselves (on audio or video) in their own time (rather than live). These files can be shared with students along with asynchronous tasks. There are many useful tools for doing this, most of which are free, at least in their basic 'freemium' version, for example: OBS Studio Screencast-O-Matic, or Screencastify. Office software designed for slideshow presentations, such as PowerPoint, Prezi or Keynote may also provide the functionality you need.

low bandwidth / high immediacy
If bandwidth is an issue, but you want the learning to be more immediate and interactive, give your students tasks to work on collaboratively – e.g. writing or presentation slides. They will develop their

soft skills as well as language skills. There are a wide range of free apps available for this, such as Google's G Suite, Slack, Asana or Basecamp.

low bandwidth / low immediacy
This represents the most basic – but still effective – form of remote learning. You can send students reading texts with questions by email, or by posting them on a discussion board (e.g. in a closed group on social media), or using a VLE – virtual learning environment – such as Moodle or Blackboard.

Ten principles for good online learning

1 Ensure that whatever approach or system you use, it should be as inclusive as possible and there should be digital equity. Make sure as many students as possible have the opportunity to access the materials.

2 Teaching online is tiring. Teachers can mistakenly think that online teaching is easier than teaching face to face. Ensure that you take breaks between sessions, and also that you don't set your expectations too high.

3 Don't use too many platforms, programs / apps, or websites. Use a small number of good ones which both you and your students are comfortable with.

4 Synchronous sessions should not be directly sequential – i.e. each session should be standalone. Students should still be able to learn something and participate effectively even if they missed previous sessions. This may not be an issue if you are able to record synchronous sessions, which students can watch or listen to later in their own time.

5 Synchronous sessions should be interactive and contain a wider range of different tasks and activities – just like a classroom lesson. They should not just be lectures. Students should do tasks in real time, either by themselves or with partners. On some online platforms, students may be able to work in their own online groups (e.g. 'breakout rooms' in online conferencing services), which you can drop into. If this is not possible, students may be able to communicate directly with each other through an instant messaging app, or speak on another device.

6 Synchronous sessions can also have an offline component, to allow students to have a break from the screen. You could set short tasks such as:
   • practise the language that you have just learned with a family member;
   • write a summary in your book;
   • read a story in the textbook;
   • draw a picture for the next activity.

7 When running synchronous sessions, you should be in control of the audio. You need to be able to mute people, otherwise lots of people may be speaking at once (which may be confusing), and some students may be in very loud locations where there is a lot of ambient noise (which makes it difficult for others to hear). However, let students decide if they want to use their video or not. That should be their decision. If the bandwidth is okay, it's better if you can use the video for yourself so they can all see and hear you.

8   If you use an open link, be careful about people from outside joining in. As a safety measure, where possible, do not put the session link on an open platform (e.g. in a social media post), but rather send it directly to participants, e.g. via email or instant message, or tell them face to face, if this is possible.

9   If providing asynchronous materials, it should not just be an 'information dump'. Think carefully about what materials you want students to use, and how they are going to use them. Think quality, not quantity.

10   If – and probably when – things go wrong, don't panic!

+1   *When teaching online, it's important not to forget the human element – you need to humanize online teaching. You are still their teacher, and need to show interest, kindness and understanding; you are not a speaking avatar. Be flexible and patient, and appreciate the difficulties which your students might be experiencing in their daily lives.*

Reflection

- Could you use technology more effectively in your teaching? Which of the websites mentioned would be particularly useful in your context?
- Do you need to convince anyone at your school (e.g. head teacher, other teachers) about the value and importance of using technology?
- What could you do to ensure students use technology (e.g. mobile phones) responsibly in lessons?

VI Teaching language with textbooks

20 Understanding textbooks

A textbook is the teacher's tool. It is to the teacher what the spade is to the gardener ... There are few better ways of wasting time and money than supplying inefficient tools to a skilled worker: conversely there are few better ways of increasing production and lessening costs than improving the instruments which the workers use.

Michael West

The short version
1 Textbooks are found in most learning environments, and are therefore very important.
2 Although important, textbooks are not the same things as a curriculum or a syllabus. However, they are often treated as if they were.
3 Language teachers are not 'textbook teachers'. They are language teachers. Textbooks can help this process, but teaching them isn't – and shouldn't be – the main teaching focus.
4 Teachers face many practical problems when using textbooks, e.g. they are out of date, they have been used before, or there aren't enough copies.
5 To maximize language learning, it's important the teachers' creativity is not restricted by textbooks.

Introduction
Answer these questions about textbooks in your language teaching environment.

1	Do textbooks help you teach more effectively?	Yes / No	_____
2	Are textbooks the main teaching resource in your school?	Yes / No	_____
3	Do your students have enough textbooks?	Yes / No	_____
4	Do your students like the textbooks they use?	Yes / No	_____
5	Are the textbooks up to date?	Yes / No	_____
6	Do the textbooks have a communicative focus?	Yes / No	_____
7	Have the textbooks been used before by students in previous years?	Yes / No	_____
8	Do textbooks allow your teaching to be creative?	Yes / No	_____

Do textbooks help you teach more effectively?

Textbooks can be very helpful to teachers, especially new and inexperienced teachers. These benefits include:
- a structure and an overview for the content to be learned;
- teachers not having to spend so much time planning;

- models of well-tried classroom routines;
- consistency between lessons, and between levels;
- advice on the best way to teach the material.

This said, using textbooks is not always simple and straightforward, and it is important not to confuse them with a curriculum or syllabus.

Your job is not to teach the *textbook*, nor is it even to teach the language. Your job is to teach your *students* how to *use* the language. Ask yourself: *What language points or communication skills am I teaching today?* rather than *Which pages in the textbook am I teaching today?*

Are textbooks the main teaching resource in your school?

In many schools, textbooks are the only language learning resource available. Teachers therefore have no choice about what to teach. Furthermore, language exams are often based on textbook content, which means that if you don't use the textbooks, students may get lower scores.

If the textbook is appropriate and well-written, this is not a problem. However, this is not always the case. For a wide range of reasons, many textbooks do not effectively support the language development of your students. In such cases, you may need to supplement the textbooks with additional material (▶ Chapter 22), create your own resources (▶ Chapter 17), use the local environment (▶ Chapter 18) or involve the community (▶ Chapter 28). If doing so, you may need to speak to key educational stakeholders in your school, and explain what you are doing and why.

If several teachers are using the same textbooks, share ideas with colleagues about your experiences. Discuss failures as well as successes. You could do this:
- informally through a conversation;
- formally in a staff meeting;
- digitally in a social media discussion group.

Note
Schools in challenging circumstances are often given free textbooks. However, these books are sometimes out-of-date, irrelevant or inappropriate for the user. Don't feel you have to use these books, just because they are a donation. If they are inappropriate or irrelevant for your students – don't use them.

Do your students have enough textbooks?

The lack of textbooks is a common challenge in many schools. Even when there is a lack of textbooks, you may still be expected to teach the textbook (for reasons mentioned above). This can make your teaching difficult and stressful. Some strategies for minimizing this challenge include:
- getting students to work in groups and share the textbooks;
- keeping all the textbooks at school, in case students regularly forget to bring them from home (however, this may be difficult if the students own the books themselves, and it means they cannot study at home);

- acting as a 'megaphone', that is you might need to read out key information and text for the whole class to make sure that everyone understands (and if you do this, make sure that students without books sit closer to you, so they can hear more easily);
- using different teaching strategies, such as dictating short texts, which minimize the challenges of fewer books.

You could also try an ▶ **information gap** activity to minimize the problem of not having enough textbooks. The following activity helps students develop speaking, listening and teamwork skills:

ACTIVITY: Jigsaw reading

1   Divide the class into groups of four (two pairs in a group). Each pair should have a book. You may need to redistribute some books around the class.

2   Pair 1 reads the first paragraph. Pair 2 reads the second paragraph. Tell them they will have to share this information afterwards.

3   Pair 1 share their information. Pair 2 can ask questions. Pair 2 then share their information, and answer questions from pair 1. To make this more challenging, don't allow them to look at the book during this stage.

Do your students like the textbooks they use?

Although difficult to make general statements about textbooks, one common complaint by students is that they don't find textbook content interesting or relevant. This is a big problem since they are less likely to be engaged. It is also a lost opportunity since research shows that when students are interested in the content, they are more likely to learn the language. Textbook writers may not understand the lives or interests of the students who they are writing for. This is also an important point for teachers. If you don't enjoy the books which you use every day, this will have a negative effect on how you perform in the classroom. This is a particular problem if you teach the same textbook every year – or indeed if you teach the same textbook to multiple classes every week.

You could try giving students the chance to personalize and contextualize textbook content. If, for example, the content is not immediately or obviously interesting to students, ask general introductory questions like: *Why do you think this topic is important?* or *Why is this topic in your book?*

Are the textbooks up to date?

Changes in the modern world happen very quickly. Textbooks, however, take a long time to research, write, print and distribute. It is also expensive to update or rewrite textbooks, meaning that the contents are often out of date. As such, it is important to not just rely on what's in your textbooks, but to supplement them (see ▶ **Chapter 22**).

If your textbooks are out of date, use this as a learning opportunity to develop your student's critical thinking skills. Ask them questions like:

What information here is incorrect?
Why is it incorrect?
If you were to rewrite the textbook, what information would you change?

Do the textbooks have a communicative focus?

Textbooks are often grammar- and vocabulary-focused, and take a very narrow view of language. Activities are often focused on written gap fill activities where there is a clear right or wrong answer. This can be boring for students, and does not promote communication, or how the student will actually use the language in their day-to-day lives.

Don't be afraid to change the focus of a textbook activity to make it more communicative, while keeping the same content. This may take slightly longer, but the learning will be deeper and more effective. Some examples of how you could do this:

Students answer the question by themselves. → Students work in pairs to answer the questions.

Students read the text → Students read the text and then perform it as a short play.

Students write the correct word in the gap. → Students work in pairs. Student 1 reads out the sentence in the book. Student 2 listens and says what they think the missing word is.

Have the textbooks been used before by students in previous years?

When textbooks are in short supply, they are often used more than once, given by sister to brother, friend to friend, Grade 5 to Grade 4. As a result, the physical quality of these books may be poor. From the teaching perspective, a further problem is that the activities and exercises are likely to have already been completed by previous students. This means that when the teacher checks if students have completed the task, and they all give the correct answer, the teacher will get a false impression about what or how much the students know. It is likely that they are just repeating what previous students have written.

Instead of asking students the exact questions in the book, you could ask them different questions which check the same language point. This might mean focusing on different parts of the text, using synonyms for key words in the question, or changing an open question into a closed question, or vice versa. For example:

Does she go to school by bus? → *How does she travel to school?*

What are her favourite subjects? → *Why are English and Maths mentioned in the text?*

How many students are in her class? → *What does the number 40 refer to?*

Do textbooks allow your teaching to be creative?

Textbooks are often prescriptive. Some teachers feel that textbooks stop them from teaching how they want to, especially if other educational stakeholders expect you to teach in a particular way, and focus only on the textbooks. Creativity, however, is an important part of the teaching and learning process, and should be encouraged.

Teachers are often afraid to use textbooks more creatively. Often, this is because they worry that the head teacher or parents (or even the students) will complain. This can be related to the pressure to do well in exams. If you work in such a school and want to be more creative, talk about this with other educational stakeholders, emphasizing how the learning experience will be more effective and more enjoyable for everyone.

Reflection
- Do the textbooks which you use focus on the kind of language you would like to teach?
- Do your students enjoy using their textbooks, or could you do something different?
- Could you use textbooks more effectively in your classroom?

21 Managing textbook bias

If TESOL teachers fail to confront textbook bias, these educators are implicitly supporting as well as possibly socializing their students into accepting it.

John Sherman

The short version

1   The contents of a textbook are not value-free; they are generally shaped by a wide range of different forces.
2   As a teacher, it's important to be able to recognize these forces, and to know how to manage them in the classroom.
3   Textbook bias can be directed towards many marginalized groups, e.g. women, minority ethnic groups, or minority religions.
4   Textbook bias can also be demonstrated by not representing particular groups and identities (e.g. gay or disabled people), or else stereotyping or presenting them negatively.
5   Where possible, teachers should combat bias and prejudice in textbooks. Even if you can't do this directly (because of your context), there may be micro-resistances you can use to enable your students to challenge textbook contents.

Introduction

1   Think about the textbook(s) which you use to teach language. If you don't currently use one, think about others you have used or seen. Mark on each line according to how these textbooks treat the following groups.

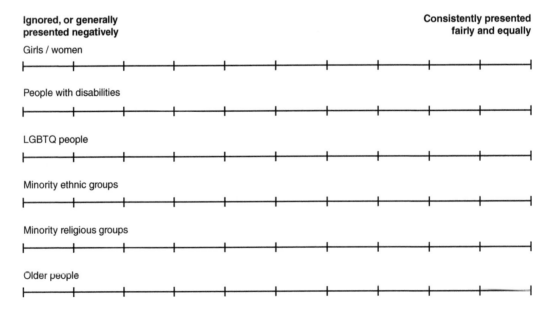

Understanding textbooks bias

As suggested in ▶ **Chapter 20**, one of the challenges of using textbooks is that they contain ▶ **bias**. Textbook contents are neither neutral, nor value-free. There are a number of reasons why this bias might exist.

- The state and government may be dominated by a particular ethnic or religious group. The education system, through textbooks, reinforces this.
- Society may have particular attitudes towards, or expectations about, certain groups (e.g. girls, people living in rural areas, speakers of particular languages). These cultural norms are treated as fixed facts.
- The writers of the textbooks have their own biases (whether conscious or unconscious).

When textbooks are biased against particular groups, it makes it much more difficult to create an inclusive classroom (see ▶ **Chapter 3**). As such, your efforts to treat all your students fairly and equally can be undermined by the textbook contents. These mixed messages can be very confusing for students.

Therefore, it is important not to ignore bias when you come across it. In thousands of classrooms around the world, the textbook may be the only resource which the students have. As such, the textbook effectively becomes the curriculum. If you don't manage or challenge the opinions or attitudes given, the students may just accept and internalize the negative views and stereotypes. You, as their teacher, are often the only person who can help guide them through this.

Note

Textbooks may contain bias regardless of whether they are published domestically or internationally. Both types may contain universal biases, e.g. against women or the physically disabled. However, whilst domestic textbooks may be biased against minority ethnic or religious groups, international textbooks might marginalize or else caricature non-native speakers of the target language.

Seven types of bias

Myra and David Sadker identified seven specific types of bias in textbooks. Sometimes this bias is conscious (i.e. it is done deliberately, for a particular purpose), or it may be unconscious (i.e. it reflects the 'normal', everyday view by most people in society). It may also be explicit (i.e. obvious and easy to see) or implicit (i.e. underneath the surface).

Invisibility

Some groups and identities are simply absent from language textbooks, especially women, people with disabilities, or gay people.

Stereotyping

When a particular group or identity are stereotyped, they are presented with a fixed set of characteristics. A common textbook stereotype for women is that their main role is as a caregiver (as a mother / wife / daughter / daughter-in-law). Stereotypes are often negative, and ignore people's individual characteristics and aspirations.

Imbalance / Selectivity

Textbooks may only present one side of an argument, or ignore important facts. Textbooks often reflect the dominant narrative in society, ignoring alternative viewpoints. For example, many language textbooks contain life stories about famous people. Very often, these people are male, from a dominant group in society, and 'respectable'. They do not accurately reflect the whole of society.

Unreality

Textbooks can sometimes present an imagined view of society, in which aspects such as racism, sexism or discrimination are ignored. This may be confusing for students, as this doesn't reflect the reality of their lives, where they encounter these challenges on a daily basis.

Fragmentation / Isolation

Information about marginalized groups is sometimes physically separate from the rest of the textbook – for example, given in boxes on the side of a page, or as a separate chapter (like *Five famous people from minority group X*). The implication is that these groups do not (or should not) interact with the dominant culture. As a result, these groups are sidelined even further. The existing hierarchy in society is thus reinforced.

Linguistic bias

The choice of language in a textbook can significantly influence how particular groups or identities are seen. For example, if disabled people are presented in the textbook, how are they referred to? It's possible that outdated negative terms like 'crippled' or 'handicapped', which suggest they are victims, may still be used. Even a term like 'the disabled' has the effect of suggesting that the entire group have the same condition.

This bias is often implicit. Consider a story in which there are six characters. Characters A, B and C are good, positive role models, whereas characters X, Y and Z are not. Although there may be no specific information given about the identity of these characters (e.g. race, ethnicity, sex, L1), the names which the characters have been given may be a clue about their background and identity. For example, characters A, B and C may have names traditionally used by prestige groups in society, while X, Y and Z may be given names generally used by the non-prestige groups.

Cosmetic bias

Don't be misled by shiny, beautiful photographs which present a particular view of society. This 'illusion of equity' (e.g. a photo of a multi-ethnic society) may not be representative of the textbook contents or society as a whole. Just because there are pictures of women doing traditionally 'male' jobs (e.g. a pilot or police officer), this doesn't mean that the contents reflect this. It's important to look beyond the pictures.

Managing bias in the classroom

Some of the most common challenges in terms of textbook bias are outlined below, along with suggestions about how they could potentially be managed in a classroom situation.

21.1 Students agreeing with textbook bias

Challenge: It is likely that some or all of your class might agree with the stereotypes presented in the textbook. In many societies, the dominant view of society is very strong, and it is difficult – even dangerous – to challenge this. Furthermore, some students may have had very little exposure to different viewpoints, and may not have met people who are different from them.

Solution: Firstly, you should recognize that it might take a long time for students to a) recognize the bias and then to b) change their views. This is understandable, as students may never have encountered any alternative view, and have been conditioned to think in a particular way. There are several different activities you can do to raise their awareness about textbook bias, whilst simultaneously improving their language ability.

- Analyse the textbook contents and then do a group or class discussion about what this means. For example, you could get students to make a list of all the jobs which men and women do in the book, and then compare which sex generally does higher-status jobs (e.g. engineers or doctors) and which lower-status jobs (e.g. secretaries or hairdressers).
- Provide students with additional material, which presents a different view about a particular issue. If the textbook contains a text about the life of a 'national hero', give the students a text about a 'local hero' from your community. Students could then do a compare and contrast activity between the two texts.
- Use ▶ flipped learning to ask students to do their own research, and find information or evidence which challenges (or contradicts) the textbook contents.

Note

It's important that you and your students take care when challenging orthodox views and values. Depending on your situation, this may be risky. If this is the case, you might consider doing some of the ▶ micro-resistances detailed below in ▶ 21.2.

21.2 Schools agreeing with textbook bias

Challenge: People in positions of authority in educational institutions are often from higher prestige groups. Therefore, head teachers, school owners and school governors may have an interest in the status quo. The biased views and opinions found in the textbooks may therefore reflect their own, and they do not want this challenged.

Solution: Try to understand the views of the school leadership, and see whether it might be possible to make changes. Explain your views about textbook bias, using examples from the book. It may be that the leadership are willing to make changes, but need you (and your colleagues) to explain the reasons to them. If this is successful, it could lead to positive changes in other aspects of policy – for example in making the whole institution more inclusive (see ▶ Chapter 3). If, however, the institution disagrees with your position, you could use micro-resistances in your classroom. Micro-resistances are small, almost unnoticeable teaching strategies which enable your students to challenge both textbook bias and their own viewpoints. Here are a few examples of micro-resistances:

- Ask open questions which don't direct people towards a particular answer, but which still allow them to share their (potentially controversial) opinion, such as *What does the text suggest about the role of women in the workplace?* rather than *Do you agree with the text's portrayal of women in the workplace?* In this case, ▶ hedging language (*suggest*) is used to soften the question, and students base their answers on the text rather than their own opinion.

- Ask students to fact-check textbook contents. They can do this in class (if electronic devices are available and permitted) or else after school. They can present alternative sources of information, or even information which contradicts what is in the textbook.
- Be more tolerant to discussions in L1 – or in a mixture of L1 and L2; see ▶ **Chapter 8** for more information about translanguaging. Students may not be able to say exactly what they want about a text in the target language.
- Don't take class feedback on some questions if you think it might cause students problems. Whilst they may feel comfortable to say what they really think in a pair / small group situation, they may be reluctant to do this in open class.

21.3 Bias in reading and listening texts

Challenge: If you don't do anything to challenge this bias, many low-status groups feel marginalized, or even ignored, by the materials they are using. Students are unable to find 'anyone like them' in the books. In such cases, education doesn't appear to provide opportunities for people to improve their situation – rather, it serves to maintain the existing hierarchies. The message which they get from school may reinforce the message they are getting, directly or indirectly, from their own family or wider community. This contributes to poorer learning experiences and lower learning outcomes. This can result in increased drop-out rates, especially at the secondary level. This may be especially problematic for students who may feel 'doubly stigmatized' (e.g. they are female *and* disabled, or from a minority ethnic group *and* blind).

Solutions: Some ideas about how you can support students in challenging bias in general terms are given in ▶ 21.1. Three ways in which to specifically address text bias are given below. Your particular context and teaching situation will determine which of the option(s) are applicable.

1 Changing the material

As noted in ▶ **Chapter 20**, you may not have a choice about the textbooks which you use, even if they are biased. This may be the case if you work in formal education. However, if you work in informal or non-formal settings, you may be able to change the textbooks which you use. The school management may only be using the textbooks because nobody has ever suggested using different ones. You may be able to find textbooks which are more appropriate and representative of your class.

2 Challenging and deconstructing the material

Even if you can't change *what* is taught, you may be able to change *how* it is taught, and the particular discussions which you have with your class. Once you have done the textbook material, you can then critically discuss (either as a whole class or in groups) questions such as:

- *What does this text say about your community / society?*
- *Do you agree? Why / why not?*
- *What are the problems of portraying your community / society in this way?*
- *What does the text not say about your community / society?*
- *Why do you think these facts have been omitted?*
- *What would be a more accurate way of portraying your community / society?*

3 Rewriting the material

This solution is valuable in both language development and psychological terms. In terms of language development, you could use either a product or process approach to the writing. Doing this can give the students agency, and can have a positive effect on their mental and emotional health, as well as enabling them to understand their social and political situation better.

If done as a piece of ▶ **product writing**, the students imitate the text, using the same essential sentence and paragraph structure. However, they replace the inappropriate information with content which is more relevant to their own social and political context.

If done as a piece of ▶ **process writing**, the textbook content is just a starting point. However, students reflect more deeply on what they are saying (rather than how they are saying it). For example, they could rewrite the text with the same characters (but a different story, more relevant to their own community), rewrite the text with the same story (but different characters, from their own community) or write a response to the text.

21.4 Other examples of bias in textbooks

Challenge: Bias can be found throughout textbooks, not just in the longer reading or listening texts, especially in dialogues and through language choice:

- **dialogues:** If males are over-represented in dialogues (as they often are), then they will get more opportunities to read these parts aloud, and act them out in role plays. Even when girls participate in the dialogues, their role is more passive and the dialogues are also frequently initiated by boys. Dialogues are presented as models, and may suggest that this model of interaction is normal.
- **language choice:** When textbooks talk about 'students in general', they often use specifically male pronouns, i.e. *he / him*. Other common gendered words found in textbooks include: *businessman, mankind, manpower*. Furthermore, the kind of words used for females may be more emotive (e.g. *kind, gentle, honest*) whilst for men be connected to dominance (e.g. *strong, powerful, confident*).

Solution: You could try the following techniques:

- **dialogues:** Change the sex of the characters, so that girls can participate equally. The act of doing this is also very empowering.
- **language choice:** Use non-gendered pronouns (e.g. mix *he* and *she*, or use *they* as third person singular, or other neutral terms like *we, students, everybody* or *a person*). Use gender-neutral terms like *businessperson, humankind* or *workforce*. When you use non-gendered language, explain to students why you are doing this.

Reflection

- Look again at your answers at the beginning of this chapter. Based on what you have read and learned, would you change your answer?
- Which of the challenges listed do you face in your classroom? How do you try and combat these?

22 Supplementing textbooks

Textbooks in every subject can be analysed from two perspectives: a content analysis that examines the areas that the textbook covers, and a didactic analysis that examines the methodological approach to the subject matter or to how the content is treated.

John White

The short version

1 Although textbooks are important, there are times when the content can be challenging for students.
2 Students may, for example, find the contents difficult, inappropriate or offensive.
3 In such situations, there are several strategies you can use, like simplifying or managing the content.
4 Another way is to make the material more directly and obviously relevant to students, for example by personalizing and contextualizing.
5 Where possible, make textbooks as student-focused as possible, and differentiate to ensure that students maximize their language learning.

Introduction

Below is a page from an English language textbook for 13–14 year old students. Their level is lower-intermediate.

1 What challenges might you face teaching this in your context?

2 How could you make the content more interesting and accessible?

Read this story silently, then answer the questions on your own. (1)

Sam lives in the city. One day, he decided to go a restaurant (2). He was feeling really hungry. Having shown him to a table, the waiter asked him what he wanted to eat. (3)

'I will have steak please.' (4)

'I'm afraid we don't have any left.'

'WHAT? I WANT TO SEE THE MANAGER IMMEDIATELY.' (5)

Sam called the manager over. She apologized to Sam, saying that they had not received their delivery of steak, but that they had lots of other food.

'I can't eat here. This restaurant is terrible. I'm never coming back.' Sam stood up, marched to the door, and walked into the street.

Questions (6)

1 Who felt hungry?

2 Where did he go?

3 Why was Sam angry?

4 What happened next?

Potential challenges of textbook materials

Of course it is difficult to make generalizations about a text. However, some of the potential problems presented by the reading text and activity in the example are outlined below.

(1) Whilst reading alone is authentic, the students will have a better learning experience and learn more if they work on questions together.

(2) Have your students ever been to a restaurant? Do they understand the concept?

(3) The sentence is a long and complex one, employing a perfect participle clause. It is too difficult for the level of most of the students in the class.

(4) Mentioning *steak* could be a trigger in that meat (in general) may be unaffordable or forbidden, e.g. for cultural or religious reasons. There may also be a specific problem with steak being from a cow.

(5) It may be hard for some students to understand why the customer is getting so angry in the situation.

(6) For some students, the comprehension questions may be too easy, and they will be finished in a very short amount of time.

22.1 Student-centred and communicative content

Textbook writers may have been taught in a traditional, teacher-centred way, meaning that the textbooks follow the same pattern. Textbooks often focus on activities which students do by themselves, which the teacher can easily manage, and where the classroom is silent. The emphasis is on *what the teacher is doing* rather than on *what the students are learning*. However, as discussed throughout this book, we should put the students at the centre of everything which happens in the classroom. This means we sometimes need to do activities differently than is suggested in the textbook.

After the students have read the text, they could perform it as a play, to show that they have understood what happens. They could work in pairs, one student playing Sam and the other student playing the waiter.

22.2 Contextualizing

Textbooks are generally written in a 'one size fits all' way. This is because they are usually created for an entire country or, in the case of internationally published textbooks, for a global audience. However, within a country there are obviously huge differences between different contexts that students live in – for example, rural or urban, rich or poor. Depending on your context, students may find some content difficult to understand because they do not have direct experience. In such cases, you will need to contextualize the content for them, building on what they already know.

Although your students might have a general understanding of what a restaurant is, they may not have any direct experience of being in one. Use similar ideas or concepts as a way of helping them understand better – e.g. if the closest example of a restaurant is a market stall where people sell food, use this as a basis.

22.3   Simplifying

As noted in ▶ **Chapter 20**, the language level in textbooks may not always be appropriate for the students. Sometimes, the words or grammar used might be too complicated, or the sentence too long and confusing. This makes it difficult for students to understand and acquire new language. Since you cannot change the textbooks, you must change the way you teach the content and make it more accessible to your students.

Some researchers say that the best way for students to acquire new language is when the input (what they hear or read) is slightly more advanced than their current level.

Explain to the class that long sentences can often be divided into shorter sentences, e.g. *The waiter showed Sam to a table. He then asked him what he wanted to eat.* Better yet, you could elicit ideas from students how they could change the long sentences to make them simpler.

22.4   Managing the content

At times, textbooks may include content which students find inappropriate, upsetting or offensive. You may have to guide them through this content. Depending on the class and the content, this might mean avoiding it, or talking about it in a responsible way.

You will need to decide the best way to deal with this issue. This kind of 'wider' knowledge can be interesting and motivating for students, but it could also be disturbing or upsetting. The way you deal with this will depend on the students in your class – e.g. you could choose to ignore it, or else explain that eating steak is normal in some parts of the world.

22.5   Personalizing

Similar to contextualizing, get students to think about the contents from their own individual viewpoint. Doing this may help them understand better what is happening. If we can link the content to our own personal experience, it gives us a platform to develop our language skills.

Although students might find it hard to understand why the customer is getting angry in the example we have seen above, they are very likely to have seen customers being angry in different situations. Thinking of the reasons in this case may help students understand the text better.

22.6   Differentiating

Another challenge of writing a textbook is to create something which is at the right level for students of different abilities. Some may find the tasks too easy, while some find them too hard. Some strategies to help students who find the tasks too hard are explained above. However, it's also important to think about what extension tasks you could give to students using the same material. This can be a way of keeping all the students interested and focused.

Additional tasks for early finishers include:

- writing their own questions on the text, and then asking other students who have also finished;
- continuing the story: *What happens next?*;
- rewriting the story from the viewpoint of another person (in the example: the waiter's).

Note

If you create additional materials which can be used with your textbook, don't distribute them until you want students to use them. As soon as you give students these materials, they will start to read them, and won't listen to your instructions.

Reflection

- Think about your last lesson. Could you have used any of the strategies described in order to make the lesson more effective?
- Think about your next lesson, and ask yourself the same question. Look through the contents which you are going to teach, and highlight any potential problems.
- Talk to colleagues about the two points above. Sharing ideas can be beneficial for both you and them.

Helping students achieve their potential

23 Motivating and empowering students

Start where you are. Use what you have. Do what you can.

Arthur Ashe

The short version

1 Students who don't feel motivated or empowered don't learn as effectively.
2 One common reason for students feeling demotivated is that they are not making progress. To address this, the idea of progress can be redefined, and different forms of assessment can be used.
3 Another reason for demotivation is that students don't see the point in learning languages, or they feel bored. You should talk to students about the value of learning languages, and ensure that your teaching style is engaging.
4 Educational role models can motivate and empower students.
5 Sometimes things which seem very minor, like valuing students' contributions in class, can have a huge impact.

Introduction

1 When you learned English, or another second language, were you motivated? Are you motivated to teach? Why / why not?

2 What do you think motivates your students to learn? How do you know this?

3 If you teach demotivated students, what do you say to them, and how do you try to motivate them?

Understanding motivation

People are motivated to do things for many different reasons. This motivation can be **intrinsic** (i.e. driven by internal rewards such as self-improvement, job opportunities and family security) or **extrinsic** (i.e. driven by external rewards such as money, praise and fear). Often, the two are combined. As a teacher, you have a huge role to play in motivating and empowering your students, for example by creating an environment and atmosphere which is conducive to this. In challenging circumstances, students' motivation for learning may be very complex, and within a single classroom, students may be motivated by very different factors.

When I learn something new, I feel proud.

School is somewhere I can be myself.

If I get a certificate, I can get a good job.

I want to live in another country.

143

Whilst a lack of motivation may be a long-term issue for some students, for others it may be short-term. Their lack of motivation may be temporary. For example, it might be caused by one of the factors identified in ▶ **Chapter 30**. It is important to differentiate those students who are just having a bad day from those who are genuinely demotivated and disempowered.

Making your students more motivated and empowered

Motivation is a state which energizes, directs and sustains action and behaviour. Empowerment is a process through which you become stronger and more confident, especially in the control you have over your life.

It is common for students in challenging circumstances to feel demotivated and disempowered. As a teacher, it can be very difficult to try and teach a class where students feel this way. Four common challenges, alongside potential ways you can help students overcome these challenges, are outlined below.

23.1   *No sense of progress*

Challenge: When students constantly receive poor marks, or get no opportunity to practise language, they might conclude that learning is a waste of time. Their negative ▶ **mindset** will raise their ▶ **affective filter**, meaning they are even less likely to feel they are making any progress.

Solutions: Three potential solutions to this significant challenge are suggested below:

Evaluate progress in class: As discussed in ▶ **Chapter 24**, students' progress should be regularly checked in the lesson. Assessment is not just something which takes place in formal exams. Students needs small, achievable goals rather than large, impossible ones to make them really feel they are making progress.

Change how progress is understood and measured: Generally speaking, in challenging circumstances, 'progress' means scoring highly in tests and exams. But progress should be considered as much more than this. It should be understood, measured and recorded in much broader terms, for example, with regard to:

- **attendance:** For some students, just getting to school is a challenge, If they are successful, it should be considered a significant accomplishment. They may have many other commitments, little family support, and might have to travel long distances and use unreliable transportation. → Put a chart in the classroom where you record attendance using stickers, or by colouring in boxes.
- **attitude:** When students have little or no experience of education, they may have neutral, or even negative feelings towards it. If, over time, their attitude becomes more positive, this is a genuine sign of progress. → Do regular questionnaires asking students about their attitude towards education. These can be quite simple and straightforward, e.g. they point to emojis which describe how they feel (see ▶ **Chapter 2**).
- **soft skills:** Students' soft skills, such as confidence, teamworking, social skills or behaviour, may initially be quite low. → Students could complete self-assessment questionnaires, at regular intervals, asking whether they feel they have made progress in these areas. Teachers can also input.

Use different forms of assessment: Testing and exams are frequently ▶ **norm-referenced**, meaning that students within a class (or year group) are measured against each other, e.g. the top 20% are given

A grades whilst the bottom 20% fail. This can be extremely demotivating for students who continually perform poorly. It also doesn't help the better-performing students much either, except to tell them that they are better than their classmates. Criteria-referenced or ipsative assessments are better, fairer and more informative ways of evaluating students' academic progress.

In ▶ **criteria-referenced** tests, progress is measured against a pre-agreed list of criteria. For speaking, the criterion might be that students must be able to participate in a simple conversation about themselves. Rather than the outcomes pass / fail, students could be placed at different levels (e.g. level 1 the lowest, going up to level 5) or placed into categories such as Competent / Nearly competent / Not yet competent. This kind of system would help capture the breadth of student ability much better (which is especially important in large classes) and doesn't demotivate those students who are branded as 'failures'. Also, if assessed on a skill-by-skill basis (rather than just getting one overall pass / fail mark), students may be able to feel they are making progress in certain areas. For example, they might be at level 1 in speaking, but at level 3 in reading.

In ▶ **ipsative assessment**, students measure their progress against themselves, comparing their performance in one test with how they did in a previous one. This is known as ▶ '**distance travelled**'. One significant challenge in using this form of assessment is ensuring consistency between tests. A student might score 65% in a test, and then get 60% in a test the following week. As such, they may feel that their language learning is getting worse. However, the first test might have been relatively easy, and the second test relatively hard. The student might actually have done better in the second test, but got a lower mark. As such, one way that ipsative assessment can help students is when they take and retake the same test.

Note

▶ **Task repetition** can be extremely useful, and develop students' confidence in using language. Whilst there is little value in redoing a test which only contains closed questions with a single correct answer, but when repeating subjective writing or speaking tasks allow students to reflect on their previous attempts, and correct their mistakes by themselves.

23.2   The reason for learning languages

Challenge: It can be difficult for students to make the link between their real lives and the abstract things they learn in the classroom. In many communities, this may be reinforced by the fact that many people learned languages (perhaps even at your institution), received a certificate or qualification, and yet are unemployed or work in jobs below their qualifications. Your students' perception may (possibly correctly) be that learning a language has not helped them get the kind of job they wanted. As a consequence, they don't see the point or value in learning languages in general. How can teachers help students overcome this challenge?

Solutions:

- **Talk about the general importance of learning languages:** Whilst language learning can – and should – be seen in instrumental terms (as in, it can help you get a good job), it is also valuable for other reasons, such as managing trauma or increasing social cohesion. These reasons can often get lost in the day-to-day focus of things like 'the past simple' and 'how to write a letter of complaint'. See ▶ **Chapter 1** for a list of why learning languages is valuable. Where possible, give examples from your own life, or ask others in the local community who have benefited from learning languages, to share their thoughts.

- **Identify what immediate value language learning can have for your students:** This can be something very simple and straightforward, such as *If my English improves, I will understand more videos on the internet*. Personalizing and contextualizing the language learning can have a very positive impact.
- **Change the way in which you are teaching the language:** As discussed elsewhere, how you teach language (e.g. teacher-centred, textbook-based, academic) may be very different from the way students learned the other language(s) they speak. If you can make the process more natural, students may respond more positively. You might also give them choices in the lesson so that they feel they have more control – e.g. *You can do the next task either by yourself, or with a partner*. Furthermore, if you can get them using the language at an early stage, they will be able to see its value.

23.3 Bored by everything being the same

Challenge: When lessons have the same structures, the same processes and the same organization, it becomes very boring for students. It can become difficult to separate one lesson from another. As such, students may already feel negative when they come into your classroom.

Solutions: Even if students feel bored by their other lessons, you have the opportunity to make your lesson stand out. Use the ideas outlined in this book to achieve this by: being student-focused (see ▶ Chapter 4), using multiple languages (see ▶ Chapter 8), changing the classroom seating layout (see ▶ Chapter 9), creating your own resources (see ▶ Chapter 17), using the local environment (see ▶ Chapter 18), involving the local community (see ▶ Chapter 28), and bringing the outside world into the classroom (see ▶ Chapter 29). You can also talk to your students about why – and when – they feel bored, and whether they have specific ideas about how to fix this. This conversation should be open and honest, and can be done individually, in groups or with the whole class.

23.4 Lack of educational role models

Challenge: Some students might be the first person in their family to go to school, or the last to go on a regular basis. The community which they live in may have few examples of people who have been educated. Indeed, in some cases, there might be disapproval or even hostility directed towards students. In these circumstances, they may feel demotivated about attending school, and in a worst-case situation, may drop out. This problem can be reinforced by some of the issues discussed in ▶ Chapter 21: if students feel that 'people like them' are ignored or negatively stereotyped, they will feel demotivated and disempowered.

Solution: Identify people who can be ▶ 'buddies' or role models for your students within the school, or potentially the wider community. You can also be a role model for your students, and talk about your own educational (or specifically language learning) experiences. If you feel comfortable doing so, you should talk about both your positive and negative experiences. Doing this will not only be motivating for your students, but they will also see you more like an actual person (rather than just their teacher).

Further techniques for motivating and empowering students

- Value their contributions in class. Acknowledge them when they make points.
- Ask them for feedback on your teaching. This obviously relies on there being trust between you and your students. Ask students questions like: *What did you (not) enjoy this week? Which activities did you (not) like?*
- Ask students to tell you what kind of things they are interested in. You can then refer to these within the classroom, or even create resources which focus on these areas (see ▶ Chapters 17 and 22).
- Ensure that, where possible, activities and tasks are multi-level. Differentiating the learning to ensure that all students will be able to accomplish something is both empowering and motivating.
- Involve students in the assessment process where possible, so that they become more responsible for their own progress. For example, students can create their own ▶ learning portfolios.

Reflection

- Which of the challenges listed do you face in your classroom? What changes do you think you could / should make?
- What resistance to these changes do you think there might be? How could you overcome this?
- What other strategies do you think could motivate or empower your students?

24 Checking what students have learned

Teacher: *Do you understand?*
Student: *Yes.*
Teacher: *Good.*

The short version

1 Checking students' understanding of the target language is something which should occur regularly throughout your lessons, not just periodically in tests and exams.

2 It's important to resist the pressure to rush through and finish the textbook. The quality, not quantity, of learning is what matters.

3 Checking students' understanding does not have to be a boring activity – there are many fun, active strategies which you can use to make it interesting as well as productive.

4 Although it's important not to 'over-check' during a lesson, checking should be a normal part of your teaching practice.

5 Asking concept checking questions is a very effective way to check students' understanding, but they can be challenging for both students and teachers.

Introduction

Think about your general day-to-day classroom practice:

1 Why do you check what your students have learned?

2 When do you check what your students have learned?

3 How do you check what your students have learned?

Checking students' understanding

Checking understanding is not something which only takes place in tests or exams. It should be a core part of your teaching practice, and what happens in your language learning classroom. However, you should also be careful not to 'over-check' as it can be quite demotivating for students to constantly be asked questions. When teaching in challenging circumstances, knowing why, when and how to test is even more important, because of the many other factors which make learning difficult.

- Classes may be multi-level (see ▶ **Chapter 10**), meaning that there is likely to be a large gap between the strongest and weakest students. Students may therefore have different levels of understanding. Some may understand the new language quickly whilst others take more time.
- Large class sizes (see ▶ **Part III**) make it more difficult to get accurate or individual data about students' levels of understanding. You may therefore need to get more general or approximate data.
- Textbook issues (see ▶ **Part VI**) lead to students facing difficulties in doing homework or checking their understanding after the class.
- Fewer learning resources (see ▶ **Part V**) mean that students may not be able to write notes and make a record of what they learn in class. This makes it more important that teachers check regularly within classes.

Why and when is it important to check students' understanding?

Checking what – and whether – students have learned what you have taught them is crucial. Many teachers often do not do this. Here are some common reasons for this:

> I don't have time to check if my students have learned what I taught them.

> If I taught it, the students learned it.

> When I ask students if they have understood, they always say yes.

> There's so much else to do in the lesson I often forget to check.

When teaching in challenging circumstances, there can be considerable pressure to get through the textbook quickly, and tell the students as many things as possible. However, it's much better to teach less and have more students understand than to teach more and have fewer students understand. You should make checking a normal part of your teaching practices (that is, something that you do every lesson).

You do not need to check the learning all the time, but it is important to do before moving on to the next stage of the lesson – e.g. there is no point moving to the production stage of a lesson if the students do not understand the target language. It is also important to do at strategic points in the lesson, e.g. after a grammar presentation or before a practice activity. It's also useful to do at the end of a lesson, so you can evaluate where students are in their learning. This can help you plan for the next lesson.

Yes is an unreliable answer to the question *Do you understand*? Students will almost always reply positively to this question, even if they don't understand. Three reasons why students might answer *yes* to the question *Do you understand*? (even when they don't):

- They may be giving a 'preferred response' – i.e. they want to please the teacher and so they answer *yes* instinctively.
- They may not want to appear stupid in front of their classmates.
- They may genuinely think they have understood something when they have not.

As such, it is best to not even ask the question. Instead, you should use some of the strategies outlined below. Remember, it may take time for your students to become familiar with these techniques – but once they do, the process will become much simpler.

Checking students' understanding in challenging circumstances

For the reasons given above, it is important to actively involve students when you check what they have learned. Checking understanding is not a passive act. It is most effective when students take the lead themselves. It is good to vary the way that you check understanding so that students don't get bored with the same techniques.

24.1   *Stand up / Sit down*
This activity works best for closed questions (true / false, or yes / no), or binary questions (when there are only two answers).

For example, imagine you have just taught a lesson about the past simple. You could say: *Listen to the following statements about the past simple. If they are true, stand up. If they are false, sit down.* Note that you might say these statements in L1 rather than the target language:

> *The past simple can be used to talk about the present.*
> *Time words like 'yesterday', '2 days ago' and 'last week' can be used with the past simple.*
> *The past simple describes a state or event which was completed before now.*
> *The past simple can be used to tell stories.*
> *To make the past simple, you add -ing onto the root form of the verb.*

Variations
An alternative way to do this is that students raise their left or right hands for each of the possible answers. This may be a better option if space in your classroom is limited.

You should be aware that some students might find this activity challenging because they prefer to hide, and don't like to do anything in public. If you are concerned about this, students could have a few seconds to decide on their answer with a partner, and they then do it together.

24.2 Four corners
This activity can be particularly useful when reviewing new language items which have been introduced over a few lessons.

ACTIVITY: Four corners

1. Identify a list of 15–20 new words.
2. Identify four categories which the words can be divided into (e.g. parts of the body, jobs, colours, and adjectives). If possible, write signs which have these categories written on them. With large classes, you could also ask students to 'be' these categories (i.e. they can repeatedly say their category name throughout the activity). Assign a corner of the classroom to each category.
3. Tell students that you will say a word, and they should stand in the appropriate corner. For example, if you say *teacher*, they should go to the 'job' corner. If you say *orange*, they should go to the 'colour' corner.
4. Read out the words one by one. Give students a specific time limit (say, five seconds) to move.
5. After each word, take feedback. You can ask students both in the 'correct corner' as well as the 'incorrect corner' to explain their answers. Ask students to give a sentence using the word correctly.
6. Repeat for the other words. Once students understand the activity, you could ask stronger students to perform your role (while you monitor the activity).

Variations
This activity could also be used for checking students' understanding of grammar: The teacher reads out a sentence / verb form / time word, and the students must go to the 'present', 'past' or 'future' corners.

It can also be used to find out what students think about a particular issue (corner 1 = strongly agree; 2 = slightly agree; 3 = slightly disagree; 4 = strongly disagree).

24.3 Spot the mistake

Create a story and read it to the students. This monologue should contain particular language items which you want students to focus on. Students need to listen carefully, and note any factual mistakes which they hear. They can do this in groups, with one person making notes. For example, if you have been learning about animals, you could say the following:

> *As I was walking my pet lion down the street, it started to bark wildly. It saw a black and white giraffe eating leaves from a tree.*

In feedback, ask students to correct what you have said. They must give reasons for this.

Teacher:	*So what's the first mistake?*
Student 1:	*It should be a 'dog' rather than a 'lion'.*
Teacher:	*How do you know?*
Student 2:	*Because a lion isn't a pet.*
Student 3:	*And because a dog barks.*
Teacher:	*OK, and what's the next mistake?*
Student 2:	*A giraffe is orange.*
Teacher:	*Good.*

Note

If you are doing this activity with weaker students, you can use L1 as well as the target language.

24.4 Order!

As discussed elsewhere (see ▶ 17.1), students are the best learning resources, and we should use them as much as possible. Dividing students into groups and then asking them to arrange themselves in an order (i.e. on a cline) is a good way to check whether they have understood differences. Some examples are given in the table below – but the activity would work with any group of words which can be compared.

Language point	Ordering criteria	Target language
comparative and superlative forms of adjectives	basic adjective to superlative	*tall, taller, the tallest* *big, bigger, the biggest*
time	past to future	*5 years ago, last year, last month, yesterday, this morning, tomorrow, in a week's time, next month, in 2050*
adverbs of frequency	low to high	*never, seldom, sometimes, often, regularly, frequently, always*
temperature	cold to hot	*freezing, cold, chilly, mild, warm, hot, boiling*

Once students have made their decisions, a good strategy is to ask the group which has identified the correct answer to try and convince the other groups that they are right. This really gets them to think deeply about their evidence, and helps you understand what they do and don't know.

24.5 3–2–1

At the end of a session, ask students to share the following. This can be done either as a whole-class activity, or in pairs or small groups:

- 3 things they learned;
- 2 things they would like to know more about;
- 1 question they still have.

24.6 Back to the board

This is a fun, competitive activity which can help you understand how much language students have understood.

ACTIVITY: Back to the board

1 Divide the class into around eight groups. In each group there are 'explainers' and 'guessers'. The ratio should be around 3:1. So in a class of sixty students you would have groups of seven to eight students, with two guessers and five or six explainers in each group.

2 In their groups, the guessers should stand opposite the explainers. The guessers should have their back to the board.

3 You should write on the board some of the target vocabulary (words which you have been studying recently). Write them big so that all the explainers can see them. You should write six to eight words.

4 Begin the activity. The explainers must describe the words without saying the word or any of its ▶ derivations, e.g. if the word was *teacher*, they could not say 'a person who teaches'. They would need to say something like a 'a person who works in a school with children'.

5 The first group to guess all the words, wins.

Note

During this activity, it's important that you keep moving around the room to check that nobody is cheating. With smaller classes, you can bring all the students to the front of the class.

24.7 Gimme 5!

Sometimes, you might want to get a quick idea about the general level of understanding in the class about a particular topic. To do this, ask all the students to hold one hand in the air. Using their fingers, they should indicate how much they have understood, where 5 = 'I have completely understood' and 1 = 'I have absolutely no idea'. Obviously this is just a guide, and is a subjective answer (without any actual evidence), but it will give you an idea.

If you are worried that students will feel pressure to show lots of fingers (even if they haven't understood), get them to close their eyes when they do it. This will give you more accurate data.

24.8 Concept checking questions (CCQs)

A CCQ is a question (or sometimes a set of questions) which the teacher asks to tell them whether a language item has genuinely been understood. The three stages to creating a good ▶ concept checking question, along with some actual examples, are given below:

1. Isolate the language item. → 2. Identify the unique aspects of the language item. → 3. Create appropriate CCQs and identify the desired response(s).

1	2	3
He <u>used to</u> play football.	modal used to talk about something <u>regular</u> which is now <u>finished</u>	How often did he play football? (regularly) Does he still play football now? (no)
She <u>may</u> go to Beirut next week.	modal to express <u>possibility</u>	Is the definitely going? (no, it's only possible) Does she have an obligation to go? (no, it's her decision)
My mother is very <u>shy</u>.	<u>adjective</u> to describe a person who <u>may not enjoy familiarity or contact with others</u>	Does she find it easy meeting new people? (no) What kind of word would 'shy' normally come before? (a noun)
My son loves <u>dolphins</u>.	a <u>sea-living</u> mammal which is smaller than most whales	Does a dolphin live on land or in the sea? (in the sea) Is a dolphin huge? (no, it's big but not huge)

A good concept checking question should:
- use simple, clear language which the students are familiar with;
- be objective, not subjective;
- try not to use function words which are negative (e.g. *not*, *never*) as this can create confusion (e.g. ask *Have you ever been there?* rather than *Didn't you go there yesterday?*)

Reflection
- Do you need to make any changes in how you check students' understanding?
- Which of the specific strategies do you think you could use in your classroom?
- How do you think your students would respond to these activities?

25 Creating assessments

If you judge a fish by its ability to climb a tree, it will live its whole life believing that it is stupid.

Matthew Kelly

The short version

1 When creating an assessment, crucial initial questions to ask are: (a) why are we assessing, and (b) what are we assessing?
2 Assessments must be both valid and reliable.
3 Assessment questions should be written as clearly and simply as possible.
4 Marking schemes are important to ensure fairness and equity within the assessment process.
5 Assessment should 'feed forward' into future learning, that is, inform our decisions about adapting our methods and approaches to better suit our learners.

Introduction

1 Why do we assess students? What is the overall purpose?

2 What is the process for creating assessments where you teach? Are you involved in the process?

3 Do you think language assessments used in your institution are fair? Why / why not?

4 Have you ever failed a test? How did you feel?

About assessment

Even if all high-stakes assessment in your institution is controlled by an ▶ education authority, you are likely to still create some kinds of assessment, e.g. formative or ▶ diagnostic assessments. This may just be the occasional test to see how students are progressing, or it may be more detailed and complex assessment. This chapter focuses on key questions which you should ask yourself when creating assessments. These questions are presented in the chronological order in which you should address them.

1 What is the assessment actually testing?

Too often, the clear purpose of an assessment is not known. Sometimes the only reason that students are assessed is because 'this is what we've always done'. Educational stakeholders often have strong expectations that assessment is a central, if not the core, component of education. Moreover, their view of what constitutes a good assessment may be very traditional – i.e. formal, written exams. However, teachers often don't know how to create good assessments, and students are just given memory tests about what they have learned in class. Furthermore, assessment results are not used to improve learning.

Before assessing students, you need to be clear about: (a) what you are assessing, (b) why you are assessing this, and (c) what you will do with the results. If you are making significant changes to common forms of assessment, you should talk to the relevant groups to explain what you are doing, and why you are doing it.

2 Will the assessment be formal or informal, or a mixture of both?

Formal assessment is when student progress is evaluated in a formal, ▶ **standardized** way, e.g. an exam. However, the most interesting and telling things in a classroom sometimes occur when the students don't realize you are watching them. You can discover a lot about a student's real progress by noticing what they are doing in regular classroom activities. Areas which you might be looking for include: How well are they working with other students? Are they listening to what other students say? Are they trying to use new language, or staying within their ▶ **comfort zone**?

Informal assessment can be a useful way of assessing how students actually use language in meaningful situations (rather than their grammatical / lexical knowledge, which is often focused on in formal assessment). Students themselves can also participate in informal assessment and this can be motivating and empowering. The result of informal assessment can be recorded in students' ▶ **learning portfolios**. Using informal assessment may represent a significant change in your institution. However, in learning situations which are time- and resource-poor, it can be very effective.

3 How do I ensure the assessment is valid and reliable?

When creating an assessment, you need to ensure it is both *valid* and *reliable*. Assessment is ▶ **valid** if it measures what it says it is measuring. For example, does the reading component really test the students' reading skills as opposed to what they can remember from the textbooks, or their general knowledge? Assessment is ▶ **reliable** if you could repeat it on a different day with the same students, or with different students, or in a different location, and get similar results.

Think of a driving test. It is only valid if it accurately assesses whether you have the ability to drive safely in public (e.g. can you stop quickly? change gear? park?). It is only reliable if you could do the test in any part of the country, with any examiner, and get the same result.

To decide whether your assessment is valid and reliable, ask yourself these five questions. Alternatively, ask a colleague to look at your assessment, and tell you what they think.
- Does it focus on what has been studied in class?
- Will the students think it is fair?
- Does it actually assess what it is supposed to?
- If a student missed several classes, would they still have a chance to perform well?
- Would the student get the same mark regardless of who marked their test?

4 What makes a good exam task?

Students in challenging circumstances may have little experience of doing formal (or even informal) assessment. It's therefore important to minimize any potential confusion. Follow the four tips below to ensure this.
- Tasks should be as short and simple as possible. However, ensure that you include all the information needed to successfully answer the questions.
- The language used in the tasks (for instructions and questions) should not be more difficult than the language that students are being tested on.
- You should indicate how many marks are available for each task. This affects how students manage their time, and the detail needed for the answers.
- Ensure that students are familiar with the task types used.

5 What should the marking scheme be?

First, you need to decide what type of assessment it is (see ▶ **Chapter 23**) as this will affect the
▶ **marking scheme**. For example, if it's criteria-referenced, you will need to identify what the criteria
are. If there are multiple components to the test (e.g. all four skills), you will need to decide on the
▶ **weighting** of each part. You might decide that each component is worth 25%, or you might decide
that you want to emphasize the speaking component, and make that part worth 40%, and the
reading, writing and listening 20% each of the overall score.

How you mark individual questions will depend on whether the task is objective or subjective.
Objective tasks (e.g. multiple choice, cloze or gap fill) are easy to mark because they are either right
or wrong. However, objective tasks only test language knowledge rather than language usage.
Subjective tasks have no specific 'correct' answer. Students give their responses in writing or speaking,
and the marker decides what their answer is worth. For these questions, there should be a clear and
unambiguous **marking scheme**, otherwise the marker may just give a mark based on the student's past
performance. A marking scheme is especially important when several people assess the same question,
in order to ensure fairness and consistency.

For example, imagine students were asked to do the following task: 'Write a short message to
someone you don't know introducing yourself.' If 3 marks were available for this task, the marking
scheme could be as follows:

3 marks:	a clear answer which focuses on key information (e.g. name, age, family, where you live), and uses appropriate and accurate language and grammar throughout
2 marks:	an answer which includes a reasonable amount of key information and mostly uses appropriate and accurate language and grammar
1 marks:	an answer which includes a small amount of key information and uses some language and grammar which is appropriate and accurate
0 marks:	does not answer the question and contains no relevant information

6 What do I do with the test afterwards?

Once you have marked an assessment, you need to think what you should do with it. You need to
decide what the marks mean, and how you report to the students. For students who do poorly, it can
be extremely upsetting if they don't know why they did poorly, and don't have any idea how to fix it.
In challenging circumstances, this kind of system can be extremely demotivating for students. When
there may already be significant barriers to education, it's important that students feel positive – not
negative – about their learning. If students are regularly failing tests, they (and their parents and
guardians) may feel there is little value in education. As a result, they might drop out of school.

There can often be considerable pressure for tests and exams to be pass / fail. It is often expected
that some students will fail a text, and that if nobody fails, the test was too easy. As such, teachers may
sometimes decide a pass mark which is arbitrary (i.e. it is not made for good pedagogical reasons).
This approach can also result in some students thinking that the main (or only) purpose of education
is to pass tests rather than to learn.

Whilst some students clearly fail tests because they did not work hard enough or were not interested in the subject, there can be many other reasons, for example, because they:

- don't have the textbook or other necessary learning resources;
- have little support at home from their parents or guardians;
- have to work or do household chores, leaving them little time to revise or prepare;
- don't have electricity at home (so can't do school work at night), or don't have pens and paper;
- are physically tired when they arrive at school because they have to travel a long distance;
- have mental or emotional health challenges which affects their performance.

Reflection

- How do you currently measure progress with your students? Is it exam-focused? Is there anything you could do to improve this?
- How can you involve students more in evaluating their own progress?

26   Helping students perform well in exams

Assessment is … the bridge between teaching and learning.

Dylan William

The short version

1   Exams should be seen as a core part of the whole educational process, not as one-off events.
2   Before exams, prepare students for what to expect, check equipment, and identify what happens to the other students.
3   During exams, ensure the physical conditions are optimized, that students are as physically prepared as possible, and that invigilators know what to do.
4   After exams, give as much feedback to students as possible, and ensure that there is systemic support for processes.
5   Create a system where students (and staff) use learning portfolios.

Introduction

1   What is your students' attitude towards exams?

2   How do you think your students' performance in exams could be improved?

3   What would be the obstacles to making these changes?

Exams are a continuous process

It's important that institutions see exams as a core part of the whole educational process. They should not be viewed as one-off events, but as part of a much bigger picture. This chapter thinks about exams from three different perspectives: how you can prepare students before exams, what you can do during exams to make the experience better, and what you can do afterwards.

Before exams

26.1   Familiarizing students with exam tasks

Students need to know what to expect in an exam, especially if it is ▶ high stakes. Knowing the type and style of tasks can help reduce anxiety and stress. If possible, share previous exam papers or tasks with the students. Another good technique is to get them to predict the kind of questions which might come. Engaging with the tasks in this critical way can result in students performing better.

26.2   Planning for the other students

During exam periods (especially for formal summative exams), it is common for the whole institution to be closed except for those doing the exams. Whilst the underlying reason for this makes sense (i.e. to minimize disruptions), the majority of students miss out on learning during this time. In situations where educational opportunities are very limited, the available time for learning has to be maximized. Teachers will need to make plans for these other students so they don't miss out on learning. For example, during these periods, teachers could base themselves in the local environment or community (rather than at the school) and do some of the activities suggested in ▶ Chapters 18 and 28. Alternatively, a ▶ double-shift system could be used so that 'regular' school occurs before or after the exams.

26.3   Checking the equipment

If the assessment depends on equipment working, it needs to be tested in advance. Ideally, this would take place several days beforehand, so that if there is a problem, there is time to fix it. This is especially important if the assessment contains a listening component. If there will be lots of students doing the listening test at the same time, some may not be able to hear properly due to ▶ ambient noise or poor acoustics in the classroom. Others might not be able to hear well because they are sitting at the back of the room. It may be that you have to do the listening test with smaller groups, or read the transcript aloud.

26.4   Supporting students with specific needs

As discussed in ▶ Chapter 3, students who have specific challenges may have particular requirements, or may be entitled to additional time in exams. If this is the case, all the relevant parties (e.g. student, invigilator, head teacher, educational authority) need to be aware what is needed.

During exams

26.5   Creating a good physical environment

Research shows that the physical environment in which students do tests is extremely important. A range of external factors can affect how well students perform, including the weather, air pollution, temperature, sound and weather. In your school, it may be difficult to find a space which meets all, or even some, of these criteria. Try to create a space which is as dry, clean, temperate, bright and quiet as possible.

The educationalist Stephen Heppell outlines several ways in which you can improve the conditions of your classroom, including:

- taking down anything (e.g. paper or posters) which is in front of the windows and prevents light from entering;
- painting classrooms with a bright white paint, which reflects more of the available light;
- advising students to dress appropriately for where they are doing their exams. If your school uses a school uniform, consider allowing students to wear their own clothes to exams, so that they feel more comfortable;
- allowing students to remove their shoes, if they wish. This can help reduce damp and mud;
- placing charcoal in the room in order to reduce air moisture.
- The presence of carbon dioxide (CO_2) make students feel tired more quickly. This is a serious problem if lots of students are crammed into a small space. It's important to keep air moving (e.g. having windows and the door open). If possible, have plants in the room, as these absorb CO_2 and provide more oxygen.

Most smartphones nowadays can give you details about the temperature in your local area. You can also download a wide range of apps to help you measure the levels of light and sound. For example, Decibel X can measure sound, while Lux Light Meter & Tools - Photometer PRO or Light & Exposure Meter can measure light.

26.6   *The role of nutrition and exercise*

Nutrition and exercise can play a significant role in student exam performance. What you are able to do obviously depends on your specific situation. Try and do as many of the following as possible:

- Advise students about the best foods to eat – e.g. vegetables, fruits, slow-release carbohydrates (such as oats, wholegrain bread) and foods with lots of protein (such as milk, yoghurt, eggs).
- Whilst food like chocolate and fizzy drinks can provide an immediate 'sugar rush', students may also experience a 'sugar crash' at the wrong time during their exam, as their blood sugar level suddenly drops which makes them sleepy and slow.
- Allow students to eat snacks during their exams.
- If possible, have 'exam breakfasts' where students can come early and eat their breakfast together. If possible, schools can also provide some suitable foods.
- Provide a place where students can sit or lie down between exams.
- Encourage students to go for walks between exams, or do some exercises or stretches.
- Provide clean, cool water for students to drink and keep hydrated.

26.7   *Briefing invigilators*

There need to be clear guidelines and instructions for exam invigilators, especially when the exams are high-stakes. Some of the key aspects of the invigilators' role include:

- distributing the exam papers;
- checking students aren't using mobile phones or other electronic devices;
- making sure that nobody is outside the room helping any of the students;
- knowing what the toilet policy is, and enforcing it;
- collecting the exam papers at the end, and making sure they are given to the right person.

After exams

26.8   *Learning from exams*

Teachers need to ensure that students can learn from exams. In challenging circumstances, you probably won't have time to give detailed feedback on all the exams you mark. It's simply not possible. However, it is important that students do get this feedback, as exams have to be linked to the learning process. This process is shown in the diagram.

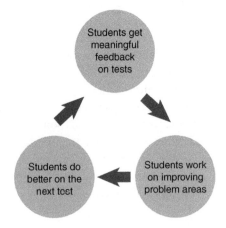

Some ideas for how you can achieve this:

- In class, feedback can focus on the most common problem areas which students faced. When you do this, don't just tell students what the correct answers were, make sure that they understand why they were the correct answers.
- Create a document containing good answers (especially for subjective tasks) so students who did badly on those tasks have the opportunity to learn. You should ask permission from students before doing this – and they can be anonymized.
- If possible, you could also provide a set of correct answers and share with students. They can then check these answers against their own.

26.9 Good systems in place

In challenging circumstances, it is common for teachers to come and go on a regular basis. In terms of assessment, this is a big problem because a lot of ▶ institutional knowledge can be lost when this happens. As such, follows the principles below:

- Make all stakeholders responsible for testing – it should not just be something which teachers are responsible for. Senior managers, head teachers and others should also be involved. Then, even if some people leave the school, some of those who remain will know about the assessment which has come before.
- If and when people who created the tests do leave, ask them to 'hand over' to other members of staff (i.e. provide all the necessary documentation to, and brief the people who take over).
- After each test, have a staff meeting to evaluate the test, identify what went well, and discuss any improvements which could be made.

To support this, it's also important to have good administrative systems in place, and for office staff to be involved in the process. This information can be collected over time to form part of learner portfolios. When new members of staff arrive, as part of their induction, they should have the opportunity to read these learner portfolios, to understand what level their students are at.

Reflection

- How could you improve the environment in which your students do exams? What resources (physical, human, financial) do you need to achieve this?
- Which of the techniques recommended here would be difficult to implement? Why? Is there anything you could do to change this?

27   Involving parents and guardians

Schools do not properly engage parents in their decisions and they rarely share critical information about what concerns the children's education, except where there arises a problem beyond the school's control.

Yakubu Anas, Kano, Nigeria

The short version

1   Parents and guardians have an important role to play in schools.

2   Some schools are supportive of parents' and guardians' involvement in schools, and have mechanisms which encourage this, such as parent–teacher associations. Other schools can be less supportive to this, or indeed hostile.

3   Some parents and guardians may feel nervous or embarrassed about getting involved, often because of their educational background or social status. Schools have to be more welcoming to those who feel like this.

4   The learning which takes place at home can be as important as the learning which takes place at school.

5   Parents and guardians can have an important role to play in the classroom.

Introduction

1   How many of your students' parents have you met, or do you know?

2   To what extent are parents and guardians involved in the life of your school, and their children's learning?

3   Below are some strategies for getting parents / guardians involved more in schools and their children's learning. What do you think they mean? How can parents and guardians be involved in them?

> parent meetings   ten-minute share   homework   teaching assistants
> parent talks   show and tell

How to involve all educational stakeholders

The first thing to say is that you cannot make the changes listed here by yourself. To fully involve parents and guardians in the life of your school, all ▶ **educational stakeholders** will need to be involved, especially head teachers and senior teachers. Strong leadership is needed to make meaningful change. Depending on your context, some of the ideas below will be more realistic than others. You will need to adapt to your local situation.

27.1   Ten-minute share

When some children begin school, they are very nervous. Indeed, they may even be scared. It's obviously important to minimize this wherever possible. One way to achieve this is to have 'ten-minute share' sessions at the beginning and/or end of the day. This can help the child feel safe and secure, and that school is a 'place for them'. These sessions should not be compulsory for parents. They should be encouraged, rather than pressured to participate. Indeed, there may be good reasons why some parents cannot come.

In these sessions, parents sit with their child in their classroom. Doing this sends a very powerful message to the child about the importance of education. During this time, children and parents and guardians can participate in different learning and sharing activities, such as:

- The child shares with their parent(s) what they learned yesterday.
- The child shares with their parent(s) what they think they are going to learn today.
- The child reads with their parent(s).
- The child introduces their parent(s) to a friend.

Of course, there may be many other things which happen, but the key point is that it is the student who is directing the activity. It is empowering and creates a very positive learning environment.

27.2   Parents' meetings

Many parents feel that they don't have a role to play in their children's education. This is particularly true if parents had negative or no educational experiences themselves. Sometimes, school makes parents feel this, directly or indirectly. They may not feel that school is a 'place for them', and that education should be left to experts.

However, academic research shows that parents are a crucial factor in children's experience of and performance at school. One way to encourage this is to have parents' meetings at the school on a regular basis. Parents' meetings provide an opportunity for teachers and parents to discuss how their child is doing, and what they are learning. The child can also be present in these meetings. This sends out a very positive message to the child, that there are many people who are interested and supportive of their educational progress.

It can be a long, challenging process to develop good relationships with parents. Ways you can make this process better include:

- making sure the first contact is positive;
- using simple, straightforward language when talking, or in written communication;
- encouraging parents to share concerns, and to see any similarities or differences between school and home life;
- encouraging students to share with their parents what they learn at school – and encouraging parents to ask these questions at home;
- being aware of parents' own attitudes towards education systems (which may be negative);
- introducing them to the language and common terms used in schooling.

A study by John Hattie (2012) in New Zealand shows that greater parental involvement in schools in low socio-economic areas leads to students being more engaged, better at reading, and more focused. There were also benefits for the parents.

27.3 Parents and homework

Learning does not only take place at school; it also takes place in the home. Parents and guardians are crucial in supporting their children with their learning outside of school. They do not need to have had a formal education in order to help their child – something that's really important for them to know. Many parents and guardians feel it's not their role to 'teach' their child, and that learning is something which only takes place at school. Parents and guardians should be aware that what they say to their child, and how they support them, is more important than what they may or may not know.

Parents and guardians can support their children's homework in many different ways:

- helping them manage their household chores (what they have to do, and when);
- providing a calm space where they can do their homework;
- asking them to explain what their homework is, and to share it with them when they finish it;
- encouraging them to 'teach' the main contents of their homework (e.g. to them, or their siblings).

27.4 Show and tell

The importance of how a classroom looks was discussed in ▶ 2.10. Putting materials made by students on the classroom walls helps to create a positive classroom atmosphere. Ideally, this display should change every month or so, as the students create new materials.

Therefore, one idea is to invite parents and guardians to the school on 'changeover day' (when the previous material is taken down). On this day, students could do informal 'show and tell' sessions. During these sessions, students explain the work which they have done. Students could also present to other year groups in the school.

27.5 Parent talks

Parents, like all people, have a unique set of skills and experiences. These can be used positively for language learning, as well as deepening parents' links to the school. One activity you can do is to ask a parent to come and talk to the class about what they do, or something that is especially interesting about them (e.g. somewhere they have been). Before they come to the class, you might brainstorm some questions from the students which they would like to ask. You can then share these with the person so that they have time to prepare.

Their daughter or son can stand alongside them and translate into English (or whatever the target language is). This is something which they could have practised beforehand, at home. When finished, you can use the material for additional activities (e.g. summarizing what was said, or eliciting what students thought was the most interesting thing they heard).

27.6 Teaching assistants

A teaching assistant (TA) is someone – often a parent or guardian – who helps the teacher in their class. The position may be paid or voluntary, depending on the situation. The role of a TA is wide and varied. Some of the common tasks which they perform include:

- providing language support to students (particularly useful if the language of instruction is different from the students' L1);
- reading with students who find this skill difficult;

- marking homework;
- managing the class, e.g. setting up and monitoring group work.

Depending on your situation, there may be parents or guardians who are willing and able to be TAs in your school. Other community members may also be interested. TAs can be very effective in the classroom, and significantly improve the quality of your language teaching.

Note

It may be useful to record the specific roles of individuals or groups in a contract. Although such a contract won't have legal status, individuals are more likely to do what they are supposed to do.

Reflection

- Which of these ideas might work in your school? What could you do to make them happen? Who should you speak to?
- Which ideas do you like, but would be difficult to implement? Is there anything you could do, or anyone you could speak to about it?

28   Involving the local community

The real challenge in resource-starved environments is to determine what the local community and society in general want from schools and then determine the most cost-effective inputs to create such effective schools.

Martin Prew

The short version

1   The involvement of the local community in the school can have a positive impact on student experiences and outcomes.

2   When the local community is more deeply involved in education, students have a richer learning experience, and marginalization is reduced.

3   Some local communities may not know or feel comfortable about being involved in the school. It such cases, it's necessary to make them feel welcome.

4   In every community there are people who have knowledge, skills and experience which can be used for language learning purposes.

5   There are many ways in which the local community can get involved – informal or formal, active or passive, long-term or short-term.

Introduction

1   To what extent is the local community active in your school?

2   Is it important for the local community to be involved in the school? Why / why not?

Why involve the local community?

Involving the local community in your school can have many benefits, such as:
- reducing marginalization;
- increasing inclusivity;
- improving school management;
- providing richer learning experiences for children;
- upholding local culture, tradition, knowledge and skills.

Participation can mean many different things, ranging from passive attendance at events, through to actual legal, statutory powers about what happens in the school.

28.1   Open days

An effective way to get the local community involved in your school is to hold an open day. Choose a day when most people will be free, and invite the local community to come to the school, where they can learn more about how it works, and how they could get involved. Organizing an open day should be a collaboration between students, teachers, parents and guardians, and school management.

Questions to ask when planning include:
- What do you want the local community to know about the school?
- What activities could you do to demonstrate the positive aspects of the school?
- How do you want the community to get involved?

28.2   School noticeboards

School noticeboards can be a useful way of updating the local community about what is happening at the school. To make them as effective as possible, noticeboards should be:
- updated on a regular basis;
- positioned outside the school boundary – some people would feel awkward about coming inside the school – so the noticeboard is then also physically 'in the community';
- written in an appropriate language or languages for the local community, to ensure that everybody can understand.

You can also give responsibility to students to share the noticeboard information with their families and other members of the community.

28.3   Language classes for the community

Running classes for the local community is a way to get them more involved in the school. Depending on your context, it may be possible that you and your students could teach language or literacy to other members of the community. These classes could be in L1 or L2, in non-formal or informal settings, with children (e.g. ▶ out-of-school children) or adults. In addition to providing a useful and valuable service to the community, it can deepen your students' understanding of what they are teaching.

Younger children may not be able to run classes themselves. Older children, however, may be able to. If younger children are involved, the classes could be led by an adult, with children supporting as teaching assistants. Although the idea of children teaching adults is an unusual and radical one, this is not a reason *not* to do it. Changing the 'natural order' like this sends a powerful message about children's ▶ agency. This process can also be very liberating for adults. As discussed elsewhere in this book, language learning can provide a safe space for people.

Note
Language classes should focus on ▶ functional language, so that participants feel like they are making quick progress, and can immediately practise what they learn. Interesting and relevant topics could include:
- introductions;
- families;
- likes and dislikes;
- jobs;
- food and drink.

28.4   Oral histories of older people

Too often, the knowledge and experience of older people is overlooked or ignored. In addition to what they can contribute in social terms, older people can add a lot of value to the classroom. In challenging circumstances, where records about the past may not be so easy to access, older people can be a gateway into history.

Oral histories can be especially rich and important in mobile communities, where students may not remember, or indeed may never have visited, their 'home' country.

ACTIVITY: Oral histories

1 Invite people into your classroom, and ask them to talk about the past. Encourage the speakers to discuss a wide range of topics (e.g. culture, society, technology, politics).

2 Make the discussion interactive. Encourage students to ask questions. It might be helpful to prompt students with questions such as:
   How have things changed in the last (*30*) years?
   What did this area used to look like?
   Are there any festivals which aren't celebrated any more?
   What were things like when (*politician*) was in charge / in government?

3 Some students should be taking notes. You could also record or video what is said (if possible). If you do, make sure you ask for and receive permission from everyone who is going to appear in the video.

4 Students create a poster / play / short video about what they have heard. From a language perspective, encourage students to use both L1 and L2 (see ▶ **Chapter 8** for more on this). For example:
   • the poster could be labelled in L1 and L2;
   • the play's dialogue could be in L1 and the narration in L2;
   • the play's dialogue could be in L2 and the narration in L1;
   • the video could be in L1, but with subtitles created in L2 (but if this is difficult technically, subtitles could be written on paper – they do not have to appear on the screen).

5 Students share what they have created with the wider community, e.g. performing the play, reading the story or displaying the poster.

6 If you have time, students could do a range of follow-up written activities in L2, like producing a summary, news report, newsletter, and so on.

Highly-mobile settings, where people have physically moved between many different places, can be used positively with students. Students could interview people, and create a map which physically represents their journeys (see an example of an oral history map on ▶ **page 170**). This could then be labelled in L2 and/or L1.

Variation

Another similar map students could create is a language or dialect map which shows how different words are expressed in different locations. If people have travelled across national borders, there are more likely to be significant language differences. However, depending on the location, even neighbouring communities may have different words for the same thing.

These activities not only provide considerable language learning and skills development opportunities, but is a way of creating deep, powerful links between the school and the community. The activities will also provide the students with a more thorough understanding of how language works in more general terms.

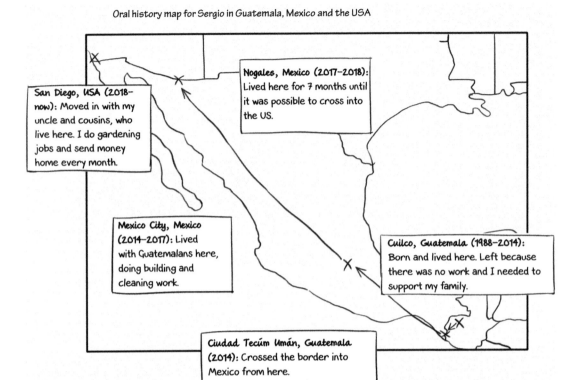

Oral history map for Sergio in Guatemala, Mexico and the USA

San Diego, USA (2018–now): Moved in with my uncle and cousins, who live here. I do gardening jobs and send money home every month.

Nogales, Mexico (2017–2018): Lived here for 7 months until it was possible to cross into the US.

Mexico City, Mexico (2014–2017): Lived with Guatemalans here, doing building and cleaning work.

Cuilco, Guatemala (1988–2014): Born and lived here. Left because there was no work and I needed to support my family.

Ciudad Tecún Umán, Guatemala (2014): Crossed the border into Mexico from here.

28.5 Parents' jobs

The work which people do can be very interesting for students, and can lead to many language learning opportunities.

ACTIVITY: Guess my job

1 Ask the guest to mime their job.
2 Students can guess the job, or ask yes / no questions about it in the target language. You (or a student) may need to be the translator.
3 After students guess the job, there can be further discussions, where students learn more about the person's work.

If possible, invite more than one person to share their job with the class. Afterwards, students can work in groups to complete a Venn diagram, which identifies the similarities and differences between the jobs they learn about. Here is an example for a comparison between a farmer and a shopkeeper.

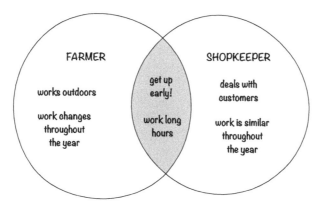

Note

Even if you know and trust the speaker well, or they have a good reputation, you should always supervise guests in your classroom. This will ensure that it remains a safe and secure place for all students.

28.6 Getting people involved

▶ Parent-teacher associations (PTAs) are organizations which provide parents with a formal structure to participate in schools. If your school has one, think about how you could work with it to support some of the other ideas listed here. If your school does not have one, you could work with interested community members to set up an informal group. These informal groups can create positive upward pressure, resulting in better educational experiences and outcomes. Whilst parents are the group who would probably be most interested in being involved, it does not have to be restricted to them. In time, if successful, the role and position of these informal groups could become more formal. Using technology, for example social media channels can be used to make these groups more effective.

For such groups to function properly and fairly, they must genuinely be representative of the entire community. PTAs can sometimes be dominated by groups which have more ▶ social capital (e.g. richer, politically active, from a more dominant social group). They should therefore:

- have very limited, and ideally no, financial expectations. People should be members because of their opinions, energy, knowledge, skills or relationships – not because of how much they can give;
- use a language in meetings which does not present a barrier. This should also be the case in any documents related to the meeting (e.g. the agenda, or minutes);
- take place at a time and in a location which does not make it difficult for people who work irregular hours, or who have no private transport, to attend;
- have appropriate toilet facilities, in case the lack of such facilities might prevent some people from coming.

Note

An example of a successful informal organization is Global Action Nepal's Child Education Concern Groups. These groups consist of parents who are responsible for monitoring school activities, supporting teachers and school governors, and holding campaigns and rallies which support child rights, health, sanitation and other relevant issues. They bridge the gap between school and community.

Reflection

- Which of these ideas would work in your school?
- What might be some of the challenges if implementing these ideas? How could you minimize these challenges?

29 Bringing the outside world into the classroom

Language is not a sterile subject to be confined to the classroom. One of two things must be done: either life must be brought to the classroom or the class must be taken to life.

Peter Strevens

The short version
1 A good starting point for connecting the global to the local is to think about what people have in common.
2 Bringing global issues into the classroom can help avoid stereotyping, and gives students a fact-based view of the world.
3 Young people are often curious and confused. These feelings can be used positively for good language learning.
4 Newspapers and magazines are fantastic resources, and they can be used many different times in many different activities.
5 Even if your school lacks technology or connectivity, you can still introduce students to new ideas and concepts, adapting them for your specific context.

Introduction
1 How much do your students know about the area where they live? Think about different topics such as: its geography, economics, society and culture.

2 How much do your students know about other communities in your region, the rest of your country or the outside world?

3 How can we use students' curiosity to develop language knowledge and skills?

29.1 Comparing life experiences
One way to connect the global to the local is to talk about things we have in common, e.g. families, festivals and food. Students can reflect on their own experiences and compare and contrast these experiences with others. Pictures (and videos) can be particularly engaging for students, and help them do this effectively.

If you have relevant contacts, you could try and establish a pen pal link with students or classes in other countries. You might be able to do this informally through social media yourself, or through a teaching association you could join (see ▶ 32.4). Alternatively, you could look into joining more formal schemes, such as the British Council's Connecting Classrooms programme.

You may be able to find pictures on the internet which help students. You might like to show students photos by the artist Peter Menzel, who has created several exhibitions which compare how people live around the world, for example, showing images of what different people eat, what they own, or how they celebrate festivals.

Note
Some readers may find some of the images in Peter Menzel's collection distressing or offensive.

29.2   *Global comparisons*

Young people are naturally very curious about the world around them, as well as the world beyond them. To avoid problems arriving from ▶ **stereotyping**, students need a clear, fact-based view of the world around them. These comparisons can be done at the local, national and international level, and in a range of different areas, such as geography, economics and culture.

There are a number of websites which you can use to give students this perspective. If your students can't get online, show them the pictures on your device, group-by-group. If your school doesn't have any online access, get students to imagine what the other information would be (e.g. *What do you think a town in that country looks like? What do you think people in (other countries) think about this issue?*). Doing this, in itself, is a very interesting and valuable speaking activity.

ACTIVITY: Our world from above

1   Find some photos online showing various communities around the world, viewed from above. (French photographer Yann Arthus-Bertrand's work is probably the best-known, but you can find other images on the internet.)

2   In groups, students discuss what they think their community would look like from above. They then draw a birds' eye-view picture of their community on a piece of paper.

3   Students display their pictures in a class gallery, and share their thoughts about them.

Stronger groups could also do comparisons in different areas (e.g. economic, social or cultural). A number of websites provide useful statistical data and reports which students can use to research a presentation or essay, including: Gapminder (gapminder.org), which provides facts and data about the world, focusing in particular on common misconceptions, and Dollar Street, a microsite within Gapminder, which imagines the world as a street, where the poor live on the left and the rich on the right. The World Values Survey (worldvaluessurvey.org) records the dominant attitudes towards particular issues (e.g. marriage, work, the environment) in various countries. You could also do a role play discussion about a selected issue. The students should pretend they are from another country, and reflect the dominant view on that issue.

Note

Humans around the world like to celebrate special days. International organizations such as the United Nations and UNESCO have a calendar of such days, which include the International Day of Happiness (20 March), International Youth Day (12 August), and World Homeless Day (10 October). Since these issues are relevant globally, they provide an opportunity for developing students' understanding across the world. A useful resource for this has been created by IATEFL's Global Issues Special Interest Group (GISIG). You can even download a series of 12 lessons about such days from their website: gisig.iatefl.org

29.3 *Spreading the news*

This is a quick and easy activity to increase students' understanding about news stories.

ACTIVITY: Spreading the news

1 Divide students into groups. Try to ensure that each group has access to either a) a printed newspaper, or b) a digital newspaper or news source. If this is not possible, you will need to provide the newspapers (for example, the website eewiki.newint.org offers offers teachers or students lots of suitable materials for free, taken from the *New Internationalist* magazine), or cut up a newspaper and circulate different articles.

2 The group reads as many of the stories as they can. Tell them that they will need to remember this information to share with others.

3 Do a mingle activity where everyone shares their stories with everyone else.

4 Ask students to say which stories they found most interesting, and why. If you have time, you can discuss in more detail.

Reflection
- How could you use – or adapt – the activities listed in this chapter in your classroom?
- What online or print resources are available in your context to help you bring the outside world into the classroom?

30   Caring for your students and for yourself

Children come into school every day and more or less do the same thing. Sometimes they behave a little better, sometimes a little worse. What makes the biggest difference is the reaction of the adults around them.

Sally Farley

The short version
1   When teaching in challenging circumstances you may want to support your students more than you are able to. For the sake of your own health, however, these relationships should be more professional than personal.
2   Managing poor behaviour is one of the major challenges teachers face. It can be managed by good classroom practices, trying to understand the underlying reasons for the behaviour, and creating a class contract.
3   Language has a specific, positive role to play in allowing students to process their anxiety and/or trauma.
4   The well-being of yourself and your colleagues is a critical factor in institutions being able to function well in challenging circumstances.
5   Where there is genuine trust between education stakeholders, the level and the degree of care is more effective.

Introduction
1   What do you understand by the term 'social, emotional and behavioural difficulties'? To what extent is this an issue in your institution?

2   How do you deal with students who display these difficulties? Does your institution have policies on what to do?

3   As a professional working in challenging circumstances, what do you do to look after yourself? Should you be doing more?

Dealing with social, emotional and behavioural difficulties

When teaching in challenging circumstances, it's important to remember that you are 'just' a teacher. When faced with students whose lives may be unimaginably hard, you might feel the pressure to be more than this. Indeed, in many cases, you might be one of the most important people in the students' lives, if not *the* most important. If you teach children or teenagers, this is even more likely. However, you might teach tens, if not hundreds, of students. You simply cannot provide the support and care which is needed for them all. You also need to think of yourself and your own well-being.

In challenging circumstances, there may be high incidence of SEBD (social, emotional and behavioural difficulties). When these difficulties come to the surface in the classroom, it can feel like you have failed. The students' behaviour feels like a verdict on your teaching, or even on you as an individual. However, in most cases it isn't. In fact, students may be more likely to 'act up' when they trust and respect you, as they see you as a safe presence.

This chapter looks at positive strategies for managing SEBD in the classroom (including the specific role of language in doing this) as well as how you can look after yourself and your own health.

Managing poor behaviour

Managing poor student behaviour is a constant, even daily, difficulty for most teachers. When working in challenging circumstances, the impact and the affect which this has on learning experiences and outcomes can be extremely serious. Four techniques for how you can manage these incidences of poor behaviour are suggested below:

30.1 SEBD-appropriate classroom practices
Many of the 'good practice' teaching techniques outlined in this book will help minimize poor student behaviour. Some of the most relevant are:
- making the classroom safe (see ▶ Chapter 2);
- being inclusive (see ▶ Chapter 3);
- giving clear instructions (see ▶ Chapter 6);
- using and respecting students' L1 (see ▶ Chapter 8);
- managing where students sit, and who they sit next to (see ▶ Chapter 9);
- motivating and empowering students (see ▶ Chapter 23);
- involving parents and guardians (see ▶ Chapter 27).

30.2 A positive, trusting classroom atmosphere
Clearly, there is no simple and straightforward mechanism for creating a positive, trusting atmosphere in class, and modelling the behaviour you would expect from your learners. How you can achieve this will depend significantly on the students in your class. However, some useful general principles include:
- **acknowledging, describing and validating good behaviour:** Sometimes teachers only talk about behaviour negatively, i.e. when a students misbehaves or does something bad. Try to talk about behaviour more positively, for example when students behave well, are helpful or show kindness. Noticing this positive behaviour, and commenting on it publicly, can motivate students and create a positive cycle. These behaviours do not necessarily need to be big – e.g. *Maria, I noticed how you shared your book with Juan*; *I liked how quickly and nicely you formed your groups*; or *It made me happy how well you listened to each other*. There is a particular power if you name the student, as others will also want to be named (see the next point below).

- **humanizing the students:** To feel empowered, people need to see themselves (and to be seen) as individuals with ▶ **agency.** Small things, which seem insignificant, can have a significant impact – like using the students' names or remembering basic information about them (e.g. where they live, or what football team they like).

- **stopping issues from escalating:** As soon as you sense a problem in the class, try to manage it. Don't ignore signs such as pushing, louder voices, or a report by another student. It can be tempting to ignore an issue and hope it goes away (and so you don't have to disrupt the whole class). Prevention, however, is better than cure – and most of the time it is quicker and decreases stress and anxiety for everyone. Quickly identify a workable solution – e.g. speak directly in their direction (to show them you are paying close attention), move the student(s) to a different seat, or ask them to take a short walk outside to calm down. Using eye contact or a gentle touch (e.g. a hand on the shoulder) can also be effective – but note that these actions may not be appropriate in all situations (see ▶ 2.4).

- **avoiding psychological triggers in textbooks:** As noted in ▶ **Part VI**, textbooks often do not understand the context in which students are learning. The contents may sometimes be inappropriate, and in serious cases may actually be ▶ **triggers.** Sometimes such content might be common ELT material (e.g. talking about family or personal issues, or discussing going on a journey), or it might be an obvious problem (e.g. a text which contains descriptions of conflict or violence). Audio / video recordings might also contain particular items which cause distress such as specific sounds (e.g. helicopters, raised voices, arguments, doors slamming) or songs. Try to look through textbook contents before the lesson, and think about whether they might negatively affect any of your students. If this is the case, you might (a) warn them, (b) skip over some things in the class, or (c) allow affected students to participate in the class in alternative ways (for example, working by themselves or with you, rather than in groups).

- **avoiding psychological triggers in the institution more widely:** In addition to some of the potential triggers indicated in ▶ 30.1 (e.g. receiving too many instructions at once, sitting too long or in a particular position, hearing unfamiliar languages), other triggers should be minimized, such as the random appearance of strangers or authority figures, bells at the start or end of lessons, fire drills, shouting and/or screaming, abrupt changes, staring, or touching. Depending on the location and context of your institution, there may be other triggers which cannot be avoided, like external noise (e.g. motorcycles), going to the toilet, crowds, or particular weather. You will need to manage these on a case-by-case basis.

- **harnessing the power of *yet*:** Students can get trapped in a cycle of negativity, especially if they are getting little or no positive support. Their response to being unable to do certain things in the classroom might be 'I can't do it' or 'I don't understand it'. When students say these things, you can add the word *yet*. This simple strategy says to students that you believe that they will be able to do, or understand, this particular thing.

- **being the change you want to see:** When faced with poor behaviour, the way you react is critical. For example, if the student shouts at you or another student, and your response is to shout back, the student will naturally conclude that this is appropriate behaviour. Clearly, in a highly-pressurized and stressed environment, it can be very difficult to respond like this. However, if you can, showing students that a different response is possible can be a very powerful message.

30.3   *Understanding students' behavioural issues*

In challenging circumstances, there are many factors which can explain why a student behaves poorly. Often, these factors may be combined. You will need to try and understand these factors before taking action. Some of the main causes are:

- *I'm hot*
- *I'm cold*
- *I'm tired*
- *I'm angry*
- *I'm hungry*
- *I'm depressed*
- *I'm worried*
- *I'm in pain*
- *I'm bored*
- *I don't understand what I have to do*
- *I can't say what I want to*
- *I'm confused*

- *I'm stressed*
- *I'm sitting in a different place than usual*
- *I'm working with someone I don't like*
- *I don't feel well*
- *I'm sad*
- *I had a bad experience this morning*
- *A teacher hit me*
- *My Mum / Dad hit me*
- *A teacher was angry with me*
- *My Mum / Dad was angry with me*
- *My Mum / Dad is ill*
- *My Mum / Dad is sad*

When teaching in challenging circumstances, it can be easy to forget these underlying causes. When faced with poor behaviour, teachers want a quick solution. Common responses include poorly-behaving students being shouted at, put into a corner, sent outside, or told to report to the head teacher. Whilst this may provide a very short-term fix for that particular lesson, it ignores the bigger picture and the underlying causes. When students are punished individually for their poor behaviour, it can feel like a personal attack: 'You are a bad student. You are always naughty in class. Why don't you behave better?'

The difficulty for the student is that they may not know why they are behaving poorly (or may not even know that they are), or they may not be able to fix the underlying causes. They may be experiencing ▶ trauma or another condition which has not been diagnosed, or other students may be bullying them, which is causing them to react in an emotional or aggressive way.

> *A child's current behaviour often reflects an essentially sane response to an untenable set of life circumstances.*

> Madge Bray

When managing poor behaviour, we need to discuss and punish the *act* rather than punish the *student*. There needs to be a full explanation about what is happening and why. Simply telling students that they should not have done something doesn't help them understand, and learn for next time. Where possible, elicit from the student what would have been a better course of action. Students always need an opportunity to fix the situation and make it better. If Student A has hit Student B, ask Student A to explain why the fight started, how they felt at the time, and how they could have acted differently. They should also have the opportunity to apologize to Student B.

Specific strategies which you might use to support students with SEBD in your classes include:

- developing a ▶ buddy system for students, so they have a reference point, a role model for appropriate behaviour.
- telling students that if they feel like this in the future, they should use their L1 to tell you. Even in their L1, you may need to give them the language they need to be able to do this.

- giving students simple strategies to try and manage their feelings – e.g. counting to ten, walking away (even if only temporarily) from the situation, getting them to think about consequences (i.e. *if* they do something, *then* what might happen), and focusing on their breathing (keeping it slow and deep). Ideally, these strategies would be turned into posters (perhaps designed and made by the students themselves) and displayed in the classroom and around the institution.
- giving students responsibility. Whilst this may sound counter-intuitive, showing trust is very important – especially if they have not experienced much trust in their own lives. Begin this with small tasks, such as cleaning the board or handing out books, and work up from there.
- referring student to agencies (where possible) if you feel that they need professional support.

Pupil behaviour is highly sensitive. It challenges teachers' sense of their own professional competence and both teachers' and parents' self-esteem. Emotions often get in the way of constructive planning.

Peter Gray and Sue Panter

30.4 A class contract

As a way of capturing some of the points listed above in ▶ 30.1–3, you could create a ▶ class contract, or a list of ▶ class norms which both students and the teacher are expected to follow. With school-age students, you might call these 'golden rules'. Depending on your context, this could even be expanded to the institutional level.

The document should contain a set of guidelines related to how people should behave in the class, as well as the responsibilities which people have to each other. It should be created jointly by teacher and students, in a language (or languages) which ensures that nobody is excluded. It is a useful way of anonymizing some of the challenges listed previously – e.g. you can include a general prohibition about staring at or touching other students, rather than saying don't stare at or touch any particular students because it is a trigger for them. The actual process of creating the document (and the discussions which take place) is extremely valuable, and to make it even more powerful and 'official', you and your students should sign it. A copy should be placed on the classroom wall for all to see.

Note

A class contract, which promotes positive behaviour, is very different from a list of school rules, which generally punish negative behaviour. It's important that the requirements of the contract are explained and justified, so that students understand the reasons for them, for example that students should not run into the classroom because this might put some students in danger, or be frightening. The requirements for the teacher should also be very clear, for example: the teacher should listen carefully to the students' answers.

The role of language

Whilst this chapter has focused mainly on general strategies for supporting students in challenging circumstances, the specific role of language, and of language learning, should not be underestimated. For, whilst the economic value of languages is widely known, the social and psychological importance is often sidelined, but is no less valuable. The language classroom can be a space in which students can learn to manage their own feelings and behaviour. There is also good evidence that the ability to switch between languages can help people manage their trauma – either to distance themselves from the traumatic event, or else to focus in on it, allowing them to ▶ **self-regulate**.

Some of the common activities and skills which are used in good language teaching can also support students who are suffering from trauma:

- working in a team;
- negotiating consensus;
- expressing your feelings;
- being inclusive;
- communicating with others;
- asking for clarification.

Language also has a huge role to play in informal and non-formal learning situations. Sometimes the language learning can be a direct, explicit target – but it doesn't necessarily have to be, as the example below about a knitting group in the UK demonstrates.

> *At Mothertongue we ran a knitting group as a way of engaging people who would be put off by an activity with mental health in the title. Besides this aim, we also wanted to help people to improve their spoken English, to feel comfortable in a supportive environment and to build trusting relationships. Although knitting was the overt activity, the by-products were often our main aims ... The group communicated in five or six languages with participants translating for each other and for the English-speaking facilitator. Eighty per cent of attendees over a period of one year felt that their English had significantly improved. As well as building sustainable, supportive relationships with each other, they had an opportunity to feel that they were productive contributors to the society in which they now lived by making and donating blankets to the Premature Baby Unit at the local hospital.*

Beverley Costa

Caring for yourself

> *I was blindsided by the emotional aspect of teaching—I didn't know how to handle it. I was hurt by my students' pain, and it was hard for me to leave that behind when I went home.*

Alysia Ferguson Garcia

Teaching can be a hugely rewarding job – but it can also be extremely challenging physically, mentally and emotionally. It's therefore important – indeed crucial – that you care for yourself, both during the school day and outside it. When teaching in challenging circumstances, and working with students who may be vulnerable, depressed, ill or in danger, you have to protect yourself. If there is a high incidence of trauma in your institution, you may be at risk of vicarious trauma. That is, through your interactions with students, and listening to their stories and experiences, you may yourself become traumatized. If you are unable to function properly because of your own mental and physical health, you won't be able to support your students effectively. Think about the following eight suggestions for caring for yourself.

1   **Be professional but not familial:** As noted before (see ▶ 6.7), it's important to keep some distance between you and your students. Be kind and compassionate, but know when and where to draw the line, otherwise the responsibility could be overwhelming.

2   **Look after yourself physically:** Drink water throughout the day, and make sure you eat something. You should also exercise – this does not have to be intensive. A few stretches or a high-intensity walk can activate the blood flow and keep you focused.

3   **Try to have some personal time during the day:** Even if this is just five or ten minutes, it can be a valuable way to recharge your batteries, and deal more effectively with the challenges you face.

4   **Lower your expectations:** You are not a miracle worker, and there is only so much that you can do. Simply being present, creating a safe space, and providing a positive learning experience is very significant for many children. There is only so much which can be achieved, so focus on what is possible and realistic.

5   **Talk to your colleagues:** They are highly likely to have similar experiences and be facing similar challenges to you. Sharing how you are feeling and what you have been doing can be hugely beneficial. This can be done formally (e.g. in periodic staff meetings), but may be more effective if done informally (e.g. a quick chat over a cup of tea). This is discussed in more detail in ▶ Chapter 32.

6   **Talk to your manager(s):** Where it's possible, and you feel comfortable to do so, talk to your head teacher or line manager about how you are feeling. They may be able to help or advise, and provide practical as well as emotional support.

7   **Talk to friends and family:** It can be hard to truly 'leave' your students at the end of the day, especially if you are worried or concerned for them. To minimize the impact of this on your personal life, make them aware (at a general level) of why you might be feeling the way you do, and the challenges which you face in your daily work.

8   **Keep a teaching diary:** A teaching diary can focus on areas where you want to develop and improve as a teacher (see ▶ Chapter 32), but it can also be a place where you record positive things. This might be a moment, a sentence, a comment, a look – in short anything which you notice, and makes you feel proud about the work you do.

> *If you don't love yourself, how in the hell you gonna love somebody else?*
>
> RuPaul

Reflection

- What changes could you make to care for your students more effectively?
- What changes could you make to care for yourself more effectively?

31   Reflecting on your own teaching

As a result of your reflection you may decide to do something in a different way. Or you may just decide that what you are doing is the best way. And that is what professional development is all about.

Julie Tice

The short version

1   Reflecting on your own teaching is an empowering process.

2   This process can help you manage some of the challenges you face on a daily basis, as well as identifying specific ways in which you can improve as a teacher.

3   In addition to reflection which can be done soon after a lesson, teachers can use Critical Incident Analysis to reflect more widely on significant teaching moments across their career.

4   A supportive school environment is one in which all educational stakeholders can give each other constructive feedback. This is difficult to achieve without trust.

5   Getting feedback on your teaching from a colleague can be very beneficial, especially if this can become systemic, and take place on a regular, ongoing basis.

Introduction

1   To what extent do you currently reflect on your own teaching? For example, do you:
   - think about whether a lesson met its objectives?
   - talk to a colleague about how a lesson went?
   - make written notes or records about your teaching?

2   Have you ever been observed in the classroom? Think about:
   - who did the observation;
   - whether the process was supportive and constructive;
   - any changes you made to your teaching following the observation.

Reflective teaching

In challenging circumstances, it may be difficult to access opportunities to improve your own teaching (see ▶ Chapter 32 for ideas on how to do this). As such, it can be beneficial to look 'inwards' rather than 'outwards' for this support. You can learn a lot about your own teaching using a few simple processes. However, if you are able to involve colleagues and even your students in this process, this will add significantly to your development. Indeed, you can use these different perspectives to triangulate the feedback. For example, you may feel that your ▶ boardwork isn't very clear and so it's difficult for students to read. If a colleague and your students give you similar feedback, then it's highly likely this is true, and you can make the necessary changes to your classroom practice.

31.1   Self-reflection

Quick, regular reflection

What you want a lesson to achieve depends a lot on your situation. Purely from a language learning perspective (▶ Chapter 5), the key question is whether you met your lesson objective. (In other words, by the end of the lesson did the students know something they didn't know before, or could they do something they couldn't do?) However, these changes are not always immediately visible, and not all 'progress' is easy to measure or even see, as it may be personal to a particular student (▶ **Part VII**). This is especially true when class sizes are large. There are many ways in which the lesson could be considered a success from a student's perspective. For example, the student may have:

- felt safe in the classroom and could 'be themselves';
- felt valued because an adult showed interest in what they had to say;
- interacted successfully with other students;
- received praise or positive feedback from the teacher or other students;
- learned something about the world which they didn't know before;
- benefited in some other personal way which the teacher has no idea about.

Reflecting on your lesson doesn't have to take a long time. It can just be a few seconds, immediately after the lesson has taken place, or when you have your next break, or at the end of the day. Reflecting on the following three questions can help you develop as a teacher, and help you become the best that you can be within your specific context:

1 Did the lesson go according to plan? If not, why not?

2 What was I pleased with?

3 What would I do differently in future?

Some teachers like to keep a **teaching diary**, in which they record some or all of their lesson observations. In addition to your evaluation of the lesson, you might also include other relevant details which might have affected the lesson, e.g. number of students, the weather, which room it was in.

Another useful, and slightly less formal, way of reflecting on your lesson is to complete a 'learning wall'. A learning wall contains similar information to a teaching diary, but it looks more like graffiti on a wall. You can write things at any time, as they occur to you. This document is, by definition, messy and unstructured. This information should not be visible to students. A learning wall can be created in a book, it can be digital (e.g. as a series of notes), or it can be something physical – e.g. a noticeboard with sticky notes on, or a large sheet of paper you keep in an office or at home.

> Had a good lesson today ...
> one child who usually finds
> it hard to participate in
> activities led a group! ☺☺
>
> Tried something new....went well! :)
>
> My instructions were not good
> today – too long and I didn't
> model... the activity didn't
> work well...
> → next time I should stop
> activity and restart.
>
> Difficult day today ... nothing quite
> worked, but MUST STAY POSITIVE !
>
> Students seemed bored ...
> stopped the lesson and ask them
> why. Did something else instead,
> which they liked! ☺

Longer, more periodic reflection

Another highly effective technique, which you can do by yourself (as either a written or a mental process) or through a dialogue with colleagues, is Critical Incident Analysis (CIA). In this approach, teachers think about moments in the classroom which have stayed in their mind, both positive and negative. The teacher analyses these individual events in order to understand them more deeply. CIA can help you understand what you do, why do it, and whether you could (or should) do it differently. The CIA process usually has two stages. In the first stage, the teacher simply describes what happened, in as much detail as they want. In the second stage, the teacher explains the meaning. CIA can be done as an individual piece of reflection, or one involving colleagues, who can perhaps give different perspectives.

> *An 'incident' need not be a dramatic event in the teaching context, just one that makes you stop and think, or one that raises questions for you.*

> Ruksana Mohammed

31.2 Peer observation and reflection

Ask your colleagues to observe you teaching. This can be done through more formalized teacher development sessions (see also ▶ **Chapter 32**) and also through a more informal ▶ **buddy** system, where you might take it in turns to watch each other teach, and then share feedback. In challenging circumstances, however, teachers very rarely have such a system. This is for several reasons, primarily the pressures of time and availability, and the strong cultural emphasis on not losing face. Furthermore, institutions generally do not have the culture of doing this either. When teachers are observed, it is usually summative, that is, they are assessed against a strict list of external criteria by an internal (e.g. head teacher) or external (e.g. inspector) authority. It is common for these observations to focus more on whether the teacher is following what they think are the 'right' (that is, teacher- and textbook-focused) procedures rather than on student learning outcomes and experience. The best kind of observation is when there is mutual trust and shared values between the teacher and the observer, and where both can be upskilled through the process.

Despite the pressures of time, if you and a colleague can find time to do peer observation, it can be hugely beneficial for both participants. The conversation afterwards doesn't have to be lengthy, and indeed can be based around the three questions presented in ▶ 31.1. In addition, you might also ask for feedback on particular areas where you want to improve (which you have identified beforehand through self-reflection). These areas could be, for example, student engagement, gender balance, group work, lesson structure, ▶ **classroom management**, or time management.

31.3 Student feedback

You could ask your students for feedback on your teaching. For this, you need to have a strong, trusting relationship with your students. If you don't have this kind of relationship, students will probably be very neutral ('Everything is fine.') or negative ('I don't like the way you...'). Neither type of feedback is particularly helpful. Student feedback is most valuable when they can tell you what went well (and why), and what could have been better (and why). This information can then be used to shape your future teaching. If it's difficult to have an open discussion with all your students, you might be able to meet four or five representatives who can summarize the views of the class. If you don't have time for this, you could put a feedback box in your classroom, where students can put messages and comments about your teaching anonymously. This box could be there on a permanent basis, or only at specific times (e.g. during a designated 'feedback week').

Reflection
- Do you think reflecting more on your teaching would be helpful? Why / why not? If yes, which of the techniques mentioned would work best in your context?
- Can you think of a colleague it would be useful to cooperate with, and observe each other's lessons?

32 Accessing development opportunities

A journey of a thousand miles begins with a single step.

Chinese proverb, attributed to Lao Tzu

The short version

1 It's important to develop as a teacher, for personal, professional and psychological reasons.
2 Although you may feel that you have no opportunities for professional development, even in the most challenging circumstances, there are things you can do.
3 Developing your language ability, particularly your spoken skills, can give you confidence and have a positive impact on your teaching ability.
4 Participating in face-to-face and/or online teacher groups, as well as joining national or international networks, is a good way of developing your pedagogical skills and to make you feel part of a community.
5 There are many online options for development, but you may need to search carefully to find ones which are relevant and appropriate for you.

Introduction

1 What skills and knowledge would make you a better teacher?

2 What development opportunities can you find in your context? Are you accessing all the opportunities which are available?

Teacher development

Developing as a teacher is important for personal, professional and psychological reasons. In becoming better as a teacher, as learning experiences and outcomes improve, both you and your students benefit. Furthermore, as you develop your own skills and abilities, you also make yourself more employable. Teachers, like students, can sometimes have a negative mindset, where professional development feels pointless, or a very high mountain to climb. You may feel that there is so much to do that there is no point in doing anything. However, in the majority of challenging circumstances, if teachers don't take responsibility for their own development, nobody else will. Although it may not be easy, it is usually possible to improve your situation.

Teacher development can be divided into three main categories:
- How can I increase my knowledge of my specific subject area? (e.g. improving your own English, or a specific aspect of it, such as speaking skills)
- How can I improve my general pedagogic skills? (e.g. using group work more effectively, or teaching writing more collaboratively)
- How can I improve a specific skill which is particularly relevant where I teach? (e.g. supporting children who have trauma, or teaching multilingual classes)

Five specific techniques about how you can develop as a teacher are outlined below. Whilst some of the options presented are digital, if it is difficult to get online in your situation, there are still many offline options, many of which may be available to you in your local area.

Note

For more detailed information about teacher development, refer to *50 Tips for Teacher Development* by Jack C. Richards, also in the Cambridge Handbooks for Language Teachers series.

32.1   *Developing teachers' language skills*

A common challenge and frustration faced by English language teachers is their own language weaknesses. Whilst this may be true for some, it might also just be their own perception. As a result, they may feel less confident in the classroom. They are also likely to be more risk-averse, and use a more textbook-focused, teacher-centred approach.

In challenging circumstances, teachers' language ability is very important. As the Knower (see ▶ Chapter 6), they may be the students' only language model and source of knowledge.

In your institution, it's possible that other teachers feel similarly to you about their own language ability. As such, you could establish a language learning club, along the same lines as ▶ 32.2 below. Whilst the club could work through a textbook, it might be more effective and motivating if it's a conversation club. Members could simply talk to each other in English (or whatever the target L2 is) on topics and subjects which have been selected by the group.

If you have good connectivity, there are also many digital opportunities for learning languages, including a wide range of mobile phone apps, such as Hello English, Duolingo, Lingbe, WordUp, Memrise, Drops and many others. There are also thousands of videos on online video-sharing platforms for learning English and other languages.

32.2   *Face-to-face teacher groups*

When teaching in challenging circumstances, it is important that you and your colleagues support each other. When facing so much change and so many variables, often the only consistent factor is the people you work with. Having the opportunity to share your experiences with people who understand your day-to-day work can be very beneficial, both psychologically and in terms of your development as a teacher.

Face-to-face teacher groups can be run and managed in several ways. When setting up such a group, consider the following questions:

How many people should it contain?

While you want to give everyone the opportunity to participate, if it's too large (e.g. twenty people or more), it might be difficult for all the participants to adequately share their views, and the group might be dominated by a few powerful voices. Smaller groups can be very effective – so even if there are just three or four of you who are interested in setting up a group, you should do it.

When should it meet?

This is obviously a question for the group itself to decide. It's important that you choose a time which reflects the range of people in the group. It's probably better if meetings are shorter and more focused (e.g. 45–60 minutes) – this may also encourage more teachers to attend. It may then be possible to do them before, during or after the teaching day. It's important that meetings are regular, but that attending them doesn't feel like a burden – e.g. two or three times a month.

How should the groups be run?

Whilst the groups could be run by a senior teacher or the head teacher at your institution, they should be fully involved and committed if this is to work. The most effective types of group are often those which are run by the members themselves on a turn-by-turn basis. Ideally, the meetings should follow the 'good practice' guidelines presented throughout this book, e.g.:

- seating members in a circle in order to encourage discussion and emphasizing the equal value of everyone's contributions;
- using multilingual techniques, according to the language demographics and abilities of the group;
- using group work and giving specific responsibilities to the members (e.g. reporting back, managing the group, timekeeping).

How formal should it be?

'Informal' does not have to mean 'unprofessional'. If the meeting also has a social focus (e.g. drinking tea, the opportunity to chat before and after the meeting), members' motivation to come will be higher.

When face-to-face groups are established, teachers are often very committed. However, after a few weeks, it is common for participation to drop. It's important to try and maintain this energy and passion over a long period of time. This is why giving responsibility and ownership to the group members is important. If the group feels they are in charge (rather it being something external which they *have to* do), its chances of success are much higher.

32.3 *Online teacher groups*

If it's difficult or impossible to meet face-to-face, a digital teacher group can provide excellent opportunities for sharing and development. In many cases, a blended approach (in which the face-to-face group is also a digital group) can be very effective. Facebook and WhatsApp are the two most common platforms for such groups, but there are a number of alternatives. Facebook groups can be open (where anyone can join and follow) or private (where people must apply and the group administrators decide who can be a member). WhatsApp groups are private by default. Whatever platform you use, consider the following general guidelines:

- Encourage members to focus on practice – i.e. what they actually do in the classroom. Some of the most effective posts are when teachers share their feedback on something new which they tried in the classroom.
- Don't let people post anything which is not relevant to the group – e.g. about the news, commercial messages, personal posts, or spam messages. Members quickly lose interest when this happens.
- Try and keep small talk to a minimum – of course be polite and pleasant, but people only have limited time to look through messages.
- If connectivity is problematic, ask members to only post text messages. Images or videos may use a lot of bandwidth and may discourage or even prevent people from participating.
- Have more than one administrator, so you can share the burden of managing the group.
- Accept that members will use the group in different ways. Most digital groups contain 'lurkers' – people who read and follow what others are saying, but do not actively participate. However, they may be benefiting from what they are reading, and in time they may feel able to share their views.

If you don't want to create your own online teacher group, there are many pre-existing ones which you could join. Whilst many of these groups are global and the language of discussion is English, there are likely to be others which are more localized.

Search social media platforms using keywords for what kind of group you are looking for. Some groups are very active, whilst some are very inactive. It may take some time before you find one which is relevant and appropriate.

32.4   Wider teaching networks

In an increasingly connected world, you can, and may want to, join an international teaching association. Being a member of, for example, IATEFL (the International Association for Teachers of English as Foreign Language) or TESOL International Association can provide you with access to high-quality learning resources as well as a ready-made network of English language teachers from all over the world. Although it can be expensive to join these associations, some discounted rates are available for people working in challenging circumstances. Whilst IATEFL is a UK-based organization, it is affiliated with around 100 national and regional teaching associations. If there isn't one in your country, you may still be able to join IATEFL through its Wider Membership individual scheme (for details, visit their website: iatefl.org). TESOL International, meanwhile, has around 10,000 members worldwide. It offers discounted rates for students and low-income professionals (for details, visit their website: tesol.org). Both these organizations have groups which focus on particular aspects of English Language Teaching, such as IATEFL's Special Interest Group on Global Issues (gisig.iatefl.org).

32.5   Online training opportunities

Several major English language providers provide a range of training materials free of charge on their websites. Cambridge University Press, for example, provides a wide range of teacher development courses. These courses and materials not only focus on areas such as pedagogy and methodology, but also on English language development. The British Council (teachingenglish.org.uk) also offers a lot of materials for both teachers and teacher educators.

Both these organizations, and many others besides, have developed MOOCs (Massive Open Online Courses). MOOCs are free, online courses which cover a vast range of topics, including language learning and pedagogy. FutureLearn, for example, provides a wide range of courses for teachers. Other major MOOC platforms include Coursera and Udemy, among others.

Applying knowledge

When you spend time developing yourself, it's important that you actually apply this knowledge in the classroom. You should adopt a practical rather than theoretical approach, and actually use your new knowledge and skills. This might feel like a challenge, and you may feel reluctant to do this, worried that you will get it wrong. The only way to find out, however, is to try. If you have a trusting relationship with your class, you might even explain what you are doing, and ask them for feedback afterwards.

Reflection
- Which of the techniques in this chapter could you implement where you teach?
- What would be some of the challenges in doing this? How you could you manage these challenges?

Glossary

accommodating: The way a speaker adjusts their accent, word choice or other aspects of language according to the way the other participant speaks.

affective filter: The concept that a language cannot be learned effectively if students have a high affective filter (which is caused by, e.g., stress and anxiety) that stops them from learning. Students have a low affective filter when they are motivated, and feel safe in the classroom.

agency: When somebody has control or power over what they want to do, they have agency.

ambient noise: Background or surrounding noise caused by external factors which may be difficult to manage.

antonym: A word that has the opposite meaning to another word (e.g. *wide* and *narrow*, *leader* and *follower*). cf. **synonym**

autonomy: The ability and desire to do something by yourself without the support of anyone else.

baseline data: Data which you gather and record at the beginning of a course or academic year. This gives you an initial idea about the level which students are at. You can measure their progress over time, and compare it against the baseline data, to identify how much progress they are making.

bias: An unfair opinion that influences your judgement, resulting in information presented in a way that it is incorrect. cf. **stereotyping**

blank slate: The idea, in education, that students have no prior knowledge before walking into the classroom.

boardwork: The way in which you write on a board, and how clear it is to follow and understand.

buddy: A classmate or colleague who may be able to provide particular support, advice or guidance to another student or professional (e.g. when they first arrive at the institution, or if they have a specific challenge or problem).

chalk and talk approach: A pedagogical approach where the teacher talks for a significant percentage of the lesson, and where the main student involvement is copying down what the teacher has written on the board. cf. **sit and listen approach**

class contract: An agreement created by the teacher and students about aspects of classroom behaviour and practice. cf. **class norms**

class gallery: A space on a wall where students can display their pictures or work for others to see.

class norms: The usual or expected behaviour in class. cf. **class contract**

classroom management: The process of creating an atmosphere in your classroom where students feel safe and secure, and understand what is happening.

cline: A way of ordering information on a spectrum, which goes from one extreme to another. An example of a cline for adjectives describing size is as follows: *tiny / small / average-sized / large / huge / enormous.*

closed question: A question asked by a teacher which has only one acceptable answer (e.g. *What is the capital city of Chile? Have you had breakfast yet?*), in contrast with open (or open-ended) questions that allow many different answers (e.g. *What would you like to see in Chile? Why is breakfast important?*). All yes / no questions are closed questions. cf. **open question**

cloze: A kind of task or test which contains deliberate gaps at regular intervals (e.g. every sixth or seventh word), which the participant is expected to fill with the correct language item. cf. **gap fill**

code switching: Alternating between two or more languages when speaking. cf. **translanguaging**

collocation: Words which commonly appear together – e.g. *fast car* (not **quick car*).

comfort zone: A place where students only use language which they have already secured. To develop their language further, they need to move out of their comfort zone.

concept checking question (CCQ): A question which genuinely and unambiguously tells the teacher whether the students have understood and acquired the target language.

conditioning: The way in which individuals or groups get used to, or are trained, to respond in a particular way. For example, in many cultures, girls and women are expected to take on traditional roles in the family, or dress in a specific way.

connotation: The way in which a word suggests a different cultural or emotional association (e.g. *skinny* is considered negative, *thin* is neutral, and *slender* is positive).

controlled practice: Language practice in which students focus on limited practice of specific language (e.g. using a gap fill activity). Once they have secured this language, they can move on to free practice. cf. **free practice**

criteria-referenced assessment: A form of assessment which evaluates whether students have competency in a particular area, as measured against a specific standard. Such assessment is commonly pass / fail (or competent / not competent). cf. **norm-referenced assessment** and **ipsative assessment**

critical consciousness: The way in which individuals and groups can apply critical thinking to examine the situation in which they live, in order to develop a deep understanding of their reality, and identify solutions to the social, political and economic challenges which they face.

curriculum: The subjects and content that are studied in a particular educational institution. cf. **syllabus**

deductive methodology: An approach to teacher grammar which begins by giving students rules, then examples, then practice. cf. **inductive methodology**

derivation: A word created from a root word by the addition of prefixes or suffixes (e.g. *re- + use = reuse*; *use + less = useless*).

descriptive: A view of language which describes how the language is actually used by speakers, as opposed to following a set of inflexible rules. cf. **prescriptive**

diagnostic assessment: Testing which is done in order to identify the level of a student, usually at the beginning of a course or module.

differentiation: The act of providing different tasks, task types, feedback etc. in the classroom according to the varied needs, interests and abilities of students.

digital equity: A situation in which all students have fair and equal access to technology for learning – and that no students are discriminated against because they lack the necessary hardware or equipment.

direct costs: The actual costs of being educated – such as fees, books, exams, food, transportation, etc. cf. **opportunity costs**

distance travelled: The improvement made by a student in assessment compared to their previous performance.

dominant language: A language which has power and importance in a particular local / national / international area.

double-shift schooling: A type of education where, due to the large number of students in the local community, there is insufficient space and capacity for them all to attend the school at the same time. In such situations, two shifts of schooling may take place (e.g. in the morning and afternoon). Double-shift schooling is often found in locations where there has been a significant and rapid increase in the number of students (e.g. mass migration).

doughnut task: A way of organizing students which can be used for speaking activities. Half the students stand in a circle, facing outwards. The other half stand in a larger circle, facing opposite them. Also known as **onion ring task.**

dyslexia: A general term which refers to difficulties in learning to read or interpret words and letters. It can affect students' ability to spell, read quickly, and write words out. Dyslexia has no impact on general intelligence.

education authority: The governmental or official body (local, regional or national) which shapes educational policy in a particular area.

educational stakeholder: An individual (or sometimes group) which has an interest in how a particular educational institution is run – student, teacher, head teacher, parent, governor, community member. etc.

eliciting: A technique through which a teacher gets information from students (e.g. using a mind map and writing on the board what students say). see also: **mind map**

evaluation: The collection of information / data about educational matters, which is then analysed and interpreted to assess whether it has been effective.

evidence base: Source of information / data which can be used to inform decision making.

face-to-face (F2F) teaching: Teaching which takes place in a classroom, where teacher and students are physically present. cf. **remote teaching**

flashcard: A piece of paper or card, often two-sided, which usually contains a picture and the corresponding word in the target language.

flipped learning: A curriculum option in which students study the course content (e.g. online) in advance of attending a face-to-face class, where, for example, they actively engage with this content by performing tasks or discussion.

form: The way a language item (word or grammar) is constructed (as opposed to its meaning). For example, the form of the present perfect is subject + *has / have* + past participle. cf. **meaning** and **use**

formal education: Education delivered in a systematic way with a specific syllabus and curriculum, e.g. at a school, college or university. cf. **informal education** and **non-formal education**

formative assessment / feedback: Feedback whose aim is to support and help the recipient. It is usually ongoing and conducted in a low-stakes manner. Students and teachers can use formative assessment to identify areas for improvement, and act on them. cf. **summative assessment / feedback**

formulaic language: Commonly co-occurring multi-word items, including idioms (e.g. *get to the bottom of*, *raining cats and dogs*), discourse markers (e.g. *what's more*, *by the way*) and set phrases (e.g. *thank you*, *you're welcome*).

fossilization: The way a second language learner's proficiency stops progressing because errors have become so deeply fixed that the teacher cannot eliminate them.

free practice: The production phase in a lesson when students can use the language in their own way, in meaningful, realistic situations. cf. **controlled practice**

functional language: Language which is needed in day-to-day situations, e.g. greetings, introductions, agreeing and disagreeing, apologizing.

gap fill: A kind of task or test which contains deliberate gaps, which the participant is expected to fill with the correct language item. It differs from a cloze activity because it focuses on a specific language point. Sometimes referred to as 'modified cloze'. cf. **cloze**

gendered language: Language which is biased towards men over women, whether directly or indirectly – for example the use of gender-specific terms such as *businessmen*.

gender-responsive pedagogy: An approach to teaching and learning in which all genders are treated equitably and fairly.

gender violence: Violence which is directed against a person specifically due to that person's gender, for example in the form of physical, sexual or psychological harm.

gesture: Non-verbal communication (e.g. by the hands or face) to communicate a particular message, either in the place of, or alongside actual speech.

ghettoizing: The process of identifying or putting people in particular groups in a way that stigmatizes them.

hedging language: Language which is deliberately indirect, used to soften the speaker's position (e.g. *That may be a terrible idea; I think you're wrong*).

heterogeneous group: A group composed of individuals with different characteristics (e.g. mixed-sex, mixed-age or mixed-ability). cf. **homogeneous group**

high stakes: Used to describe an important exam or test which has significant consequences for the student. Passing a high stakes exam can lead to, for example, a certificate, scholarship or progressing to the next level of education, or gaining access to a particular institution. cf. **low stakes**

homogeneous group: A group composed of individuals with similar characteristics (e.g. same-sex, same-age or same-ability). cf. **heterogeneous group**

identity: The qualities or beliefs which define a person or group.

inductive methodology: A discovery approach to teaching grammar which begins with examples, and then asks students to develop the rules themselves. cf. **deductive methodology**

informal education: Learning which is neither formal, nor non-formal. There is no specific objective to informal learning, and it can be interpreted very broadly. Self-directed learning, or teachers running their own professional development group, are examples of informal education.

information gap: A task in which each student lacks all the information to complete it by themselves. Students must work with their classmates and share information to do this, making the activity highly communicative.

institutional knowledge: The combination of data, experience, information, values and processes possessed by a specific educational institution.

instruction checking question (ICQ): A type of question which is used to check whether students have understood what they have to do in a particular activity.

internally displaced person: A person who has been forced to leave their home because of the threat of violence or due to natural or human-made disasters, but who has not crossed a national border. cf. **refugee**

ipsative assessment: A form of assessment where a student's current performance is compared against their previous performance, to assess what progress (if any) has been made. cf. **criteria-referenced assessment** and **norm-referenced assessment**

L1: The mother tongue, or home language, spoken by an individual.

L1 interference: When the student's L1 negatively affects the acquisition of L2.

L2: A second language, which is usually learned as a foreign language (but not always, especially in multilingual communities).

language of instruction (LOI): The language which is used in the classroom for teaching purposes. Also known as vehicular language.

learning portfolio: A printed or digital collection of documents (e.g. feedback, samples, exam scripts) about the progress a student has made.

lexical bundle: A sequence of two or more words that commonly occur together in a language (e.g. *the end of the*, *the fact that*, *is due to*). Also known as **lexical chunk**.

lexical set: A group of words in a particular category. For example, the lexical set for jobs includes words such as *teacher*, *builder*, *waiter*, *cook*, *driver*, *lawyer*, *pilot* and *nurse*.

losing face: To become less respected by others.

low stakes: A type of testing which has little impact on a student's grades, and is generally used to provide formative feedback – e.g. a fun vocabulary quiz. cf. **high stakes**

marking code: A set of abbreviations which teachers can use in formative feedback to help students correct their own writing. For example, *V* may indicate that a verb error has been made, with *SP* for spelling mistakes, or *art.* for article misuse.

marking scheme: Description of different levels of performance in a test / exam, to help examiners decide how many points to award for a student's answers.

matching task: A checking activity where students have to match two items, e.g. a word and its definition, or a word and a picture.

meaning: The sense of an item of language (word, grammatical structure etc.) as opposed to its form. cf. **form** and **use**

mental coding: The idea that visual and verbal information is processed in different ways in the human mind.

metalanguage: Specialized language or terms used to analyse or describe the structure of a language.

micro-resistances: Small acts of breaking with the expected procedures in the classroom through which you can challenge the status quo, and advocate for change.

mime: Acting out a story using the body, and without the use of speech.

mind map: A technique for brainstorming ideas. One central idea is written in a circle, and different, related ideas radiate out from the centre. see also: **eliciting**

mindset: The view or attitude which you have towards change and personal development.

mingle: A type of task in which students move about the room and speak to other students at random. This type of task can be used in many different situations, and presents a natural and authentic opportunity for using the target language.

minimal pair: Two words which are identical except for one aspect of their pronunciation (e.g. *cat* and *bat*, *bin* and *bean*, *hat* and *had*, *sink* and *think*).

model answer: An answer to a question, which would receive full marks for the task. A model answer, created by the teacher or included in exam / test samples, helps students understand what kind of extended response is expected of them.

monitoring: The process by which a teacher assesses how well an individual, group or class is performing a particular task (e.g. by walking round and listening to people talking). Teachers may also provide on-the-spot assistance as necessary during monitoring, or note ideas for a follow-up or feedback stage.

nomination: The practice of asking a student by name to answer a question, report on a task, give feedback about a particular activity, etc.

non-formal education: A form of education which is structured (or semi-structured) but lacks the curriculum, syllabus or certification found in formal education. cf. **informal education**

norm-referenced assessment: A form of assessment which compares the relative performance of students on a scale, or by ranking. cf. **criteria-referenced assessment** and **ipsative assessment**

noticing: The theory that students have to notice the grammatical features of a language before they are able to acquire them.

onion ring task: See **doughnut task**.

open question (or **open-ended question**): A longer and more detailed question which the student is expected to answer (in comparison to a closed question). Open questions may begin with words such as *how* and *why* rather than *when*, *what*, *where* and *who*. cf. **closed question**

opportunity costs: The monetary benefit given up when a student attends school – e.g. being at school means that they are not working for the family business. cf. **direct costs**

orthographic skill: The skills needed in order to be able to write in a particular language.

out-of-school children: Children who are unable to attend school. This can be for a wide range of issues, including: poverty, poor performance, lack of educational culture in the community, behavioural reasons, poor sanitation facilities at school, early marriage, etc.

paraphrasing: Saying or writing what somebody else has said or written, but using different words or grammatical structures.

parent–teacher association (PTA): Usually a group in a formal education situation consisting of parents who support their children's school in a range of different ways, e.g. raising funds or helping with events.

part of speech: see **word class**

peer-to-peer (P2P) learning: The process through which students teach each other.

PPP method: PPP stands for Presentation Practice Production. It is a deductive approach in which the teacher initially presents the target language. Students then practise the language through controlled activities. Finally, they participate in freer activities to produce the target language.

prescriptive: A view of language which argues that there are socially-approved standards of correctness (of grammar, vocabulary and pronunciation) that should be followed. cf. **descriptive**

process writing: An approach to teaching writing that focuses on the production processes involved (planning, drafting, revising, sharing, etc), where self-expression and the ability to say what you want is emphasized. The teacher is a 'reader' rather than a 'marker'. cf. **product writing**

production stage: The stage when, having practised a new item of language, the students use it more freely and creatively.

productive skills: Speaking and writing, where students actively produce and create language. cf. **receptive skills**

product writing: A traditional approach to writing, where students note and then imitate the features of a model text. cf. **process writing**

realia: Real objects, which can be particularly useful when teaching vocabulary.

receptive skills: Reading and listening, where students receive and understand language. cf. **productive skills**

recycling: The educational process of repeating or revising information on an ongoing basis, in order to help students secure their learning.

refugee: A person who has been forced to leave their country to escape conflict, violence, natural disasters or persecution. cf. **internally displaced person**

reliability: Refers to the capacity of a test to be repeated, and to produce consistent results each time it is done.

remote teaching: Teaching which takes place online, where teacher and students are not physically present. cf. **face-to-face (F2F) teaching**

restricted practice: see **controlled practice**

role play: A type of speaking activity where students play a particular role rather than speaking 'as themselves'.

root form: The base form of a word, which does not have either a prefix (at the start) or suffix (at the end).

rote learning (or **rote production**): When students produce language by copying what the teacher has said.

scaffolding: The support provided, typically verbally and by a teacher, to students to learn new skills or knowledge.

school charter: An agreement between all different educational stakeholders which concerns what they are supposed to do, and how they are supposed to behave.

schwa: The most common vowel sound in the English language: /ə/. It is always short and unstressed. It can be spelled using a variety of different letters, as highlighted in the following words: *about, written, pencil, random.*

secure: When a student has understood something to the extent that they are highly unlikely to forget it in the future.

self-regulate: The ability to act in your own self-interest and make decisions which are not personally detrimental – e.g. managing your short-term desires.

sequence words: Words which helps the reader or listener understand the order in which something takes place (e.g. *firstly, subsequently, then, afterwards, finally*).

service provider: Agencies who can provide support in specific areas (such as physical health, mental well-being, counselling, etc.).

show and tell: An activity in which students bring an object or item from their home, and explain what it is (and why it is important) to the class or in a group.

sit and listen approach: A pedagogical approach where the teacher dominates and the students are generally passive. cf. **chalk and talk approach**

social capital: The resources possessed by an individual or group, which come from their social networks and relationships.

soft skills: The umbrella term for the useful set of life skills which students can develop in the language learning classroom. Soft skills are difficult to assess, but they can be very valuable not only in the workplace, but in general life. Examples of soft skills include: confidence, communication, empathy, flexibility, interpersonal skills, motivation, social skills, teamwork, timekeeping.

standardization: The procedure in assessment which ensures that although different people are marking an exam, they are giving comparable marks. The process of standardization ensures reliability. see also: **reliability**

step change: A significant change, larger and more significant than usual.

stereotyping: A mistaken idea which people have about a particular group, which may be based on, e.g., their sex, ethnicity, nationality, age, sexuality, religion or social class. cf. **bias**

student-focused (or **student-centred**): An approach to learning where the active involvement of the student is prioritized.

substitution drill: A classroom procedure for practising new language. The teacher models the target language, and then provides a piece of language which the students have to substitute, as well as make further necessary adjustments. For example: T: *How many eggs are there? Potatoes.* SS: *How many potatoes are there?* T: *Sugar.* SS: *How much sugar is there?*

summative assessment / feedback: An exam or test which evaluates how well a student has done at the end of a topic, course, term of year. It is often linked to an official grade or mark. cf. **formative assessment / feedback**

superdiversity: A social landscape in which many different cultures, ethnicities, races and/or language speakers live together.

syllabus: A summary or outline of a course of study. cf. **curriculum**

synonym: A word which has a similar (but not identical) meaning to another word (e.g. *wide* and *broad, speak* and *talk*). cf. **antonym**

target language: 1. The sounds, words, phrases or structures which you want the students to acquire during a lesson / week / module / course. Target language includes areas of language such as lexical sets (e.g. sports, parts of the body, classroom objects), functional language (e.g. ways of asking permission, talking about the future, saying how you feel) and grammatical structures (e.g. comparative and superlative adjectives, prepositions of movement, talking about future plans). 2. In a broader sense, we also use **target language** to talk about L2, i.e. the language that the students are aiming to learn. cf. **L2**

task repetition: Doing a particular activity for a second (or more) time, often so that a student can correct the mistakes which they made the first time.

teacher's guide (also **teacher's book**): A book or booklet which may be provided alongside a textbook, which provides ideas and methods for teaching the contents.

Total Physical Response (**TPR**): A method of teaching language which involves using physical movements (e.g. the teacher says 'jump', and the teacher and students jump).

translanguaging: A similar communicative practice to code switching, in which people use the resources they have from different languages together, using elements of each language to communicate more effectively. cf. **code switching**

trauma: A deeply disturbing or distressing experience which can affect the way an individual behaves, feels or presents themselves to others.

trigger: An event or memory which makes a person remember a previous traumatic experience. The trigger itself is not necessarily frightening, and it may only be of general relevance to what happened – e.g. a smell or a sound which the individual associates with the traumatic event.

use: How language or grammar gets used – e.g. some words are more common in written rather than spoken English. cf. **form** and **meaning**

validity: Criteria which evaluate whether a test measures what it is supposed to measure. For example: Is a particular reading test genuinely testing the students' ability to read, or their general knowledge, or their ability to remember what was in the textbook? cf. **reliability**

visual aids: Items such as flashcards, photographs or newspapers which can be used to help you teach language.

weighting: Different questions / parts of an assessment are weighted according to how important you consider them to be, determining how many marks are available for completing them.

word class: A group of words which have the same grammatical properties. Also known as **part of speech**.

zone of proximal development: A term coined by Soviet-Russian psychologist Lev Vygotsky to describe the cognitive gap between what learners can do unaided and what they can do with the assistance of a more skilled expert. According to Vygotsky, teaching is most effective when it targets this gap.

Index

AAA (accessible, appropriate, accurate) 107, 113
ABC order of English 49 (lower case), 89
ability
    autonomy 190
    communicate meaningfully with others
    dividing students by 68
    dyslexia 192
    factors directly affecting of institution or
        teacher to be effective 4
    language 11, 66, 135, 186, 187
    linguistic 52
    organizing classes by 67, 69
    process writing 197
    teachers'/ students' 4
    to get through a text 78
    to learn 13, 16
    to produce language 87
    to recall words 100
    to remember words 117
    to self-regulate 198
    to switch between languages 180
    to use grammar 93
    to use languages 5
    to use or understand just a few words 99
absenteeism 4
abstract ideas 95
academic research 164
academic skills 48
academic subjects 55
academic year 14, 16, 60, 190
accent 11, 79, 80, 88, 108, 190
access
    educational 2
    equal, to technology for learning 192
    for all potential students 22
    learning and training opportunities 10

    online 173
    seats 59
    temporary, to instruction and instructional
        support 123
    to 3G, 4G, Wi-Fi 113
    to books in school library 83
    to high-quality learning resources and ready-
        made network of English language teachers
        from all over the world 189
    to education 2
    to electronic device 123
    to internet and a printer 106
    to mobile phones or computers from
        home 122
    to online learning materials 125
    to opportunities to improve teaching 182
    to particular institution 194
    to printed newspaper or news source 174
        (activity)
    to records about the past 168
    to resources 40, 107
    to television, radio, internet 84
    wider development or training opportunities 7
accommodating 59, 190
activities
    allow students to deepen and embed
        knowledge of a new language 36
    categorizing 124
    cloze 101
    communicative 30
    controlled 195
    demonstrate positive aspects of school 168
    determined by time of day 32
    doughnut / onion 30, 60
    environment-based learning 47
    freer 196

fun, interactive 43, 93
grammar 87
grammar and vocabulary 108
group 59
learning and sharing 164
listening 79
longer 67
mingle 30
multi-level 147
online 123
outdoor language learning 72
physical 24
reading 41
reading / listening 65
regular, energetic 37
school 171
share 30
short 37, 38
skills development 169
speaking 45, 70, 192
speaking / writing 65
spoken ranking 67
teaching grammar 98
textbooks, which students do by
   themselves 139
to develop students' ability to recall words 100
to retrieve and use new language 103
to support students suffering from trauma 180
traditional, controlled 28
vocabulary 101
whole-class 29
within school grounds 72
writing / written 112, 130, 169
zero-resource 6
acoustics 23, 159
actions
   eye contact or gentle touch 177
   student 78
   to help students secure language 96
acquiring language
   acquiring L2 52
   language divided into 'lexical bundles' 103

oral to written 35
   student-centred approach 27
adjective + noun combinations 73
adjectives 73, 102, 110, 117, 150
   comparative and superlative 151
   cline for adjectives 190
   opinion 117
adverbs
   adverbs of frequency 95, 119, 151
   high-frequency suffixes
adverse weather 32
affective filter 16, 58, 152, 198
age
   difference 19
   different breaks for different ages, age
      difference between learners 19
   experience of young females in many
      societies 25
   heterogeneous group 194
   homogeneous group 194
   inclusivity 21
   learning English at young age and associated
      L1/L2 reading skills 78
   mixed-age classroom 21, 69, 78
   mixed-age students of similar ability 63
   organize classes by ability rather than age 67
   school-age students 179
   stereotyping according to age 198
agency
   children's 168
   individuals 176, 190
   students' 5, 6, 43, 120, 137
agreeing
   functional language 193
   schools agreeing with textbook bias 135
   students agreeing with textbook bias 135
air pollution 167
alphabet
   alphabetical sequence 49, 89
   differences between L1 alphabet and that of
      English 78
   English 89

alienation 55
ambient noise 23, 77, 79, 125, 159, 190
American
    English 11
    nationality 88
American Red Cross 16
anger 50
anti-inclusive 21
antonym 99, 108, 190, 198
anxiety
    associations with learned helplessness 44
    caused by seating arrangement 58
    causing high affective filter 16, 190
    decreased due to prevention of problematic
        issues 177
    developing L2 to lessen anxiety 11
    faced by students 31
    processing 175
    reduced by type and style of tasks 158
approach
    blended 188
    'chalk and talk' 4
    Critical Incident Analysis (CIA) 184
    deductive 93, 95, 196
    direct translation from L1 to L2 100
    focused 89
    gender-responsive pedagogy 193
    inductive 93, 94, 95, 194
    learn language similar to how L1 was
        learned 11
    lexical 103
    'listen and sit' 27, 57, 190
    methodological 76, 138
    'one size fits all' 34
    'one too many' 123
    open and welcome approach to different
        languages 51, 55
    pedagogical 76, 77, 190
    positive, dynamic approach to education 46
    PPP (Presentation Practice Production)
        93, 196
    pragmatic, practice-oriented pedagogy 1
    product or process 137, 197

'snowball' 67, 112
staged 65
student-centred / student-focused 27, 40,
    102, 198
teacher-centred / teacher-fronted 36, 94, 187
teaching 28, 57
textbook-focused 187
theoretical 189
variety 101
area
    conflict or post-conflict 13, 51
    different areas of the classroom 96
    Learning walk 115
    local 107, 110, 111, 113, 114, 160
    low socio-economic 164
    map 119
    national 192
    playground 72
    risky 14
    rural 133
    sports area 72
articles
    definite 11, 50
    different uses in different languages 94
    indefinite 11
    non-standard use 12
asking for clarification 59, 66, 180
Ask me anything 98
assessment
    affected by changes in teaching staff 161
    assessment-focused culture 1
    college and university entrance tests 93
    criteria-referenced 191, 194, 196
    curriculum 9
    deciding on type 156
    depends on equipment working 159
    diagnostic 154, 192
    dictating type of English taught 11
    different forms 143, 144
    dominant language of 56
    formal 155
    formative 193, 198
    higher than level of student 89

high-stakes 154
informal 155
institution 93
involving students in process 147
ipsative 145, 191, 194, 196
language 52
marks received by student, not actual
    comments 49
national exams 93
norm-referenced 191, 194, 196
pass / fail (competent / not competent) 191
poor performance 34
reliable 155
self-assessment questionnaires 144
small, achievable goals 144
standardization 198
student 21
summative 91, 193, 198
valid 155
weighting 156, 199
what to do with marks 156
association
    international teaching 189
    national and regional teaching 189
    parent–teacher 163, 171, 196
    teaching 172
asynchronous
    learning 123
    materials 126
    tasks 124
atmosphere
    classroom 93
    classroom management 190
    conducive to motivating and empowering
        students 143
    differences in classroom 57
    negative 6
    peaceful classroom 31
    positive 45, 87, 97
    positive classroom 165
    positive learning 101
    positive, trusting 176

where emphasis is on comprehensibility 88
where mistakes are tolerated 87
attendance
    chart for recording 144
    irregular 38
    passive 167
attitudes
    changing long-held 22
    conditioned to believe incorrect attitudes are
        facts 24
    dominant towards particular issues in various
        countries 173
    mindset 195
    of different stakeholders 10
    parents' towards education systems 164
    questionnaires about attitude to
        education 144
    societal towards certain groups 133
    to education, positive 47
    to education, neutral or negative 144
    to learning and impacts on this, such as
        sympathy 24
    towards exams 158
    towards institution, negative 70
    towards mixed-age classrooms 70
audio
    conferencing 124
    control of 125
    difficulties in teaching listening 79–80
    ensuring appropriate model of pronunciation
        is used 108
    flexibility 37
    no choice in teaching 77
    on a machine 23
    recordings 177
    sufficient quality for deaf and hard-of-hearing
        students 25
    teachers recording themselves 124
authentic
    context of textbook grammar not felt as
        authentic by students 97
    language used in real-life situation 75

mingle 195
stories 90
students working on questions together 139
using different voices, actions, props when not
  having books 78
way of developing L2 59
autonomous users of language 102
autonomy 66, 102, 190
background or surrounding noise 190
Back to the board 101, 152
backup plan 37, 38
behaviour
  acknowledging, describing and validating
    good behaviour 176
  appropriate 177, 178
  bad 46, 58
  class contract 190
  classroom 190
  expected 190
  good 176
  issues 28, 40, 178
  managing poor behaviour 175
  motivation to energize, direct and sustain
    behaviour 144
  negative 179
  poor 16, 17, 45, 46, 49, 59, 176, 177, 178
  poor student 176
  positive 176, 179
  positive impact, monitoring playtime 20
  problems 59
  reasons 196
  SEBD (social, emotional and behavioural
    difficulties) 175, 176
  students' behavioural issues 178
  techniques for dealing with behavioural
    issues 40
  understanding and correcting poor
    behaviour 4
bandwidth
  high 124
  low 124, 125
base form 197
baseline data 190

bench 57, 58, 72, 83
bias, text
  against girls/ women 23
  avoiding, being inclusive 108
  classroom 134
  cosmetic 134
  gender 24
  gendered language 193
  linguistic 134
  non-biased 24
  own 15
  reading and listening texts 136–137
  stereotyping 189, 198
  teacher's guides 24
  textbook 6, 15, 132, 133
  unconscious 23
  universal 133
  unreality 134
  views about groups or identities 22
binary
  educational contexts 3
  questions 149
bisexual 21
blank slates 27, 29
blended approach 188
blind 21, 23, 136
blob tree 19
'blocks', learning 6, 36
board 23, 27, 28, 53, 57, 59, 60, 61, 86, 87, 90,
  95, 97, 98, 100, 179, 192
boardwork 23, 182, 190
bodily changes 71
body language 43, 49
brainstorming 64, 66, 195
'breakout rooms' 125
British
  English 11
  nationality 88
British Council 52, 84, 172, 189
breaks 19, 125
buddy 47, 190
  system 178, 184
bullying 15, 178

calendars 54, 173
Cambridge University Press 95, 189
capacity
    lack of 22, 192
    to repeat a test and produce consistent
        results 197
carbon dioxide (CO_2) 159
categorizing 103
CD 79
    player 37
certification 10, 196
certificate 9, 143, 145, 194
'chalk and talk' approach 4, 27, 34, 57, 190, 198
challenges
    age range 69–71
    common classroom 33
    creating written resources 107
    faced by students 21, 25, 31, 46, 47
    faced by multilingual students 94
    faced on daily basis 182
    fixed-desk classrooms 58
    gender-related 23
    implementing ideas in schools 171
    making students more motivated and
        empowered 144–146
    managing 51
    managing poor behaviour 175
    mental or emotional health 157
    minimizing, fewer books 129
    of teaching receptive skills, productive skills,
        grammar and vocabulary 6
    online learning 123
    physical 22
    planning for specific challenges in
        classroom 34
    promoting language diversity 55
    reading and listening 77–83
    social, political and economic 191
    speaking and writing 85
    teaching students new vocabulary 99
    timing and minimizing these 39
    to student-focused teaching 27

typical challenges faced in classroom and
    techniques to address them 7
using English alphabet at primary level 89
using textbooks 133, 134–137, 139–141
'changeover day' 165
Changing places 98
chants 45
characteristics
    heterogeneous 194
    individual 47
    special 91
    specific, of local area 114
    stereotyping 133
charcoal 159
checking activity 195
child rights 171
class contract 23, 175, 179, 190
class gallery 14, 99, 173, 190
class norms 55
class sizes
    benefits of large classes 66
    changes in class and visibility of these 182–183
    difficulties 3, 31, 141
    noise in large classes 79
    preventing students speaking and writing
        in L2 85
    teachers' feelings of insecurity with large
        classes 27
classroom
    atmosphere 31, 93, 176
    behaviour 190
    challenges 34, 39
    decorating 101
    environment 77
    extension of students' everyday lives 28, 45
    fixed-desk 57–8
    furniture 76
    inclusive 15, 21, 25, 133
    interactions 27
    language 49, 54, 55
    language of instruction 194
    language policy 56

language (learning) classroom 5, 42, 52, 79, 90, 148, 180
language-friendly space 52
lessons 25, 125
level 4, 55
management 185, 190
management issues 27
managing bias in 134–137
micro-resistances 195
mixed-age 21, 69–71
model for positive social change 6
multilingual 21, 51–2
norms and protocols, unfamiliarity with 48
objects 54, 100, 102
outside 72–75
performativity 1
practice 1, 6, 25, 148, 175
routines 128
safe 13–18
seating 57, 146
segregated 24
setting 7
skills 47–8, 63
tasks 28
teacher-centred 29
teacher roles in 40
techniques 86
time 17, 82, 94
unsafe 13–18
CLIL (Content and Language Integrated Learning) 55
cline 99, 100, 151, 190
closed questions 29, 44, 130, 145, 149, 191, 196
cloze 11, 28, 96, 101, 156, 191, 193
    modified 193
code switching 51, 52–53, 191, 199
cognate words 79
cognitive
    gap 199
    level 52
collaborative tasks 61, 88, 124
Collective story writing 88, 89
college and university entrance exams 93

collocation 99, 101, 103, 191
comfort zone 70, 88, 155, 191
comic books 54
common words 78, 89
communication
    lack of confidence in 87
    making easier through seating arrangement 61
    non-verbal 193
    promoting between disparate groups 51
    soft skills 198
    spoken 122
    textbooks not promoting 130
    use of English as tool of international 11
    written 164
community
    as a resource 111
    -based learning activities and student interest in these 47
    classroom as vision for 22
    gap between school and community 171
    groups 52, 60
    lack of educational culture 196
    languages 51
    local 72, 107, 111, 145, 146, 167–168, 192
    mapping 114, 118–119
    members 166, 192
    perceptions of education 48
    wider 25, 108, 136, 146
complaints procedure 19
comprehensibility 1, 88
comprehension 28, 37, 44, 65, 66, 79, 112, 113, 139
concept checking question (CCQ) 148, 152, 153, 191
conditioning 47, 191
connectivity 123, 124, 172, 187, 188
connotation 3, 99, 101, 191
constructive feedback 40, 182
content analysis 138
contextualizing 29, 138, 139–140, 146
controlled practice 35, 36, 90, 94, 191, 193, 197
Conversation basket 72, 74
'core components' in lesson planning 37

cosmetic bias 134
cost-effective inputs 167
counselling 198
countability 94
crises 120
criteria-referenced assessment 145, 156, 191
critical analysis 111
critical consciousness 191
Critical Incident Analysis (CIA) 182, 184
critical thinking 129, 191
culture
    different 94
    dominant 134
    educational, lack of 196
    human 90
    local 41, 167
    of learned helplessness 6
    school 25
curriculum
    content 85
    flipped learning 193
    hidden 2
    in a particular educational institution 191
    in non-formal education 196
    primary school 115
    wider 1
data
    accurate 148, 152
    baseline 190
    evaluation 192
    individual 148
    institutional knowledge 194
    statistical 173
decentralizing the learning 28
deductive
    approach 93, 94, 95, 196
    methodology 191, 194
deficit model 3
depression 31, 44
derivation 152, 191
descriptive 191, 196
development
    accessing opportunities 186

cognitive 71
economic 5
emotional 19
equitable individual 5
formalized teacher development sessions 184
human 5
language 128, 189
language learning 137, 169
personal 195
physical 19, 69
professional 34, 182, 194
pronunciation skills 117
psychological 22
sexual 71
skills 169
social 19
societal 5
teacher 186–189
zone of proximal 52, 199
diagnostic assessment 154, 192
dictation 72, 73, 86
Dictogloss 86
didactic analysis 138
differentiate 63, 64, 88, 138, 144
differentiation 192
digital equity 113, 125, 192
direct costs 46, 192, 196
disability 15, 21
Disappearing words 43
disasters
    human-made 194
    natural 16, 119, 123, 197
discipline problems 59
discourse markers 193
discrimination 15, 20, 134
disparate groups 51
displaced people 10
disruptions 120, 158
'distance travelled' 145, 192
dominant groups 22, 134, 171
dominant language 54, 56, 192
dominant narrative 134
double-shift schooling / system 26, 159, 192

doughnut 30, 38, 58, 60, 92, 192, 196
drill(s), drilling 40, 43, 52, 90, 94
drop-out rates 136
dyslexia 25, 192
earthquake 16, 123
economics 172, 173
education
    authority 192
    experience 24, 25, 76, 144
    formal 25, 46, 47, 77, 136, 165, 193, 196
    gap between sexes 25
    GDP spend 2
    importance 164
    informal 194, 196
    non-formal 196
    quality of 24, 46
    significant barriers 156
    stakeholders 175
    students' 123
    systems 5, 10, 11, 23, 48, 55, 133, 164
    traditional 27
educational
    access 2
    achievement 48
    advice 24
    authority 159
    benefit 120
    bodies 4
    contexts 93
    culture 196
    experiences 33, 34, 63, 171
    institutions 3, 7, 135, 191, 194
    landscape 2
    language policy 55
    massification 2
    models 4
    non-specialists 4
    process 6, 158, 197
    progress 52, 164
    role models 143, 146
    stakeholders 4, 9, 12, 21, 24, 56, 70, 96, 128,
       130, 131, 154, 163, 182, 197
electronic devices 113, 120, 136, 160

eliciting 63, 64, 117, 165, 192, 195
embarrassment 46, 49, 50
EMI (English as a Medium of Instruction) 52, 55
empathy 198
emojis 19, 144
emotional support 45, 181
empowerment 144
encouragement 47
English
    ABC order 49, 89
    alphabet 89
    American 11
    British 11
    developing language skills 26
    EMI (English as a Medium of Instruction)
       52, 55
    language providers 189
    language specific podcasts 84
    multilingual perspective 11
    phonological representation of 48
    spoken 199
    sounds 88
    teaching in informal or non-formal
       situations 12
    top 100 words of written English 79
    written 78
entrepreneurism 10
environment
    -based learning activities 47
    classroom 57, 77
    exam 25
    friendly, non-judgemental 26
    good 6
    highly pressurized and stressed 177
    language teaching 127
    learning 127, 164
    local 10, 107, 110, 111, 114, 115, 118,
       128, 146
    physical 159
    resource-light 41
    resource-starved 167
    safe, welcoming 24
    supportive 180, 182

teaching 56
virtual learning 125
ethnicity 15, 21, 134, 198
evaluation
  educational matters 192
  lesson 183–184
  self-evaluation 46, 49–50
  students' learning 44
everyday lives 11, 28, 120, 121
evidence 44, 135, 151, 152, 180, 192
exercise
  cloze 96
  gap fill 94
  grammar practice 28
  practice 95
  repetitive 96
  review 96
  written 1
exhaustion 31
expectations
  financial 171
  low educational 34
  low homework 31
  lowering 181
  societal 133
  stakeholders' 10, 96, 154
external factors 159, 190
eye contact 15, 177
eye movement 49
eyesight 21, 23, 25
face-to-face teacher groups 186–187
face-to-face (F2F) teaching 120, 123, 192, 197
fairness 23, 154, 156
feedback
  applying 91
  asking for 147, 189
  class 136
  constructive 40, 182
  detailed 44
  formative 49, 86, 92, 193
  from parents 25
  giving 42, 63, 64, 158, 160
  individual 44

  peer 44
  positive 34, 44, 183
  receiving 65
  sharing 185, 188
  student 117, 184–185
  summative assessment / feedback 91, 184, 193
  written 92
flashcards 79, 122, 199
flexibility 12, 37, 77, 85, 122, 123, 198
flipped learning 112, 122, 135, 193
fluency 11, 50
folk tales 85, 91, 92
formulaic language 49, 193
fossilization 193
'found objects' 107, 111
fragmentation 134
free practice 35, 90, 191, 193
'freemium' 122, 124
frustration 46, 49, 59, 187
function words 153
functional language 168, 193, 199
functional literacy 5
functionality 122, 124
gap fill 28, 44, 93, 94, 96, 100, 101, 130, 156, 191, 193
gay 21, 132, 133
gender
  balance 184
  bullying 15
  hierarchy 24
  inclusivity 21
  violence 24
gendered
  language 193
  words 137
gender-fair strategies 23
gender-neutral
  language 24
  terms 137
gender-related challenges 23
gender-responsive pedagogy 23, 193
general knowledge 135, 199
geography 117, 172, 173

gestures 15, 41, 49, 193
ghettoizing 54
global literacy 2
global South 2, 3, 55
governors 52, 135, 171
gradeable words 100
grammar
    activities 87, 108–109
    -based syllabus 85
    complex 73
    complicated 140
    correctness of 196
    developing students' 98
    explaining 94
    knowledge about 93
    managing 94
    practising 97
    presentation 149
    producing 94, 97
    reading about 122
    students' understanding 150
    target 94, 96
    teacher 191
    teaching 93, 95, 110, 194
    textbooks 97, 130
    traditional 95
    'translating' grammar, problematic 94
    understanding 94
    usage 199
grammatical
    choice 112
    construction 94, 103
    differences 94
    knowledge 89
    patterns 49
    presentation 28
    points 53
    properties 199
    structures 35, 66, 93, 97, 196, 199
group
    cultural 51
    discussions 55
    ethnic or social 10, 15, 51

project 56, 61
    work 27–29, 31, 37, 41, 59, 66, 166, 184–185
harnessing the power of 'yet' 177
health, mental and emotional 137, 157
health benefits 72
hearing
    difference from listening 77
    hard-of-hearing 23, 25
    unfamiliar language 177
hedging language 136, 194
heterogeneous
    groups 67, 70, 82, 194
    pairs 67
    rows 59
    students 66
'hidden curriculum' 2
higher prestige groups 135
high-frequency
    collocations 101
    lower-case letters 89
    nouns 79
words 77, 78, 95
high stakes
    assessment 154
    exams 48, 158, 160, 194, 195
HIV status 15, 21
homework
    being sensitive in giving 69
    collecting 15
    conflicts with other duties 71
    difficulties 148
    expectations 31
    flipped 122
    marking 166
    parents and guardians supporting 165
    pressure 25
    setting 36
homogeneous groups 63, 66, 67, 70, 194
hormones 71
host country 26
household chores 157, 165
humanizing 176
hunger 31

hurricanes 123
IATEFL (International Association for Teachers of English as Foreign Language) 173, 189
identity
  bias 134
  ethnic 21, 63
  racial 21
  religious 21
  stereotyping 133
idioms 192
imbalance 72, 134
immediacy 124, 125
implementation/ transition plan 72
'in and out' approach 80
inclusive
  approaches 125
  being 108, 176, 180
  classrooms 15, 21, 22, 25, 26, 133
  institutions 22, 135
  policies 21
  systems 125
inclusivity 21, 22, 26, 167
inductive
  approach 93, 94, 95
  methodology 191, 194
inequity 2
inexperienced students
  building confidence 60
  challenges / difficulties faced 47
  general academic skills 48
  poor behaviour 49
  providing additional classes for 48
  teaching 6, 46–47
informal methodology 194
information, visual and verbal 195
information gap 129, 194
institutions
  assessment 93
  context 177
  culture 184
  educational 135
  educational stakeholders 9, 21, 70, 192
  formal 4, 12, 46

head teacher 187
inclusive 21, 22, 26, 135
informal 4
lack of support for 2
language assessments 154
local environment 110
location 177
mentors in 25
non-formal 4
part of whole educational process 158
psychological triggers 177
role models in 25
subjects and content 191
well-being of members 175
institutional knowledge 161, 194
instruction checking question (ICQ) 194
interaction
  between male and female students 24
  classroom 27
  patterns 37
  real-world 28, 75
  'safe' 58
  with students 180
interactive activities 43, 93
internally displaced
  person 194, 197
  refugees 46
international communication 11
International Day of Happiness 173
international teaching association 189
International Youth Day 173
interpersonal skills 198
intonation 64, 82, 91
intransitive verbs 73, 109
invigilators 158, 160
invisibility 133
isolation 90, 120, 134
I spy 72, 75
Knower 40, 42, 187
L1 10, 11, 14, 28, 29, 31, 38, 41, 43, 46, 48, 49, 51, 52, 53, 54, 55, 65, 78, 79, 80, 87, 88, 89, 91, 94, 97, 100, 101, 110, 115, 116, 117, 118, 134, 136, 150, 151, 165, 168, 169, 176, 178, 194

L2 11, 29, 31, 38, 41, 49, 51, 52, 53, 58, 59, 60,
    65, 78, 82, 84, 85, 86, 87, 88, 91, 94, 96, 97,
    100, 101, 110, 112, 136, 168, 169, 187,
    194, 199
language
    ability 11, 63, 66, 135, 186
    acquiring 28, 35
    assessments 52, 154
    benefits 29
    body 43, 49
    class 31, 168
    classroom 49, 54, 79, 180
    classroom language policy 56
    complex 73
    contextualizing 41
    demographics and abilities 188
    development 49, 128, 137
    diversity 55
    dominant 10, 54, 55
    educational policy 55
    exams 128
    experiences 110
    first 48, 60
    foreign 88, 194
    formulaic 46
    functional 168, 193
    gender-biased 24
    gendered 24, 193
    groups 55
    hedging 136, 194
    home 15, 194
    international 14, 51
    items 85
    knowledge 11, 156, 172
    learning 9, 10, 11, 24, 41, 58, 61, 70, 72, 75,
        85, 91, 111, 112, 113, 114, 115, 122, 127,
        138, 145, 165, 167, 168, 169, 179,
        189, 198
    learning classroom 52, 90, 148
    learning process 58, 87
    learning resources 107
    local 51
    minority 14, 51, 52, 55

    multiple 53
    national 14, 51
    of business and commerce 10
    of instruction 10, 24, 52, 165, 194
    of playground 52
    outdoor 72
    practice 111, 144, 191
    podcasts, English language 84
    producing 87
    rhythms 82
    school language policy 52
    second 48, 143, 194
    skills 26, 59, 64, 83, 99, 125, 140
    specialized 195
    spoken 35
    target 14, 24, 35, 36, 97, 98, 110, 112, 115,
        122, 133, 136, 148, 149, 150, 151, 170,
        190, 193, 195, 196, 199
    teaching 37, 52, 85, 93, 109, 110, 111, 145,
        166, 168, 199
    teachers 127
    textbooks 96, 130, 132, 133, 134, 138
leadership
    school 135
    skills 16
    soft skills 16
    strong 163
learned helplessness 6, 40, 44
learner portfolios 161
learning
    activities 47, 111
    aims 82
    areas 24
    asynchronous 123
    atmosphere 101
    children's 163
    classroom 52, 90, 148
    day-to-day 25
    differentiating 65, 147
    digital equity 192
    disruptions 76
    environments 127
    evaluating 44

experience 23, 29, 58, 95, 131, 136, 138, 167,
181, 184–185
flipped 112, 122, 135, 193
from exams 160
from mistakes 81
grammar 102
informal education 194
language 9, 10, 11, 13, 24, 31, 41, 42, 58, 61,
70, 75, 85, 87, 91, 94, 102, 111, 112, 113,
115, 122, 127, 138, 145, 146, 165, 168,
169, 172, 179
materials 51, 84, 115
negative atmosphere for 16
online 120, 123
opportunities 10, 14, 119, 129, 170
outcomes 36, 52, 53, 136, 184, 185
outside 72
outside lessons 120
peer-to-peer (P2P) learning 196
personalize 81
perspective, language learning 182
points 36
poor behaviour when 45
portfolios 155, 158, 195
positive environment 164
positive impact on 22
process 130
recycling 196
remote 125
resources 56, 107, 108, 111, 148, 151,
157, 189
situations 38, 66, 85, 110, 180
skills 48
soft skills 198
student 40, 62, 177
student-centred / student-focused 27, 96
students as equal partners 21
students' motivation for 143
synchronous 123
tasks 57
to learn 46
vocabulary 99, 102
walk 115, 117

legal status 166
lesbian 21
lesson
    learning outcomes 36
    objective 35, 36, 37, 38, 182
    plan, planning 33–35, 39
    structure 185
    template 36
lexical
    approach 103
    bundles / chunks 49, 99, 195
    grammar 95
    knowledge 155
    set 99, 101, 199
life
    chances 51
    experiences 29
    skills 10
linguistic
    ability 52
    bias 134
    difficulty 88
listening
    accuracy 75
    activities 65
    apps 122
    comprehension 37, 66
    developing 11, 90
    differences from hearing 77
    in class 82
    in L2 84
    skills 58
    tasks 77, 81
    teaching 6, 79
    test 159
    texts 78, 101, 108, 136, 137
loneliness 44, 49
losing face 70, 87, 97, 184, 195
low socio-economic
    areas 164
    background 46
low stakes 193, 195
managing the seating 41, 57

marginalization
  cultural 5
  economic 5, 34
  political 5, 34
  reduced 167
  social 5, 34
marking code 64, 92, 195
marking scheme 154, 156, 195
matching task 11, 195
maximum value 108
meaningful production 85
'mechanics' of the lesson 28
'megaphone' 129
memorization 11, 52
menstruate 71
mental
  coding 46, 48, 195
  well-being 198
mentors 25
metalanguage 77, 80, 93, 94, 195
methodology
  'chalk and talk' 27, 34
  curriculum 9
  deductive 93–95, 191, 194
  inductive 93–95, 191, 194
  'listen and sit' 27
  teacher-centred 29
micro-resistances 132, 135, 195
Millennium Development Goals 2, 5
mime 41, 99, 101, 170, 195
mind maps 81
mindset
  changing 61, 195
  negative 6, 25, 34, 144, 186
  of learned helplessness 6
mingle 30, 58, 60, 174, 195
minimal pairs 88, 98
minority
  ethnicity 21
  language 2, 4, 14, 51, 52, 54, 55
mobile phones 117, 120, 121, 122, 126, 160
mobility
  restricted 24
  socioeconomic 10

model
  answer 92, 195
  classroom 6
  classroom routines 128
  dialogues 137
  educational 4
  'freemium' 122
  institution 25
  language 186
  of inclusivity 26
  pronunciation 43, 108
  role 83, 134, 137, 143, 146, 178
  sentence 93, 94, 95, 97
  teacher-centred 28
  teaching 28
  text 197
modelling 176
MOOCs (Massive Open Online Courses) 189
mother tongue 46, 51, 54, 90, 194
motivation
  decreasing 36
  lack of 144
  low levels 16
  maximizing 121
  understanding students' 143
multilingual
  classes 186
  classroom 21, 51–52
  communities 193
  multilingualism 34
  perspective 11
  space 14
  strategies 24
  students 94
  techniques 188
mutual trust 184
nation state 3, 10
national
  border 169, 194
  exams 93
  unity 10
nationality 15, 198
natural disasters 16, 119, 123, 194, 197
natural instincts 28

natural order 168
negotiating consensus 180
networks
    national or international 186
    social 198
    teaching 189
nervous 15, 16, 18, 20, 46, 47, 87, 122, 163, 164
noise, ambient 23, 77, 79, 125, 159, 190
nouns
    concrete 79, 100
    high-frequency 79
nutrition 160
official government agencies 56
Onion ring /Doughnut 30, 38, 192, 196
online
    dangers 123
    groups 125
    learning 125
    library 56
    materials 113
    platforms 54, 56, 125
    teacher groups 186, 187, 188
    video-sharing 187
open
    day 167
    link 126
    platform 126
questions 29, 130, 135, 191, 196
opportunity costs 46, 192, 196
Organizer 40, 41
'othering' 51
out-of-school children 168
outdoor space 3, 72
'over-check' 148
overprotective 48
overworked 31
oxygen 159
paragraph structure 112, 137
paraphrase 53, 82
parental involvement 164
partners in learning 21
partially sighted 25

passive acceptance 2
pedagogy
    gender-responsive 23, 193
    global South 2
    pragmatic, practice-oriented 1
    teacher-fronted 3, 96
    textbook-free 115
peers 3, 46, 90
peer-to-peer (P2P) learning 123, 196
persecution 197
personalizing 29, 103, 138, 140, 146
phobias 44
physical
    activities 23, 117
    attributes 118
    challenging 180
    checks 20
    conditions 158
    connection 96
    dangers 14
    development 19, 69, 71
    disability 21, 22, 23, 133
    environment 159
    fitness 75
    health 198
    movement 15
    objects 110
    presence 15
    quality 130
    resources 161
    safety 13
    space 10
    tired 157
    uncomfortable 72
    violence 16
'playground friends' 20
playtime 13, 19, 20
pluralization 12
podcasts 84
policies
    formal 52
    inclusive 21

informal 52
school-wide 24
social, emotional and behavioural
  difficulties 175
positivist 3
potentially unfamiliar words 41
poverty 5, 22, 120, 196
power
  agency 190
  dominant language 192
  imbalance 72
  naming students 176
  of students 2
  of 'yet' 177
PPP (Presentation Practice Production) method
  93, 94, 196
'preferred response' 149
prefixes 102, 103, 191
pre-listening 80, 81
pre-reading 80, 81
prejudices 22
prescriptive 130, 191, 196
pressure
  availability 186
  economic and social 21
  homework 25
  positive upward 171
  time 184
prior knowledge 35, 80, 190
private schooling 55
process writing 137, 197
product writing 137, 197
production stage 149, 197
productive competence 85
  skills 85, 91, 197
  tasks 88, 90
professional development 34, 182, 186, 194
programs/ apps 125
prompting 40
pronouns
  female 24
  male 24, 137
  non-gendered 137

pronunciation
  consistent model 43
  listening texts/ audios 108
  main features of L1 110
  minimal pair 88, 98, 195
  skills development 117
  source 40
props 78
protocols
  classroom 48
  school 46
punctuation rules 110
qualifications 10, 145
race 15, 21, 134, 198
racism 134
radio 84, 100
reading
  ability 1, 78
  activities 41, 65
  aloud 80
  comprehensions 66, 82, 112
  confidence 78
  corner 83
  exams 25
  extensive 51, 54, 82
  group 83
  Reading in interesting places 72
  skills 6, 78, 80, 83, 88, 90, 155
  teaching 77
  texts 65, 101, 103, 108, 110, 125, 136, 137
realia (real-life objects) 28, 99, 100, 112, 197
real-world interaction 28
receptive skills
  improving 82
  lacking 80
  teaching 77
  using 35, 197
recycling
  educational process 197
  material(s) 30
  new language / words 1, 100
reflection 11, 182, 183, 184, 185
refugees 26, 46, 120

reliability in assessment 155, 197

religion 15, 21, 132, 198

remote

    learning 125

    teaching 120, 123, 192, 197

repetition 11, 70, 73, 85, 91, 145, 199

representation, phonological vs visual/

    conceptual 48

restricted practice 66, 197

retention, student 21

rewriting 137, 140

role play 28, 38, 81, 88, 137, 173, 197

root form 95, 150

rota 18, 20

rote

    learning 11, 197

    production 197

rules

    class list 55

    deductive methodology 190

    grammar 94, 95

    inductive methodology 194

    playground 47

    punctuation 110

    school 46, 179

Running dictation 72, 73, 86

rural 133, 139

safe space 13, 53, 97, 119, 168, 181

'safe talk' 52

sanitary/ bathroom requirements 24, 71

sanitation facilities 196

scaffolding 52, 65, 197

scholarship 194

school

    activities 171

    boundary 168

    charter or agreement 26, 197

    curriculum 115

    governors 135

    leadership 135

    library 83

    management 13, 21, 22, 69, 76, 136, 167

    noticeboard 19

    owners 135

    protocols 46

    skills 47

    uniform 159

schwa sound 75, 197

seating

    arrangement 57, 58, 62, 71

    circle 188

    classroom 60, 146

    fairness 23

    layout 60–61

    managing 29, 41, 57, 60

    plan 32, 57, 59, 60–61, 76, 85

SEBD (social, emotional and behavioral

    difficulties) 176, 178

selectivity 134

self-directed learning 194

self-esteem 43, 179

self-evaluation 46, 49

self-regulate 180, 198

sentence structure 96, 110, 112, 137

sequence words 110, 198

service provider 4, 45, 198

set phrases 54, 193

settings

    highly mobile 169

    informal or non-formal 136, 168

sexism 134

sexuality 198

sexual orientation 15

'show and tell' 28, 112, 163, 165, 198

shy 46, 47, 60, 87, 153

silence or 'thinking time' 88

'sit and listen' approach 27, 57

skills

    basic 48, 89

    classroom 46, 47–48, 63

    collaboration 29

    critical thinking 129

    L1 skills 48

    language 16, 49, 59, 64, 87, 125, 140, 169,

        172, 187

    leadership 66

learning 48
life skills 10
listening 50, 58, 77
necessary 52
orthographic 47, 48, 85, 196
productive 35, 85, 90, 197
pronunciation 117
reading 54, 78, 82, 83, 88, 90, 155
receptive 35, 77, 80, 82, 85
soft skills 16, 75, 111, 125, 144, 198
speaking 85, 186
spoken 185
sub- 66, 80
specific 49
team-working 29
teamwork 129
vocabulary 99
writing 85, 91
smartphones 74, 122, 160
snowball approach 67, 112
Snowman 104
social capital 171, 198
social class 15
social divisions 10
social skills 144, 198
social status 163
soft skills 16, 75, 111, 125, 144, 198
songs 45, 122, 177
standardization of assessment 155, 198
status quo 135, 195
step change 28, 85, 198
stigmatized 136
stopping issues from escalating 177
sub-skills 66, 80
substitution drills 94
substitution table 97
subject
   area 41, 186
   knowledge 52
subjective
   answer 152
   task 156, 161
   writing 145

suffixes 102, 111, 199
summative
   assessment / feedback 91, 193, 198
   exams 158
   teacher observation 184
superdiverse 55
superdiversity 198
Sustainable Development Goals 5
'swimming against the tide' 78
syllable stress 43
syllabus 11, 85, 115, 127, 128, 191, 193, 196, 198
synchronous
   learning 123
   sessions 125
synonym 99, 100, 130, 190, 198
target
   language 14, 35, 36, 52, 88, 94, 96, 97, 98, 99,
      110, 112, 115, 119, 122, 133, 136, 148, 149,
      150, 151, 165, 170, 191, 193, 195, 196,
      198, 199
   vocabulary 152
tasks
   asynchronous 124
   collaborative 88
   common 165
   exam 158
   extension 140
   household 25
   language 155
   listening 77
   matching 11
   multi-level 147
   objective 156
   productive 88, 90
   setting 63, 65
   speaking 87, 122
   student ability 52
   student-centred 28
   student interest 52
   subjective 161
   synchronous 125
   writing 58
   while-listening 80–81

while-reading 80–81
writing 87
task repetition 85, 91, 145, 199
teacher
-centredness 1
-fronted approach 94
-fronted stage 28
involvement 24
professional development 7, 34, 182,
185–189, 194
teaching
association 172
assistants 163, 165–6
British English or American English 11
classroom after disasters 123
diary 181
different strategies 129
dominant style 102
face-to-face (F2F) 120, 123, 192
focus on non-linguistic features involved in
developing language skills 49
gender-responsive pedagogy 193
good practice techniques 176
grammar, transmissive, teacher-fronted 94
in challenging circumstances 148, 175, 178,
180, 187
in resource-light environments 41
language 122, 166, 180
language of instruction 194
materials 3
model 28
multilingual classes 186
multilingual strategies 24
online 123, 125
perspective 130
reading and listening 80–81
reflective 182–185
remote 123, 197
resources 107
rewarding 180
situation 9, 136
speaking and writing 85
student-focused 27

style 143
Total Physical Response (TPR) 72, 75, 96,
117, 199
vocabulary and grammar 110
teaching strategies
encouraging students' use of local languages in
classroom 51
greater use of appropriate and effective
teaching strategies 52
multilingual 24
using different 129
teamwork 111, 129, 144, 198
teasing 16
technology
digital equity 192
face-to-face teaching integrating
technology 123
lacking technology and response to this 172
outside of lesson 122
provides opportunities for accessing
resources 107
using effectively 120, 171
television
access to 84
temperature 57, 159
'ten-minute share' sessions 163–164
TESOL International Association 189
textbooks
accompanied by teacher's guide 34
avoiding psychological triggers 177
bias 137
changing 136
determining what English is taught 11
dominated by grammar 96
inappropriate content 140
insufficient 4
language learning opportunities when not
using 72
language level 140
making student-focused 138
minimizing the problem of not having enough
textbooks 129
no access to 113

not providing many details about words 101
'one size fits all' 139
out of date 127
prescriptive 130
presenting imagined view of society 134
reinforcing how state and government is
    dominated by particular ethnic or religious
    group 133–134
supplementing 128
teaching lacking without 6
uninteresting 36
using gender-biased language 24
using in class 41
vocabulary-focused 130
writers and biases 133
time
    affecting kind of activities undertaken by
        students 32
    classroom 5, 17
    dividing 24
    homework 71
    lack of 91
    limit 98, 117
    management 39, 184
    need for additional time 25
    playtime 13, 20
    real 123, 125
    students' speaking time 66
    thinking 88
    timekeeping 28, 187, 198
    time-consuming activities in class 28, 65, 85
timing 39
toilet policy 160
tolerance
    need for greater tolerance for mistakes 97
    towards using L1 in classroom 51
topic or subject area 41
topics
    boring 86
    choosing appropriate 70
    identifying relevant 97
    interesting 74, 168

sensitive and difficult 53
triggers 31
Total Physical Response (TPR) 72, 75, 96, 177, 199
touching 15, 177, 179
tradition(al)
    activities 28
    classroom practices 52
    classroom techniques 86
    PPP (Presentation Practice Production) 93
    product writing 197
    teaching grammar 94
    understanding grammar 95
    views of what constitutes a good
        assessment 154
    way textbook writers were taught 139
    women's roles 24, 191
traditions
    local 45
    regional 91
'transform' information 81
translanguaging 51, 53, 136, 191, 199
translate
    L1 into classroom language 54
    texts into English 78
translation approach / method 100
transportation
    direct costs 192
    lack of 123
    unreliable 144
trauma
    cause of poor behaviour 16
    experiencing 178, 199
    managing 10, 145, 180
    processing 175
    supporting 186
    trigger 15
Treasure hunt 72, 82
trigger
    avoiding through anonymizing challenges 179
    depression 31
    psychological 177
    traumatic experience 15, 199

turn-by-turn basis 188
understanding
  checking in lessons 41
  checking and clarifying 52, 109, 122, 149
  context 94
  correcting weaker students' understanding 64
  critical consciousness 191
  deeper / deepening 16, 100, 168
  developing understanding of basic school
    skills and school norms 47
  difficulties 24
  general 139, 152
  limited 49
  local environment 110
  of different sanitary/ bathroom requirements
    of students 71
  of prefixes and suffixes 102
  not having real understanding 58
  scaffolding 80
  securing 99
  showing more advanced understanding 43
  showing to students 126
  structure of language 85, 89
  students' behavioural issues 178
  target language 148
  'top up' 100
unreality bias 134
urban 139
validity in assessment 154–155, 199
values
  orthodox 135
  shared 184
  institutional knowledge 194
Venn diagram 170
verb form 15, 64, 92, 96, 150
verb usage, simplified 12
verbs
  fun, active, interesting 75
  general 11
  intransitive 73
  irregular 95
  regular 95
  transitive 109

videos
  engaging for students 172
  online sharing platforms' range 84, 187
  using a lot of bandwidth 188
visual aids 41, 199
violence
  descriptions in texts 177
  gender 24, 193
  low-level 16
  physical 16
  threat of and results, such as being forced to
    leave home 194
VLE (virtual learning environment) 125
vocabulary
  active 99, 102, 103, 106
  activities 87, 101, 108
  building 103
  choice, random 101
  distinction with grammar 95
  general vocabulary items, practising 74
  list 122
  long lists 11
  passive 106
  students' lack of 49
  target 152
  teaching 110, 196
  wide 85
Vocabulary tag 72, 73
voice
  directing 23, 79
  louder or raised 177
  of authority 2
  passive 109
  recording apps 122
  students 78
  teacher 15
  variety 108
weaker students
  advising 65
  asking first 41, 64
  checking instructions 64
  experiencing frustration and boredom, leading
    to poor behaviour 59

feeling lost and confused 63
giving feedback 64
giving opportunity to answer 64
grouping with stronger students 66–67
lack of participation 59
weather conditions 36, 159
weighting 156, 199
well-being 175, 197
whole-class discussion 18
'wider' knowledge 140
Wi-Fi 113
Word Bingo 104
'working with a new friend' 59
World Homeless Day 173
writing
    activities 65
    challenges 85
    collaborative 89–90, 124

difficulties, such as students lacking basic orthonographic skills 48
giving feedback 64
lack of skills 89, 91–92
making interesting 86–87
marking code 195
on the board 28
paraphrasing 196
pieces 44
prioritized 58
process 137, 197
product 137, 197
students lacking confidence 87
subjective 145
textbooks 140–141
written texts 77, 78
zone of proximal development 52, 199